Beginning HTML5 Media

Make the most of the new video
and audio standards for the Web

■ ■ ■

Silvia Pfeiffer
Tom Green

Apress®

Beginning HTML5 Media

ISBN-13 (pbk): 978-1-4842-0461-0

ISBN-13 (electronic): 978-1-4842-0460-3

Trademarked names, logos, and images may appear in this book. Rather than use a trademark symbol with every occurrence of a trademarked name, logo, or image we use the names, logos, and images only in an editorial fashion and to the benefit of the trademark owner, with no intention of infringement of the trademark.

The use in this publication of trade names, trademarks, service marks, and similar terms, even if they are not identified as such, is not to be taken as an expression of opinion as to whether or not they are subject to proprietary rights.

While the advice and information in this book are believed to be true and accurate at the date of publication, neither the authors nor the editors nor the publisher can accept any legal responsibility for any errors or omissions that may be made. The publisher makes no warranty, express or implied, with respect to the material contained herein.

Managing Director: Welmoed Spahr
Lead Editor: Ben Renow-Clarke
Technical Reviewer: Chris Pearce
Editorial Board: Steve Anglin, Louise Corrigan, Jonathan Gennick, Robert Hutchinson,
 Michelle Lowman, James Markham, Susan McDermott, Matthew Moodie, Jeffrey Pepper,
 Douglas Pundick, Ben Renow-Clarke, Gwenan Spearing, Steve Weiss
Coordinating Editor: Mark Powers
Copy Editor: Lori Jacobs
Compositor: SPi Global
Indexer: SPi Global
Artist: SPi Global

Distributed to the book trade worldwide by Springer Science+Business Media New York, 233 Spring Street, 6th Floor, New York, NY 10013. Phone 1-800-SPRINGER, fax (201) 348-4505, e-mail orders-ny@springer-sbm.com, or visit www.springeronline.com. Apress Media, LLC is a California LLC and the sole member (owner) is Springer Science + Business Media Finance Inc (SSBM Finance Inc). SSBM Finance Inc is a Delaware corporation.

For information on translations, please e-mail rights@apress.com, or visit www.apress.com.

Apress and friends of ED books may be purchased in bulk for academic, corporate, or promotional use. eBook versions and licenses are also available for most titles. For more information, reference our Special Bulk Sales–eBook Licensing web page at www.apress.com/bulk-sales.

Any source code or other supplementary material referenced by the author in this text is available to readers at www.apress.com/9781484204610. For detailed information about how to locate your book's source code, go to www.apress.com/source-code/.

Contents at a Glance

Contents

About the Authors

Dr. Silvia Pfeiffer has worked on novel media technology for more than 20 years and is an internationally renowned expert in new web video standards. Silvia was an editor of the HTML5 standard and continues to edit the WebVTT specification and several other specification documents at the W3C. Silvia has in the past worked on accessibility at Mozilla and Google and contributed code to the Google Chrome browser. She was a Xiph and open media technologies contributor long before these technologies made it into the Web. In fact, she helped the progress of open web media technology not only through technical contributions but also by making sure the communities would work together productively by organizing the annual "Foundations of Open Media Standards and Software" Workshop.

Silvia has a PhD in Computer Science in the field of automated audio and video content analysis. During her academic phase, Silvia published more than 50 academic papers, journal articles, and book chapters and has spoken at many international conferences. Since moving out of academics, Silvia has pursued the creation of standards and startups. The latter is currently taking her to the creation of a new company focused around WebRTC (web real-time communications) technology, a new web standard for real-time video, audio, and data conferencing.

Tom Green is a Professor of Interactive Media in the School of Media Studies at Humber College Institute of Technology and Advanced Learning in Toronto. He has written 12 previous books on media and web technologies, and many articles for numerous magazines and web sites, including About.com, Layers Magazine, video2brain, and Lynda.com. Finally, he has spoken at numerous international industry conferences including FITC, Web Design, Digital Design World, and Adobe Max.

As an educator, Tom has delivered expert lectures and seminars dealing with a variety of digital media technogies and trends at a number of major universities throughout China such as the Central Academy of Fine Arts in Beijing and Shenzhen Polytechnic in Shenzhen. Tom was also instrumental in the establishment of the Adobe Education Leaders program whose sole aim is to bring the leading K–12 and postsecondary educators from around the world together in a collaborative and networking environment to share their best practices with each other. As well, Tom has contributed over 200 tutorials and lessons to the Adobe Education Exchange—`https://edex.adobe.com/member/93c2256a9a/resources`—which is a web resource, open to educators for the sharing of knowledge around teaching digital media. Tom also participates in a regular series of online seminars designed to keep educators current with changing technologies such as those that are the subject of this book.

About the Technical Reviewer

Chris Pearce is a software engineer working at Mozilla on the HTML5 audio and video playback support for the open-source Firefox web browser. He is also the creator of the keyframe index used by the Ogg media container and contributes to the Ogg/Xiph community. Chris has also worked on Mozilla's text editor widget, and previously worked developing mobile software developer tools. Chris works out of Mozilla's Auckland office in New Zealand, and blogs about matters related to Internet video and Firefox development at `http://pearce.org.nz`.

Acknowledgments

Working with a coauthor can be a tricky business. In fact, it is a little like a marriage. Everything is wonderful when things are going well but you never discover the strength of the relationship until you are deep into it. Having always been fascinated with video and audio technologies it should come as no surprise that Silvia's first book—*The Definitive Guide to HTML5 Video*—never really left my desk. Thus it was huge surprise when I was asked to work on an update of this book with her. As we got deep into the book I discovered I was working with one of the great minds of the Internet. I also realized I had been handed the opportunity to learn more than I ever expected around the subject of this book. It is not often a teacher is given this experience and for that I am both grateful to Apress for asking me to work with her and to Silvia for her patience and for helping me to become a better teacher.

—Tom Green

I am positively surprised that I am able to hold this book in my hands. When Apress asked me to author an update of *The Definitive Guide to HTML5 Video*, I knew that it was necessary: the web APIs (application programming interfaces) had changed so fundamentally that about half of that book didn't reflect reality any longer. I also knew that I was busy writing standards and creating a new startup and didn't really have the time that was necessary to rewrite the book. Apress suggested a coauthor and introduced me to Tom and we made it work! Thanks to the modern Internet, we still haven't met face to face, and yet were able to pull it off. If it wasn't Tom's continued enthusiasm and his more engaging writing style, I'm sure I would have given up. I hope you all enjoy it!

—Silvia Pfeiffer

Preface

When it comes to the Internet, the pace of change can be both breathtaking and overwhelming. This is especially true when it comes to the subject of this book.

In 2003, Tom was in Seattle getting ready to do a presentation on Flash Video at Digital Design World when Jim Heid, the Conference Organizer, saw the title slide of the presentation and mentioned that he might be facing a rather tough crowd. Tom looked out over the audience, sized them up, and told Jim he had his back covered. Jim said he wasn't too sure about that and pointed at the title on Tom's screen: "QuickTime is dead." Looking out into the darkened room, Tom watched about 400 people in the audience open their Powerbooks; hundreds of bright white Apple logos staring back at him. It was indeed going to be a tough crowd.

Nobody really expected the stranglehold that Apple, Microsoft, and Real had on the web streaming market in 2003 to be broken. Yet by Spring 2005, just 18 months after that presentation, that is exactly what had happened. Those three web video delivery technologies practically vanished, replaced almost entirely by Flash Video. This is not to say QuickTime and Windows Media were dead technologies. But when it came to putting video on the Web, the Flash Player, thanks, in part, to YouTube, had become the only game in town.

Two years later when the iPhone arrived, Flash as a video delivery platform, lost its stranglehold on video and audio content delivery. In fact Flash essentially disappeared in 2011 when Apple banned Flash from its devices. It was at that point the market changed its focus to HTML 5 encoding and playback solutions. With a single standard that was "ubiquitous" one would think the dust had settled. Not quite.

Sivia's opening paragraphs from the Preface of the first version of this book were written in 2010 and still resonate today:

> *"It is ironic that I started writing this book on the exact day that the last of the big browsers announced that it was going to support HTML5 and, with it, HTML5 video. On March 16, 2010, Microsoft joined Firefox, Opera, Google Chrome, and WebKit/Safari with an announcement that Internet Explorer 9 will support HTML5 and the HTML5 video element. Only weeks before the book was finished, the IE9 beta was also released, so I was able to actually include IE9 behavior into the book, making it so much more valuable to you.*
>
> *During the course of writing this book, many more announcements were made and many new features introduced in all the browsers."*

As we proceeded through this book we discovered things haven't much changed since Sivia's Preface. As we were writing this book the browsers introduced new features and updates. Microsoft announced a revamp of Internet Explorer. Video and audio formats used by the browsers were starting to settle around a single format. Third-party video streaming services have appeared. Live streaming and mobile delivery of audio and video content is becoming more and more important. The streaming of Ultra HD 4K video is starting to appear. And so it goes . . .

Understandably, browsers and technology are continuing to evolve and what doesn't work today may work tomorrow. As you start using HTML5 video—and, in particular, as you start developing your own web sites with it—we recommend you check out the actual current status of implementation of all relevant browsers for support of your desired feature.

Approaching This Book

This book is written for anyone interested in using HTML5 media elements. It assumes an existing background in writing basic HTML, CSS, and JavaScript, but little or no experience with media.

If you are a beginner and just want to learn the basics of how to include video in your web pages, the **first three chapters** will be sufficient. You will learn how to encode your audio and video for the web, how to create cross-browser compatible markup in HTML to include audio and video into your web pages, and how to use the JavaScript API for media elements. This will allow you to replace the default controls of web browser with your own: "skinning" your media player. You will also learn how to style the display of your audio and video elements in CSS to make them stand out on your site.

The **remaining three chapters** are about a more in-depth use of media content. We start with accessibility and internationalization of media elements, which includes captions, subtitles, and audio descriptions. Then we give you an introduction on how to manipulate video and audio content through Canvas and the Web Audio API. You will learn how to play with a green screen in JavaScript or make your music sound like you're in a cathedral and many other awesome effects.

Notation

In the book, we often speak of HTML elements and HTML element attributes. An element name is written as <element>, an attribute name as @attribute, and an attribute value as *value*. Where an attribute is mentioned for the first time, it will be marked as bold.

Downloading the Code

The source code to the examples used in this book is available to readers at http://www.html5videoguide.net, as well as www.apress.com/9781484204610.

Contacting the Authors

Do not hesitate to contact either author at silviapfeiffer1@gmail.com or tomgreen17@gmail.com

We can also be reached on Twitter: @silviapfeiffer or @TomGreen

Silvia's Blog: http://gingertech.net

Tom's YouTube Channel: https://www.youtube.com/channel/UCCjDB7XASezB9lERBF1qwbA

■ ■ ■

CHAPTER 1

Encoding Video

The "art" of encoding video for HTML5 is, in many respects, a "black art." There are no standards other than file format and everything else from data rate to audio is left to your best judgment. The decisions you make in creating the MPEG4, WebM, and Ogg files are therefore "subjective" not "objective." Before you can play the video and audio content in HTML5 you need to clearly understand how these files are created and the decisions you will need to make to ensure smooth playback. This process starts with a rather jarring revelation: video is not video. The extensions used to identify video and audio files are more like shoeboxes than anything else. The file formats—MPEG4, WebM, and Ogg—are the names on the boxes and inside the boxes are a video track and an audio track. The box with the file format label is called a "container."

In this chapter you'll learn the following:

- The importance of containers and codecs.

- The audio and video codecs used to encode the audio and video files used by HTML5.

- How to use Miro Video Converter to create .mp4, .webm, and .ogv files.

- How to use the Firefogg extension to create .webm and .ogv files.

- How to use the Adobe Media Encoder to create an .mp4 file.

- The commands used by FFmpeg to encode the various audio and video formats used by HTML5.

Containers

Though you may regard video files as say, an .mp4 file, in reality, it is nothing more than a container format. What it does is define how to store what is in the container, not what types of data are stored in the container. This is a critical distinction to understand.

If you were able to open the box labeled MPEG4 you would see a video track (without audio), plus one or more audio tracks (without video), which is exactly what you see when you edit a video file in a video editor as shown in Figure 1-1. These tracks are usually interrelated. For example, the audio track will contain markers that allow it to synchronize with the video track. The tracks typically contain metadata such as the aspect ratio of the images of a video track or the language used in the audio track. The containers that encapsulate the tracks can also hold metadata such as the title of the video production, the cover art for the file, a list of chapters for navigation, and so on.

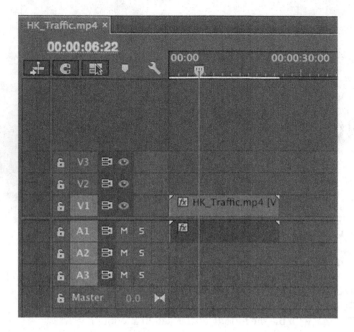

Figure 1-1. You can see the video and audio tracks in a video editor

In addition, it is possible that video files contain text tracks, such as captions or subtitles, or tracks that contain programming information, or tracks that contain small thumbnails to help users when using fast forward to a jog control to find a particular point in the video. We call these tracks "timed metadata" and will talk about them later. For now, we'll focus on creating video files that contain a video and an audio track.

Similar to video files, audio files also consist of a container with tracks of content inside them. Often, the same container formats are used for creating audio files as for creating video files, but some simpler containers exist also for audio alone.

Video and audio signals are put into container formats by encoding to binary form and compressing the bits. This process is called encoding and the process of returning the binary data to audio/video signals is called decoding. The algorithm for encoding and decoding is a codec (COder/DECoder). We'll talk about codecs in a bit; first we need to understand the container formats that browsers support.

Video Containers

Though there are a lot of container formats out there, thankfully browsers only support a limited set and there really are only three you need to know.

- **MPEG4** which usually contains a .mp4 or a .m4v extension. This container, which typically holds an H.264 or H.265 encoded video track and an AAC (Advanced Audio Codec) audio track, is based on Apple's older .mov format and is the one most commonly produced by the video camera in your smartphone or tablet.

- **Ogg** which uses the .ogg or .ogv extension. Ogg, as pointed out in the "Introduction," is an open source format unencumbered by patents. This container holds Ogg video (the Theora codec) and Ogg audio (the Vorbis or Opus codec). This format is supported, "out of the box" by all major Linux distributions and is also playable on both the Mac and Windows platforms using the VLC player which is freely available at www.videolan.org/vlc/index.html.

- **WebM** which uses the .webm extension. As pointed out in the "Introduction," WebM is a royalty-free open source format designed specifically for HTML5 video. This container holds a VP8 or VP9 encoded video track and a Vorbis or Opus encoded audio track. This format is supported natively by many of the modern browsers except for Internet Explorer (IE) and Safari for which you need to install Media Foundation or Quicktime components, respectively.

All browsers that support the Ogg container format also support the more modern WebM container format. Therefore, this book focuses on WebM and we only cover Ogg in this chapter for completeness.

■ **Note**   For more information regarding video and browsers, check out http://en.wikipedia.org/wiki/HTML5_Video#Browser_support.

Audio Containers

Most of the video containers are also applicable to audio-only files, but then use different MIME types and different file extensions. HTML5 supports the following audio file formats:

- **MPEG4** files that are audio-only have an AAC encoded audio track and an .m4a extension.

- **Ogg** files that are audio-only have either a Vorbis encoded audio track and an .ogg or .oga extension, or an Opus encoded audio track and an .opus extension.

- **WebM** files that are audio-only have a Vorbis or Opus encoded audio track but also a .webm extension.

- **MP3** files contain the MPEG-1 audio layer 3 defined codec as a sequence of packets. While MP3 is not really a container format (e.g., it cannot contain video tracks), MP3 files have many features of a container, such as metadata in ID3 format headers. MP3 audio files are found in files with the extension .mp3.

- **RIFF WAVE** files are containers for audio tracks that are typically raw PCM encoded, which means that the audio data is essentially uncompressed, making for larger files. The RIFF WAVE file extension is .wav.

Each of these five audio files formats are supported in one or more of the Web browsers natively in their audio or video elements. Since there is no format that all browsers support equally, you will need to pick, at a minimum, two to cover all browsers (e.g., .m4a and .webm with Opus). (See also http://en.wikipedia.org/wiki/HTML5_Audio#Supported_audio_codecs.)

Codecs

When you watch a video in a browser there is a lot going on under the hood that you don't see. Your video player is actually doing three things at the same time.

- It is opening the container to see which audio and video formats are used and how they are stored in the file so they can be "decoded."

- Decoding the video stream and shooting the images to the screen.

- Decoding the audio and sending that data to the speakers.

What you can gather from this is that a video codec is an algorithm which encodes a video track to enable the computer to unpack the images in the video and shoot them to your screen. The video player is the technology that actually does the decoding and display.

Video Codecs

There are two types of video codecs: lossy and lossless.

Lossy video is the most common type. As the video is encoded, increasingly more information is, essentially, thrown out. This process is called compression. Compression starts by throwing away information that is not relevant to the visual perception of the human eye. The end result is a seriously smaller file size. The more you squeeze down the size of a video file, the more information you lose and the more the quality of the video images decreases.

Similarly, compressing a file that has already been compressed with a lossy codec is not a "good thing." If you have ever compressed a .jpg image a few times you would have noticed the quality of the image degrade because jpg is a "lossy" image compressor. The same thing happens with video. Therefore, when you encode video, you should always keep a copy of the original files in case you have to re-encode at a later stage.

As the name implies, "lossless video" loses no information and results in files that are simply too large to be of any use for online playback. Still, they are extremely useful for the original video file especially when it comes to creating three versions of the same file. A common lossless codec is Animation available through QuickTime.

There are myriad codecs out there all claiming to do amazing things. Thankfully when it comes to HTML5 video we only have three with which to concern ourselves: H.264, Theora, and VP8.

H.264

If H.264 were a major crime figure it would have a few aliases: MPEG-4 part 10 or MPEG-4 AVC or MPEG-4 Advanced Video Coding. Regardless of how it is known, this codec's primary purpose was to make a single codec available for anything from the cell phone in your pocket (low bandwidth, low CPU) to your desktop computer (high bandwidth, high CPU) and practically anything else that has a screen. To accomplish this rather broad range of situations the H.264 standard is broken into a series of profiles, each of which defines a number of optional features that trade off complexity for file size. The most used profiles, for our purposes, are

- **Baseline:** use this with iOS devices.

- **Main:** this is mostly an historic profile used on standard definition (SD) (4:3 Aspect Ratio) TV broadcasts.

- **High:** use this for Web, SD, and HD (high definition) video publishing.

You also should know that most non-PC devices such as iPhones and Android devices actually do the decoding piece on a separate chip since their main CPU is not even close to being powerful enough to do the decoding in real time. Finally, the only browser that doesn't support the H.264 standard is Opera.

While H.264 is still the dominant codec in the MPEG world, a new codec called H.265/HEVC (MPEG High Efficiency Video Coding) is emerging. The tools to create content in H.265 will likely be the same as for creating H.264, except that the resulting files will be smaller or of higher image quality.

Theora

Theora grew out of the VP3 codec from On2 and has subsequently been published under a BSD-style license by Xiph.org. All major Linux installations and the Firefox and Opera browsers support Theora while IE and Safari as well as iOS and Android devices don't support it. While being royalty-free and open source, it has been superseded by VP8.

VP8

This is the "New Kid On The Block." Technically VP8 output is right up there with the H.264 high profile. It also works rather nicely in low bandwidth situations comparable to the H.264 baseline profile. As pointed out in the "Introduction," Apple is not a huge supporter of this codec, which explains why it isn't supported in Safari or iOS devices. You can, however, get support by installing a QuickTime component (see https://code.google.com/p/webm/downloads/list). Similarly, installation of a Microsoft Media Foundation component from the same site enables support in IE.

While VP8 is still the dominant codec in the WebM world, a new codec called VP9 is emerging. It is comparable in quality to H.265 but is royalty-free. As both of these codecs are starting to take the stage at around the same time, new hardware for hardware-accelerated encoding and decoding seems to focus on supporting both codecs. This is good news for users and publishers of HTML5 video content, in particular if you are interested in very high resolution video such as 4K.

Audio Codecs

Video without audio is a lot like watching Fred Astaire dance without Ginger Rogers. It just doesn't seem natural.

When an audio source is digitized, this is called sampling, because a sound pressure value is sampled every few microseconds and converted into a digital value. There are basically three parameters that influence the quality of audio sampling: the sampling rate (i.e., how often is the pressure sampled during a second), the number of channels (i.e., how many locations do we use to sample the same signal), and the precision of the samples (i.e., how exact a value do we sample, or how many bits to we use to store the sample—also called bitdepth). A typical sampling rate for phone quality sound is 8 kHz (i.e., 8,000 times per second), while stereo music quality is 44.1 kHz or 48 kHz. A typical number of channels is 2 (stereo), and a typical bitdepth is 8 bits for telephone quality and 16 for stereo music quality. The resulting sampled data is compressed with different codecs to reduce the storage or bandwidth footprint of digitized audio.

Like video, audio codecs are algorithms that encode the audio stream, and like video codecs, they come in two flavors: lossy and lossless. Since we're dealing with video online, where we want to save as much bandwidth as possible, we need only concern ourselves with lossy audio codecs. Note that the RIFF WAVE format is uncompressed and is supported natively in all browsers except IE, so should you need uncompressed audio, this would be your choice. For compressed audio, there really are only three codecs you need to be aware of.

Before we start let's get really clear on audio. Just because you can sit in your living room and watch a video with six or more speakers of glorious surround sound doesn't mean web viewers get the same privilege. Most content on the Web is mono or stereo and your typical smartphone or mobile device will not offer you more than stereo output anyway. It is, however, possible to create Ogg Vorbis and MPEG AAC files with six or more channels and get these played back in your browser as surround sound, always assuming that your surround system is actually available to your web browser through your operating system. There will be occasions where you simply want to add an audio file to a web page. In this case, the three audio codecs you need to be aware of are MP3, Vorbis, and AAC.

MP3: MPEG-1 Audio Layer 3

The heading may be confusing but this is the official name for the ubiquitous MP3 file.

MP3 files can contain up to two channels—mono or stereo—of sound. There is a backward-compatible extension of MP3 for surround sound, which might also work in your browser of choice. MP3 can be encoded at different bitrates. For those who may be encountering the term "bitrate" for the first time, it is a measure of how many thousand 1s and 0s are transferred to your computer each second. For example, a 1 k bitrate means 1,000 bits, or kilobits (kb), move from the server to the MP3 player each second.

For MP3 files the bitrates (Kbps) can range between 32, 64, 128, and 256 up to 320 Kbps. Simply "supersizing" the bitrate does nothing more than supersize the file size with a marginally noticeable increase in audio quality. For example, a 128 Kbps file sounds a lot better than one at 64 Kbps. But the audio quality doesn't double at 256 Kbps. Another aspect of this topic is that MP3 files allow for a variable bitrate. To understand this, consider an audio file with 5 seconds of silence in the middle of the file. This audio section could have a bitrate of 32 Kbps applied to it, and as soon as the band kicks in, the bitrate jumps to 128 Kbps.

All of the modern browsers except for Opera 10.0+ support the MP3 format on the desktop. For smartphones, the decoder is, in many cases, device dependent; though you can reasonably expect an MP3 file to play, it doesn't hurt to have an Ogg Vorbis fallback. MPEG's MP3 has generally been superseded by the more modern and more efficient AAC.

Vorbis

Though commonly referred to as Ogg Vorbis, strictly speaking, this is incorrect. Ogg is the container and Vorbis is the audio track in the container. When Vorbis is found in WebM, it's a WebM audio file, but with a Vorbis encoded audio track. Vorbis has, generally, a higher fidelity than MP3 and is royalty-free. There is no need to choose from a set list of fixed bitrates for Vorbis encoding —you can request the encoder to choose whichever bitrate you require. As is the case for all the Ogg codecs, neither Safari nor IE supports Vorbis out of the box and you need to install extra components to decode them.

Advanced Audio Coding

This format, more commonly known as "AAC," was dragged into prominence by Apple in 1997 when it was designated as the default format for the iTunes store. AAC has been standardized by MPEG in MPEG-2 and in MPEG-4.

In many respects AAC is a more "robust" file format than its MP3 predecessor. It delivers better sound quality at the same bitrate but it can encode audio any bitrate without the 320 Kbps speedbrake applied to the MP3 format. When used in the MP4 container, AAC has multiple profiles for exactly the same reasons—to accommodate varying playback conditions.

As you may have guessed, there is no magical combination of containers and codecs that work across all browsers and devices. For video to work everywhere you will need a minimum of two video files—mp4 and webm—and stand-alone audio will require two files—mp3 and Vorbis. Video is a little more complicated, especially when audio is found in the container. If you are producing WebM files, the combination is VP8 and Vorbis. In the case of MP4, the video codec is H.264 and the audio duties are handled by AAC.

Encoding Video

Now that you understand the file formats and their uses and limitations, let's put that knowledge to work and encode video. Before we start, it is important that you understand why we are using four different pieces of software to create the video files.

The main reason is the skill level of many of you reading this book. It ranges from those new to this subject to those of you who feel comfortable using command lines to accomplish a variety of tasks. Thus the sequence will be Miro Video Converter, Firefogg, the Adobe Media Encoder (AME), and finally FFmpeg. The only commercial product is Adobe's and we include it because, as part of the Creative Cloud, AME has a significant installation base. As well, it gives us the opportunity to explore a critical aspect of MP4 file creation. You will also be asked to make some fundamental decisions while encoding the video file and each of these applications gives us the opportunity to discuss the decisions made.

Finally, other than FFmpeg, you will need to use a combination of encoders because none can be used for everything and the four applications demonstrated contain features common to many of the other products out there.

We start with an uncomplicated encoder: Miro Video Encoder. Alternative open source encoding software with a GUI (graphical user interface) include Handbrake (http://handbrake.fr/) and VLC (www.videolan.org/vlc/index.html), both of which are available in Linux, Mac, and PC versions.

Encoding with Miro Video Converter

If all you are looking for is a dead-simple, easy-to-use encoder then Miro is for you. Having said that, Miro does produce reasonable quality output, but, thanks to its overly simple interface, if you are unhappy with the end result you might want to try one of the other applications presented.

Miro Video Converter is an open source, GPL-licensed application available for Macintosh, Windows, and Linux computers. It is free and you can download the installer at www.mirovideoconverter.com.

Take the following steps to create either the WebM, MP4, or Ogg Theora versions of a video:

1. Run the Miro Video Converter application. When the application launches, you will see the home screen shown in Figure 1-2. Next you will need to add your original video file to the converter queue. Do this by dragging the video file to the drop area, or choose the file through the file selector. Once added, it will appear in the drop area with a thumbnail as shown in the top of Figure 1-3.

Figure 1-2. *The Miro Converter home screen*

2. The plan is to create the WebM version first. To do this, click the Format button and, as shown in Figure 1-3, select WebM HD from the Video selection. The Convert Now button will turn green and change to read Convert to WebM HD. Click it.

Figure 1-3. *Creating a WebM version of a video*

3. As the video is converted you will see a progress bar beside the video thumbnail at the top of the interface. Depending on the size of the video this could be a rather slow process so be patient. The encoder tries to maintain the duration of the original video file, its resolution, its framerate, its audio samplerate, and the number of audio channels that were used in the original audio file.

4. When it finishes you will see a green check mark. Miro places the completed files in a separate folder on a Mac. The easiest way to find any conversion is to click the Show File link and move the file to your project's video folder. Miro also adds the format name to the resulting filename. Feel free to remove it.

You can follow the same process to encode MP4. Just select MP4 from the Video menu in step 2 instead of WebM HD and repeat the same process. Similarly for Ogg Theora, if needed.

This is a great place to demonstrate just how powerful these codecs are when it comes to compression. In Figure 1-4, we have placed the original .mov version of the file above the WebM, MP4, and Ogg Theora versions just created. Note the significant difference in file size—about 180 MB—between the original and its compressed versions. Due to the lossy nature of the codecs there will be a slight loss of quality but not one that is noticeable. In fact, the Miro WebM and MP4 encodings are of comparable quality, maintaining all video parameters except for WebM having resampled the 48 kHz audio to 44.1 kHz. The Ogg Theora version is of much poorer quality because the default Miro encoding setting for Ogg Theora is suboptimal.

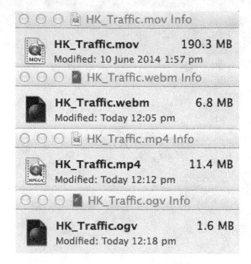

Figure 1-4. *The drop in file size is due to the "lossy" codec*

For you "Power Users": Miro uses FFmpeg under the hood. It calls the FFmpeg command line via python scripts. If you want to make changes to your default encoding of Miro, it is possible to change the python scripts (see www.xlvisuals.com/index.php?/archives/43-How-to-change-Miro-Video-Converter-3.0-output-quality-for-Ogg-Theora-on-OS-X..html). If you make these changes and re-encode Ogg Theora, this will result in a 12.4 MB file of comparable quality to the WebM and MP4 files.

If you open one of the files in a browser, it will expand to the full size of your browser window. This can look a bit fuzzy if your video resolution is smaller than your current browser window. You will need to reduce the size of the browser window to the resolution of your video and the image will become sharper.

As pointed out earlier, you can convert practically any video file to its WebM, Ogg Theora, and MP4 counterparts. You are also given the choice to prepare the file for a number of iOS and Android devices.

In Figure 1-3 you will notice the Apple button on the left side. Click this and you can prepare the file for playback on the full range of Apple iOS devices. When the file is converted, Miro will ask if you want this file placed in your iTunes library. The choice is up to you.

COMPRESSION SCORE CARD FOR MIRO VIDEO CONVERTER

- Original file: 190.3 MB.

- WebM: 6.8 MB.

- MP4: 11.4 MB

- OGG: 1.6 MB.

Encoding Ogg Video with Firefogg

Firefogg is an open source, GPL-licensed Firefox extension whose sole purpose is to encode a video file to WebM or Ogg Theora. To use this extension you will need to have Firefox version 3.5 or higher installed on your computer. To add the extension, head to http://firefogg.org/ and follow the installation instructions.

Follow these steps to encode video using Firefogg:

1. Launch Firefox and point your browser to http://firefogg.org/make/. You will see the Make Web Video page shown in Figure 1-5. Click the Select File ... button and navigate to the file to be encoded.

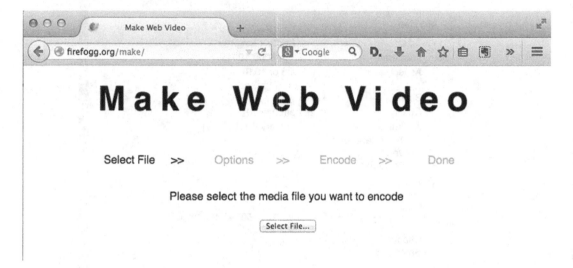

Figure 1-5. *We start by selecting the video to be encoded*

2. When you select the file to be encoded the interface changes to show you the specifications of the original file and two pop-downs for Format and Preset. You can choose between WebM with the VP8 and Vorbis codecs, WebM with the VP9 and Opus codecs, and Ogg Theora with Vorbis. Also choose a Preset adequate to your input file format, which is usually pre-selected for you. If this is as far as you choose to go with adapting encoding parameters, then feel free to click the Encode button. It will ask you what to name the encoded file and where to store it.

3. In this instance, we want to exert a lot more control over the encoding parameters. Click the Advanced Options button. The interface changes to that shown in Figure 1-6. It shows you the most important encoding parameters for WebM (VP8/Vorbis) video. This is actually a subset of the FFmpeg encoding parameters, which—as in the case of Miro Video Encoder—is the actual encoding software used under the hood by Firefogg.

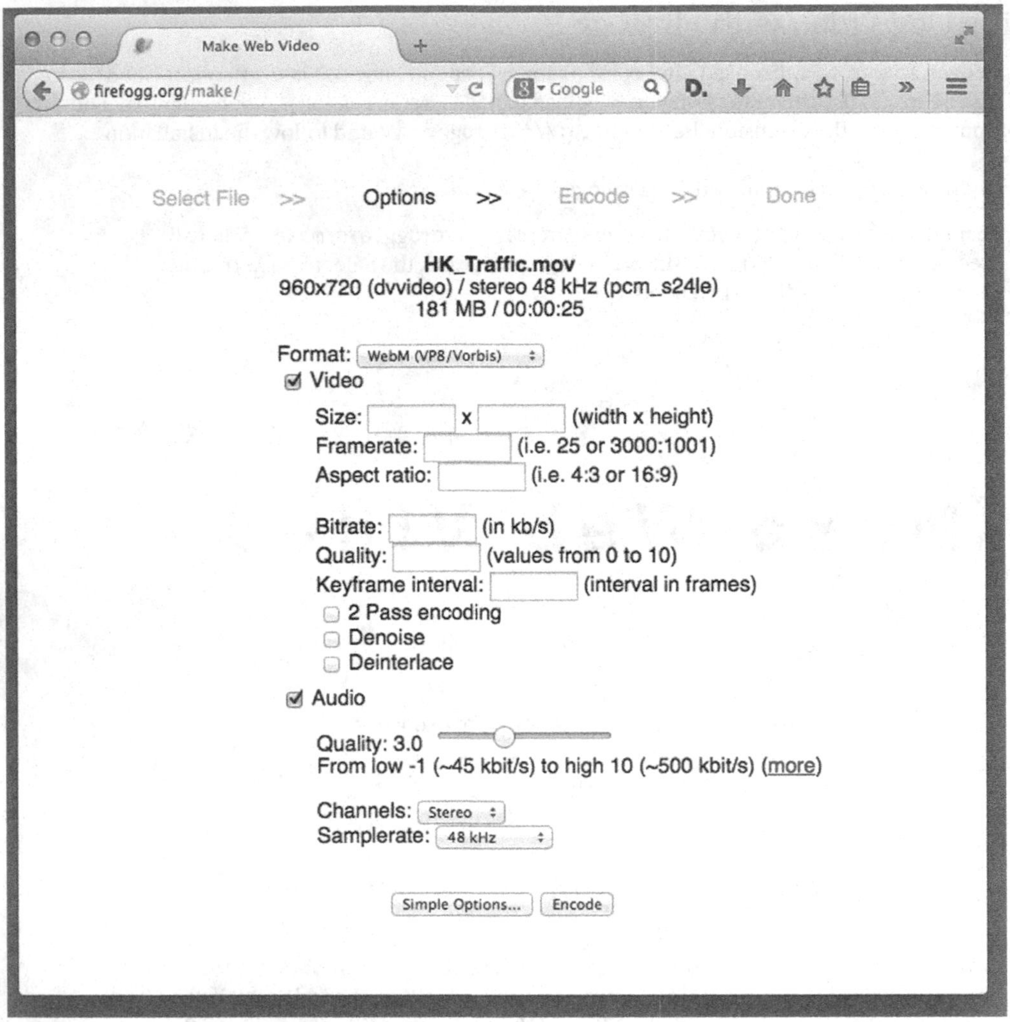

Figure 1-6. *The Firefogg Advanced Options dialog box*

The choices presented here give you absolute control over the quality of the video. Let's go through them.

- **Format:** You are given three choices. The WebM (VP9/Opus) selection offers you the opportunity to use the latest version of the codecs for the WebM format. The WebM (VP8/Vorbis) selection is the most common format and the final choice Ogg (Theora/Vorbis) lets you create an Ogg Theora version of the file. We chose Ogg (Theora/Vorbis).

- **Size:** You can change the resolution of the video but just keep in mind that changing this value without maintaining the aspect ratio will distort the final product or place it in a letterbox. Also, increasing the physical dimensions of the video does nothing more than stretch the input pixels over more output pixels and thus has to create new pixels from the existing ones. This upsampling actually reduces quality through anti-aliasing and should be avoided. We chose to resize this video to 50% and change the width and height values to 480 x 360.

- **Framerate:** If you leave this section blank, the encoding video's framerate will be used. A common framerate is 30 frames per second (fps). If there is not a lot of motion in the video, reducing the fps to 15 will not have a noticeable effect on playback quality. We enter 30 as the value, since our example video is of road traffic and thus has a lot of motion.

- **Aspect Ratio:** If the video is standard definition, enter 4:3. If it is HD, enter 16:9. Our example video is 4:3.

- **Bitrate:** In many respects this is where the "rubber hits the road." There is no magic number here but studies have shown the average US broadband speed is 6.6 megabits per second (Mbps). Don't become attached to that number because those same studies have shown the average mobile broadband speed is 2.7 Mbps. If you are streaming HTML5 video, you may want to target the lowest common denominator, so a good place to start is 2,000. Even then this choice could be dangerous. Bitrate for any video is the sum of the audio and video bitrates. If you decide to use 2,700 Kbps for the video and 700 Kbps for the audio you can pretty well guarantee that the user experience on a mobile device will involve video that starts and stops. In our case, because the physical dimensions of the video are small, we decided to use 1,200 Kbps for the video track which leaves plenty of bandwidth for the audio track.

- **Quality:** Your choices are any number between 0 and 10. The choice affects file size and image quality. If the video was shot using your smartphone, a value between 4 and 6 will work. Save 10 for high-quality studio productions. Our video was shot using a Flip video camera so we chose 6 for our quality setting.

- **Keyframe interval:** This is the time interval between two full-quality video frames. All frames in between will just be difference frames to the previous full video frame, thus providing for good compression. However, difference frames cannot be accessed when seeking, since they cannot be decoded by themselves. By default, Firefogg uses 64 frames as a keyframe interval, which—at 30 fps—means you can basically seek to a 2-sec resolution. That should be acceptable for almost all uses. Leave this blank and let the software do the work using its default setting.

- **2 pass encoding:** We always select this option. This feature, also called "2 pass variable bitrate encoding," always improves the output quality. What it does is to hunt through the video on its first pass looking for abrupt changes between the frames. The second pass does the actual encoding and will make sure to place full-quality keyframes where abrupt changes happen. This avoids difference frames being created across these boundaries, which would obviously be of poor quality. For example, assume the video subject is a car race. The cars will zip by for a few seconds and then there is nothing more than spectators and an empty track. The first pass catches and notes these two transitions. The second pass will reset the keyframe after the cars have zoomed through the frame and allow for a lower bitrate in the shot that has less motion.

- **Denoise:** This filter will attempt to smooth out any artifacts found in the input video. We won't worry about this option.

- **Deinterlace:** Select this only if you are using a clip prepared for broadcast. We won't worry about this option.

The audio choices, as you may have noticed, are a bit limited. Our video contains nothing more than the noise of the traffic on the street and the usual background street noise. With this in mind, we weren't terribly concerned with the audio quality. Still some choices had to be made.

- **Quality:** This slider is a bit deceiving because it actually sets the audio bitrate. We chose a value of 6. If audio quality is of supreme importance select 10. If it is simply unimportant background noise a value of 1 will do. Other than that, only trial and error will help you get the number set to your satisfaction.

- **Channels:** Your choices are stereo and mono. We choose mono because of the nature of the audio. If this file were professionally produced and only destined for desktop playback then stereo would be the logical choice. Also keep in mind that choosing stereo will increase the file size.

- **Sample rate:** The three choices presented determine the accuracy of the audio file. If accuracy is a prime consideration then 48 kHz or 44.1 kHz are the logical choices. We chose 22 kHz since our audio is not that important to be reproduced exactly.

4. With our choices made we clicked the Encode button. You will see the Progress Bar twice as it completes its two passes and the video, Figure 1-7, will launch in the Firefox browser.

Figure 1-7. *The Ogg Video file plays in the Firefox browser*

The previous options are almost identical when encoding WebM. This is because these are rather typical options of any video encoder. There are many more options that you can use in Firefogg when using the Firefogg Javascript API (application programming interface) (see `www.firefogg.org/dev/`). It allows you to include the encoding via the Firefogg Firefox extension in your own Web application.

COMPRESSION SCORE CARD FOR FIREFOGG

- Original file: 190.3 MB.

- WebM (VP8/Vorbis): 14.4 MB.

- WebM (VP9.Opus): 7.6 MB.

- Ogg Theora (default settings): 11.4 MB.

- Ogg Theora (our custom encode): 4.2 MB.

Encoding an MP4 File with the Adobe Media Encoder CC

Encoding an MP4 file involves many of the same decisions around bitrate, audio quality, and so on, as those encountered in the previous example. Though there are a number of products out there that will encode an .mp4, ranging in complexity from video editors to Miro—they are all remarkably similar in that you will be asked to make the same decisions regardless of the product. In this example we are using the Adobe Media Encoder to present those decisions. As well, the Media Encoder adds another degree of complexity to the process outlined to this point in the chapter. So let's get started.

1. When the Media Encoder launches, drag your video into the queue area on the left, as shown in Figure 1-8. Over on the right side of the interface are a number of preset encoding options. We tend to ignore them, preferring, instead, to set our own values rather than use ones that may or may not fit our intention.

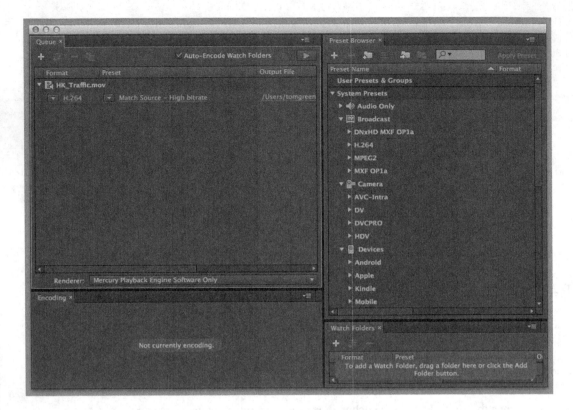

Figure 1-8. *The file to be encoded is added to the Encoding Queue*

2. When the file appears, click on the "Format" link to open the Export Settings dialog box shown in Figure 1-9.

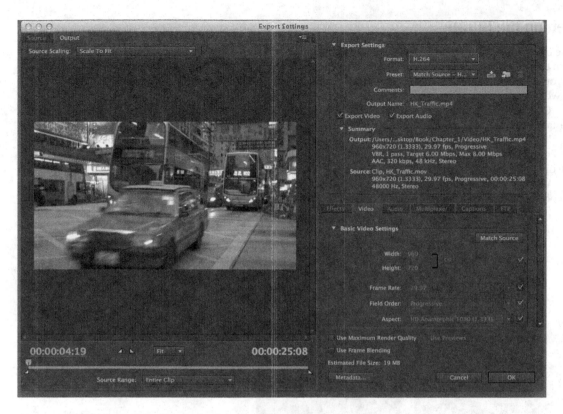

Figure 1-9. *The Export Settings dialog box is where the magic happens*

The left side of the dialog box allows you to set the In and Out points of the video and not much else. The right side of the dialog box is where you make some fundamental decisions.

3. The first decision is which codec to use. We clicked the format pop-down and selected the H.264 codec from the list. You don't need to select a preset but make sure the output name includes the .mp4 extension.

■ **Note** Any output created by the Adobe Media Encoder is placed in the same folder as the source file.

---

4. Select Export Video and Export Audio if they are not selected. Leaving these unchecked will have the obvious consequences.

5. Click the Video tab to edit Basic Video Settings. This is where we set the values for the video part of the MP4 container.

6. Clicking a check box will allow you to change the values in the Basic Video Settings area. If you do need to change the physical dimensions, be sure the chain link is selected and the width and height values will change proportionally.

7. Click the check mark beside "profile" and, as pointed out earlier in this chapter, select the "High" profile, which is used for Web video. If our target included iOS devices, then "Baseline" would be the profile choice.

Setting the Bitrate

The next important decision to be made involves bitrate. If you click the pop-down you will be presented with three choices: CBR (constant bitrate), VBR (variable bitrate),1 Pass, and VBR,2 Pass. You will notice, as you select each one, the Target Bitrate area changes to include an extra slider for the two VBR choices. So what are the differences?

CBR encoding applies the set data rate to your setting to the entire video clip. Use CBR only if your clip contains a similar motion level—think a tree in a field—across the entire clip.

VBR encoding adjusts the data rate down and to the upper limit you set, based on the data required by the compressor. This explains the appearance of that extra slider. Unlike the Ogg Theora example, you get set the upper and target limits for the bitrate.

When it comes to encoding mp4 video, VBR 2 pass is the gold standard. This is the same as the 2 pass encoding that we used for Ogg Theora.

1. Select VBR,2 pass from the pop-down menu.

2. Set the Target Bitrate to 1.2 and the Maximum Bitrate to 1.5 as shown in Figure 1-10. Remember, bitrate is the sum of the audio and video bitrates. We know our bandwidth limit is around 2 Mbps so this leaves us ample room for the audio. Also note, the projected file size is now sitting at 4 MB.

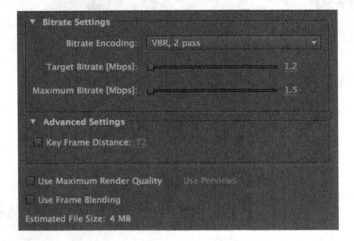

Figure 1-10. *The bitrate targets are set for the H.264 codec in the .mp4 container*

3. Ignore the keyframe distance setting. Leave that to the software. Now we can turn our attention to the audio track in the mp4 container.

Setting the Audio values for the AAC Codec

The mp4 container uses the H.264 codec to compress the video track and the AAC audio codec to compress the audio track in the container. In this example we are going to apply AAC encoding to the audio track in the video. Here's how.

1. Click the Audio tab to open the Audio options shown in Figure 1-11.

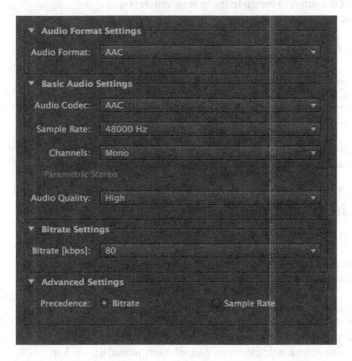

Figure 1-11. *The Audio Encoding options*

2. In the format area select AAC. The other two options—Dolby Digital and MPEG—can't be used for the Web.

3. Select AAC as the audio codec. Though there are two other options—AAC+ Version 1 and AAC+ Version 2—these are more applicable to streaming audio and radio broadcasting.

4. Reduce the Sample Rate to 32000 Hz. The reason is that the audio track is more background noise than anything else and reducing its sample rate won't have a major effect on the audio quality.

5. Select Mono from the Channels pop-down.

6. Set the Audio Quality to High though; with the audio contained in our clip, a quality setting of medium would not be noticeably different.

7. Set the Bitrate value to 64. If this video were to contain a stereo track, then anything between 160 and 96 would be applicable. In our case it is a Mono track and 64 Kbps is a good medium to aim for. Also be aware that bitrate does affect file size. In our case simply selecting 160 Kbps increased the file size by 1 MB.

8. Advanced Settings offers you two choices for Precedence for playback. Obviously, since we are running this file through a browser, Bitrate is the obvious choice.

9. With our choices made, click the OK button to return to the queue. When you arrive click the Green Start Queue button to start the encoding process. When it finishes, you will hear a chime.

COMPRESSION SCORE CARD FOR ADOBE MEDIA ENCODER

- Original file: 190.3 mb.

- MP4: 4 MB.

Encoding Media Resources Using FFmpeg

In this final section of the chapter, we focus on using an open source command-line tool to perform the encoding.

The tool we will be using is FFmpeg, which is also the tool of choice for many online video publishing sites, including, allegedly, YouTube. This software is available to everyone, on every major platform and is vendor-neutral.

Install Windows builds from `http://ffmpeg.zeranoe.com/builds/`. On Mac OS X we recommend using Homebrew (make sure to install it with the following command-line options: `-with-libvorbis`, `–with-libvpx` for WebM support, and `–with-theora` for Theora support). On Linux, there should be a package built for your distribution. Even if you have an exotic platform, you are likely to make it work by compiling from source code.

We start with encoding MPEG-4 H.264 video.

Open source tools for encoding MPEG-4 H.264 basically all use the x264 encoding library, which is published under the GNU GPL license. x264 is among the most feature-complete H.264 codecs and is widely accepted as one of the fastest with highest-quality results.

Let's assume you have a video file from a digital video camera. It could already be in MPEG-4 H.264 format, but let's assume it is in DV, QuickTime, VOB, AVI, MXF, or any other such format. FFmpeg understands almost all input formats (assuming you have the right decoding libraries installed). Running `ffmpeg --formats` will list all the supported codec formats.

To get all the options possible with libx264 encoding in FFmpeg, run the following command:

```
$ ffmpeg -h encoder=libx264
```

There is up-to-date information on command-line switches at `https://trac.ffmpeg.org/wiki/Encode/H.264`.

The following are some of the important command-line switches:

- The -c switch specifies the codec to use. ":v" specifies a video codec and libx264 the x264 encoder. ":a" specifies the audio codec and libfaac the AAC encoder.

- The -profile:v switch specifies a H.264 video profile with a choice of baseline, main or high.

- To constrain a bitrate, use the -b [bitrate] switch, with ":v" for video and ":a" for audio.

- To specify the run in a multi-pass, use the -pass [number] switch.

- To specify the number of audio channels, use -ac [channels] and the sampling rate, use -ar [rate].

Following is a simple command line that converts an input.mov file to an output.mp4 file using the main profile:

```
$ ffmpeg -i input.mov -c:v libx264 -profile:v main -pix_fmt yuv420p -c:a libfaac output.mp4
```

The pixel format needs to be specified because Apple QuickTime only supports YUV planar color space with 4:2:0 chroma subsampling in H.264.

Here is a two-pass encoding example. The first pass only needs video as input because it creates the temporary log files required for input to the second pass.

```
$ ffmpeg -i input.mov -c:v libx264 -profile:v main -b:v 1200k -pass 1 -pix_fmt yuv420p -an
temp.mp4
$ ffmpeg -i input.mov -c:v libx264 -profile:v main -b:v 1200k -pass 2 -pix_fmt yuv420p \
-c:a libfaac -b:a 64k -ac 1 -ar 22050 output.mp4
```

COMPRESSION SCORE CARD FOR FFMPEG MP4

- Original file: 190.3 MB.

- MP4 (unchanged encoding settings): 9.5 MB.

- MP4 (first pass w/o audio): 3.8 MB.

- MP4 (second pass): 4 MB.

Encoding Ogg Theora

Open source tools for encoding Ogg Theora basically use the libtheora encoding library, which is published under a BSD style license by Xiph.org. There are several encoders written on top of libtheora, of which the most broadly used are ffmpeg2theora and FFmpeg.

The main difference between ffmpeg2theora and FFmpeg is that ffmpeg2theora is fixed to use the Xiph libraries for encoding, while FFmpeg has a choice of codec libraries, including its own Vorbis implementation. ffmpeg2theora has far fewer options to worry about. To use FFmpeg for encoding Ogg Theora, make sure to use the libvorbis and vorbis encoding library; otherwise your files may be suboptimal.

Because ffmpeg2theora is optimized toward creating Ogg Theora files and has therefore more specific options and functionality for Ogg Theora, we use it here.

The following command can be used to create an Ogg Theora video file with Vorbis audio. It will simply retain the width, height, and framerate of your input video and the sampling rate and number of channels of your input audio in a new Ogg Theora/Vorbis encoded resource.

```
$ ffmpeg2theora -o output.ogv input.mov
```

Just like MPEG H.264, Ogg Theora also offers the possibility of two-pass encoding to improve the quality of the video image. Here's how to run ffmpeg2theora with two-pass.

```
$ ffmpeg2theora -o output.ogv -- two-pass input.mov
```

There are a lot more options available in ffmpeg2theora. For example, you can include subtitles, metadata, an index to improve seekability on the Ogg Theora file, and even options to improve the video quality with some built-in filters. Note that inclusion of an index has been a default since ffmpeg2theora version 0.27. The index will vastly improve seeking performance in browsers.

You can discover all of the options by calling

```
 $ ffmpeg2theora -h
```

Encoding WebM

Open source tools for encoding WebM basically use the libvpx encoding library, which is published under a BSD style license by Google. FFmpeg has many command line options for encoding WebM. The most important are described here: https://trac.ffmpeg.org/wiki/Encode/VP8.

If you enter the following command, you should be able to create a WebM file with VP8 video and Vorbis audio. It will simply retain the width, height, and framerate of your input video as well as the sample rate and number of channels of your input audio in a new WebM-encoded resource:

```
$ ffmpeg -i input.mov output.webm.
```

Strangely, FFmpeg tries to compress the WebM file to a bitrate of 200 Kbps for the video, which results in pretty poor picture quality.

Following is a command line that targets 1,200 Kbps:

```
$ ffmpeg -i input.mov -b:v 1200k output.webm
```

COMPRESSION SCORE CARD FOR FFMPEG WEBM

- Original file: 190.3 MB.

- WebM (unchanged encoding settings): 1.7 MB.

- WebM (1200Kbps bitrate): 4.2 MB.

Using Online Encoding Services

While you can do video encoding yourself, and even set up your own automated encoding pipeline using FFmpeg, it may be easier to use an online encoding service. There are a large number of services available (e.g., Zencoder, Encoding.com, HeyWatch, Gomi, PandaStream, uEncode), with different pricing options. The use of online encoding services is particularly interesting since they will run the software for you with already optimized parameters, and the cost will scale with the amount of encoding you need to undertake.

Encoding MP3 and Ogg Vorbis Audio Files

As you may have guessed, encoding audio is far easier than encoding video. Several programs are available for encoding an audio recording to the MP3 container format, including lame or FFmpeg (which incidentally uses the same encoding library as lame: libmp3lame). Though most audio-editing software is able to encode MP3, let's use FFmpeg. Here's how.

1. Enter the following command:

    ```
    $ ffmpeg -i audiofile -acodec libmp3lame -aq 0 audio.mp3
    ```

    The aq parameter signifies the audio quality with potential values ranging between 0 and 255 with 0, used in this example, being the best quality. There are further parameters available to change such as bitrate, number of channels, volume, and sampling rate.

    To encode an Ogg Vorbis file

2. Enter the following command:

    ```
    $ ffmpeg -i audiofile -f ogg -acodec libvorbis -ab 192k audio.ogg
    ```

    The ab parameter signifies the target audio bitrate of 192 Kbps. There are further parameters available to change, such as, the number of channels, volume, and sampling rate.

3. You can also use oggenc to encode to Ogg Vorbis. This command is slightly easier to use and has some specific Ogg Vorbis functionality. Enter the following command to create an Ogg Vorbis file with a target bitrate of 192K:

    ```
    $ oggenc audiofile -b 192 -o audio.ogg
    ```

    The oggenc command also offers multiple extra parameters, such as the inclusion of skeleton—which will create an index to improve seeking functionality on the file—a quality parameter -q – with values that range between -1 and 10, with 10 being the best quality. The command also includes parameters that let you change channels, audio volume, the samplerate, and a means to include name-value pairs of metadata.

    Oggenc accepts input the audio input file only in raw, wav, or AIFF format, so it's a little more restricted than the ffmpeg command.

Summary

We won't deny this has been a rather "tech heavy" chapter. The reason is simple: You can't really use audio and video files in HTML5 if you don't understand their underlying technologies and how these files are created. We started by explaining container formats and then moved into the all-important codecs. From there we started encoding video. Though we showed you a number of free and commercial tools used to encode video, the stress was on the decisions you will have to make at each step of the process. As we pointed out, these decisions are more subjective than objective and regardless of which software you use to encode video, you will be making similar decisions.

We ended the chapter by moving from GUI-based encoding to using a command line tool—FFmpeg—to create audio and video files. Again, you will have to make the same subjective decisions regarding a number of important factors that have a direct impact on the audio and video output.

Speaking of output, now that you know how the files are created let's play them in HTML5. That's the subject of the next chapter. We'll see you there.

■ ■ ■

CHAPTER 2

Using and Manipulating HTML5 Video and Audio Elements

With the video files encoded we can now turn our attention to the HTML5 markup that plays and controls the video files. In this chapter we will thoroughly review the <video> and <audio> elements introduced in HTML5. We will also be reviewing the various user interfaces used by the modern browsers because they do change from browser to browser. As we move through the chapter you can find all of the examples presented at http://html5videoguide.net.

One final note: HTML5 video continues to be a work in progress. If you discover something isn't quite working as you expect, you really should check the actual specification for any updates that have been added. The HTML5.0 specification can be found at www.w3c.org/TR/html5/. The next version is being developed with new features at www.whatwg.org/specs/web-apps/current-work/multipage/.

■ **Note**   The authors would like to thank the School of Media Studies at Humber College in Toronto for permission to use the Vultures video clip presented in this chapter. We would also like to thank Joseph Labrecque for permission to use the audio clip used in the audio portion of this chapter.

Before we get going, let's keep in mind that the modern browsers, as shown in Figure 2-1, only support specific codecs. This is important for you to know because there will be occasions where you look at a blank screen wondering why the video is missing. The odds are almost 100% the browser doesn't support the codec or file format used.

Browser	WebM	Ogg Theora	MPEG- H.264
Firefox	•	•	•
Safari	--	--	•
Google Chrome	•	•	•
Opera	•	•	--
Internet Explorer	--	--	•

Figure 2-1. *Browser support*

As is so typical with the Web, standards don't remain static. On the horizon are two new codecs—VP9 and H.265—specifically designed to exist in a world slowly moving toward 4K or ultra HD (high definition) video. H.265 is being designed to be a better compressor than H.264 rather than a compressor designed to squash more data into a small space with the inevitable loss of quality.

Another on the horizon is VP9. Unlike H.265, VP9 is open source and royalty free. Developed by Google as the successor to VP8, this also explains why Google has quietly added VP9 support into Chrome and . YouTube. Firefox has also added VP9 support.

Though the new codecs may seem quite different, VP9 and H.265 have something in common: both halve the file size of 720p and 1,080p content, making it far easier to download or stream HD video over relatively slow connections.

The <video> element

HTML5 introduced the <video> element, which allows you to place your video content in a web page without the use of complicated code or <object> and <embed> tags. This element can be placed directly on a page or within a CSS-driven <div> on the page. Throughout this chapter we will be demonstrating the use of the various properties and attributes that apply to HTML 5 video. The markup template used throughout this chapter is really quite basic, as shown in Listing 2-1. Please note that the listing numbers relate to the example files that we have published on http://html5videoguide.net/ so you can more easily locate them.

Listing 2-1. A Bare Video Element

```
<body>
<div class=".container">

    <h1>Beginning HTML5 Media</h1>
    <h2>The basic code:</h2>
    <p>Here is an example of the Video element:</p>

    <video></video>

</div>
</body>
```

The video "magic" all happens between the <video></video> tags. As it stands right now, you will see absolutely nothing because there is no video content being pointed to.

Fallback Content

You may have noticed the <video> element has an opening and closing tag. There are two reasons for this.

First, other elements can be introduced as children of the <video> element—in particular the <source> and <track> elements. We will introduce you to the <track> element in Chapter 4, which deals with accessibility.

Second, anything found inside the <video> element that is not inside a specific child of the <video> element is regarded as "fallback content." By that we mean if the browser doesn't support an element, it will ignore it and, instead, display its contents—in this case the content in the audio and video element. It could be something as simple as the message shown in the code block in Listing 2-2.

Listing 2-2. A Video Element with Fallback Text

```
<video src = "Vultures.mp4">
        Your browser doesn't support the HTML5 video element.
</video>
```

If this were to be loaded into the old Internet Explorer (IE) 6 browser the user would see that message in the block set aside for the video. In fact, it is a best practice to always include fallback content in any page containing HTML5 video.

You can add any HTML markup inside the <video> element including, as we said, <object> and <embed> elements. Thus, for example, you could provide a fallback that displays a Flash Video file that uses the mp4 or flv format, always assuming that a legacy browser without media element support will at least have Adobe Flash support.

Such video plug-ins will not support the JavaScript API (Application Programming Interface) of the HTML5 <video> element, but you can get JavaScript libraries that emulate some of the JavaScript API functionality and can be used to provide fallback under a variety of conditions. Example libraries, two of which we explore in the next chapter, are

> mwEmbed: https://github.com/kaltura/mwEmbed
>
> Video For Everybody: http://camendesign.com/code/video_for_everybody
>
> Sublime Video: www.sublimevideo.net/
>
> VideoJS: www.videojs.com/
>
> JW Player: www.jwplayer.com/

Also keep in mind that even though you may be using a modern browser, if it does not support ogv, for example, it will not display the fallback content. You have to use JavaScript to catch this error and we'll get into how to catch this load error in Chapter 3. This really is relevant only if you intend to use a single-media format and want to catch errors for browsers that don't support your choice.

So much for introducing the <video> element; let's move on to a review of all the content attributes of the <video> element to explore just how robust the <video> element has become.

@src

At its most basic form, all the <video> element needs is to be pointed to a video file and it takes over from there. Here, Listing 2-3, shows the code.

Listing 2-3. A Video Element with an @src Attribute

```
<video src="video/Vultures.mp4"></video>
```

By simply adding the @src attribute and pointing it to a folder on the site containing the Vultures .mp4 file, we can include a video file on a page. Figure 2-2 shows the result.

The basic code:

Here is an example of the Video element embedding an .mp4 file with @src:

Figure 2-2. *A <video> element with only an @src attribute*

As you may have noticed, the video looks like a simple image. It won't play and only the first frame in the video is displayed—thus the look of an image. Use of the <video> element in this manner only makes sense if the video is to be controlled with JavaScript or your intention is to have the video start playing immediately after loading.

@autoplay

To have the video start automatically you only need to add the @autoplay attribute. Without being set to autoplay, a browser will only download enough bytes from the video to decide whether or not it is able to decode the video and the header. When you talk about HTML5 video, the header really is the video file's metadata, containing information such as the resolution and framerate which we talked about in the last chapter.

When you supply the @autoplay attribute, the video will request more audio and video data after setting up the decode pipeline, buffering the data, and starting playback when sufficient data has been provided and decoded. This explains why some videos take a while to load and others start almost immediately. The browser is making sure it can play the video at the given data rate without draining the buffer.

When you get right down to it, adding an @autoplay attribute with the @src attribute is the bare minimum needed to play a video. The code, shown in Listing 2-4, would be as follows:

Listing 2-4. A Video Element with @autoplay

```
<video src="video/Vultures.webm" autoplay></video>
```

The @autoplay attribute is a "Boolean" attribute, meaning it only has two possible values: True or False, where "True" means that the attribute exists and "False" means it doesn't. By adding @autoplay to the markup, the True value is enabled. With @autoplay enabled, a video will start playing immediately (see Figure 2-3) and stop at the end of the video. Be careful with this one: using @autoplay="false" also enables the attribute through its sheer existence. If you don't want @autoplay, you have to remove it. Give it any value at all and it is enabled.

The basic code:

Here is an example of the Video element playing a .webm file with @autoplay:

Figure 2-3. *A webm file with @autoplay enabled*

The other thing to be aware of is that if the download speed of the video is not fast enough to provide smooth playback or the browser's decoding speed is too slow, the video will stop and start as the buffers are refilled before continuing playback.

Finally, using @autoplay is not regarded as an industry best practice. If you have ever arrived at a site where an annoying video starts playing, you'll understand this. Use this attribute carefully. One place where it can be used freely is in situations where the video is used as a full-page background video without audio and is more of a design element than media.

@muted

It is a best practice to leave the choice of whether or not to play the audio track in a video to the user. However, there will also be occasions where you simply don't need the audio to play. This is accomplished through the @muted attribute as shown in Listing 2-5.

Listing 2-5. A Video Element with @muted

```
<video src="video/Vultures.webm" muted autoplay></video>
```

@muted, like @autoplay, is a Boolean attribute. If muted is present, the value is true and the audio track is turned off. If it isn't, the audio track plays.

If you want to give the user control of the audio, use either the @controls attribute or the JavaScript API.

@loop

The @loop attribute enables a video to automatically restart after it has finished playing. Obviously, this attribute turns the video into a continuous loop. Listing 2-6 shows the code,

Listing 2-6. A Video Element with @loop

```
<video src="video/Vultures.webm" autoplay loop></video>
```

@loop, like @autoplay, is a Boolean attribute, which will play and replay the video continuously until the user either leaves the page or quits the browser. If the video is more of a design element (e.g., full-screen background video) or is relatively short, then feel free to use it. Otherwise this attribute should be used sparingly.

If you want to put a limit on how many times the video loops, you will need to use the JavaScript API.

@poster

When a video loads, the browser typically displays the first frame in the video. Sometimes this first frame has color bars or is all black or all white and is not a good representative for your video. HTML5 allows you to define an image, usually picked from further into the video, as the poster image for the video. You can see this in Figure 2-4. We have gone a few minutes into the video, extracted a picture of a baby vulture, and saved it as a .jpg image for use as the poster frame. When we add this picture in the @poster attribute, Figure 2-4 is the image the user will see when he loads the video.

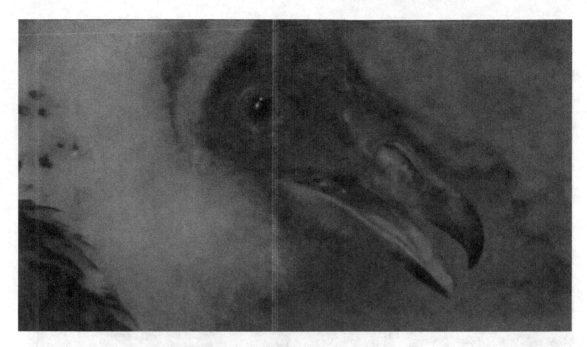

Figure 2-4. *The screenshot to be used as the poster frame*

Poster frames are especially useful for videos that will take some time to load and play back. This way the user isn't staring at a blank area of a page. The neat thing about poster frames is they don't have to be taken from the video. Provided the image has the same physical dimensions as the video, it could be any `.jpg` or `.png` image you create, including a picture with a title text for the video. Some web sites even choose to use a looped animated `.gif` to display a brief video summary.

Listing 2-7 shows the code that loads the `BabyVulture.jpg` image as the poster frame.

Listing 2-7. A Video Element with @poster

```
<video src="video/Vultures.mp4" poster="img/BabyVulture.jpg"></video>
```

There are some differences in the way that the various browsers work with a poster frame. Firefox, Chrome, Opera, and Safari will display the poster (see Figure 2-5) instead of the video and pause if there is no @autoplay attribute. IE is a bit more problematic. IE will display the poster while it is setting up the decoding pipeline, but, as soon as the pipeline is established, it will display a black frame and then transition to the first frame of the video.

The basic code:

Here is an example of the Video element using the @poster attribute to display a poster frame:

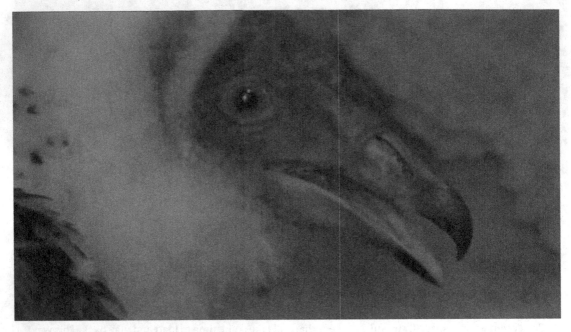

Figure 2-5. *The .jpg image used as a poster frame*

If you use the @autoplay attribute, the poster image will only appear briefly while the video's metadata is loaded and before playback starts. A good rule of thumb is not to use the @poster attribute in conjunction with @autoplay.

@width,@height

To this point in the book we have been displaying the same two videos in the browser and you may have noticed the physical dimensions of the video mirror those of the original source file. How do browsers do that?

Essentially the dimensions are calculated from the first picture of the video resource, which could be obtained from the @poster attribute or the video itself. In the case of the HK_Traffic video used in this example the dimensions are 1,066 x 600 (this is the video's intrinsic size).

If there are no poster or video dimensions available—video load errors or no @poster attribute—the video display area or "viewport" is displayed at 300 x 150 (the minimum display) or at its intrinsic size.

If the poster dimensions and the video dimensions are different, the video will initially display at the poster dimensions and later adapt to the video dimensions.

What you can gather from this is that there is a lot of scaling going on by default. This can actually create a performance bottleneck in the browsers and a disruptive display when the viewport suddenly changes size between a differently scaled poster image and the video. To avoid this, we recommend the use of the @width and @height attributes in the <video> element—or even better, the use of width and height CSS attributes.

What values should be used? The @width and @height attributes can be expressed as either pixels (px) or percentages (%). The only browser that won't accept a percentage value is IE9, which interprets the percentage as a px value (subsequently fixed in IE10). In a responsive web environment, where percentages reign supreme, our suggestion is to use CSS for percentage.

Listing 2-8 shows the code that uses the @width and @height attributes.

Listing 2-8. A Video Element with @width and @height Percentages

```
<video src="video/HK_Traffic.mp4" width="50%" height="50%"></video>
```

If we were to use numbers instead of percentages the code line would be as shown in Listing 2-9.

Listing 2-9. A Video Element with @width and @height in Pixels

```
<video src="video/HK_Traffic.mp4" width="533px" height="300px"></video>
```

Though you can use px, a more common application is to simply forget the px and use numbers instead. Listing 2-10 shows an example.

Listing 2-10. A Video Element with @width and @height with No Measurement Units

```
<video src="video/HK_Traffic.mp4" width="533" height="300"></video>
```

The result, as shown in Figure 2-6, is a video scaled to one-half of its size in the viewport.

The basic code:

Here is an example of the Video element changing the @width and @height attributes:

Figure 2-6. *The video is scaled to 50% of its original size*

Naturally, there are issues and the bulk of them relate to the inclusion of percentages. Let's look a little deeper. When a percentage value is used for both the poster and the video, Firefox will scale both the video and the poster to the value required. Not Safari and Chrome. They scale to the value of the height of the poster image.

Sizing by giving fixed pixel values doesn't come without its "issues" because CSS pixels, not screen pixels, are used to define pixels. A CSS pixel is a unit of measurement that establishes an optical standard for the length of a pixel and is totally independent of the size of the screen of a device. In the W3C standard for CSS3, this unit is described as roughly 1/96th of an inch (before CSS3, a pixel was defined as one device pixel on a standard 96 dpi monitor positioned roughly arm's length from the observer, which is now called a reference pixel (see www.w3.org/TR/css3-values/#absolute-lengths). This explains why content on devices is sometimes rather fuzzy. The CSS pixel, in this case, may just be larger than the device pixel on the screen.

Another pain point you may encounter with the @width and @height attributes is the aspect ratio. If a video with an aspect ratio of 16:9 (1280 x 720) is reduced to a 4:3 ratio (640 x 480) the video will be placed in a letterbox or pillarbox. Note that IE9 uses black bars instead of the transparent ones used by the other browsers.

@controls

The ease of adding video to web pages has made the use of video somewhat ubiquitous. Along with ubiquity comes responsibility. To this point with @autoplay, the video starts playing and plays right through to the end. This is not a best practice. The user should have the ability to choose when to play the video.... not you. Which brings us to the most useful attribute in the arsenal: @controls.

Like @autoplay this one is a Boolean attribute. If specified, controls are displayed when the video is loaded. During playback, the controls are displayed when the user mouses over the video and hidden otherwise.

Listing 2-11 shows the code that uses the @controls attribute.

Listing 2-11. A Video Element with @controls

```
<video src="video/HK_Traffic.mp4" controls></video>
```

The result, shown in Figure 2-7, is that the video now sports a spiffy control bar at the bottom and will not play until the user clicks the Play button.

The basic code:

Here is an example of the Video element with the @controls attribute:

Figure 2-7. *The @controls attribute, shown here in Chrome, adds user controls to a video*

@preload

The final attribute we need to look at is `@preload`.

`@preload` replaces an earlier attribute called `@autobuffer`, which was a Boolean attribute and was thus unable to distinguish between several different buffering requirements of users. This is why the `@preload` attribute was introduced. It allows web developers to give the browser more detailed information about what they expect regarding the user's buffering needs.

The `@preload` attribute is an attribute that you will not ordinarily want to use unless you have very specific needs. Thus, the following paragraphs are only meant for advanced users.

When a web browser encounters a <video> element, it needs to decide what to do with the resource that it links to.

If the <video> element is set to `@autoplay`, then the browser needs to start downloading the video resource, set up the video decoding pipeline, start decoding audio and video frames, and start displaying the decoded audio and video in sync. Typically, the browser will start displaying audio and video even before the full resource has been downloaded, since a video resource is inevitably large and will take a long time to download. Thus, as the web browser is displaying the decoded video, it can, in parallel, continue downloading the remainder of the video resource, decode those frames, buffer them for playback, and display them at the right display time. This approach is called progressive download.

In contrast, if no `@autoplay` attribute is set on <video> and no `@poster` image is given, the browser will display only the first frame of the video resource. It has no need to immediately start a progressive download without even knowing whether the user will start the video playback. Thus, the browser only has to download the video properties and metadata required to set up the decoding pipeline, decode the first video image, and display it. It will then stop downloading the video resource in order not to use up users' bandwidth with data that they may not want to consume. The metadata section of a video resource typically consists of no more than several kilobytes.

A further bandwidth optimization is possible if the <video> element actually has a `@poster` attribute. In this case, the browser may not even bother to start downloading any video resource data and may just display the `@poster` image. Note that, in this situation, the browser is in an information-poor state: it has not been able to discover any metadata about the video resource. In particular, it has not been able to determine the duration of the video, or potentially even whether it is able to decode the resource. Therefore, most browsers on laptop or desktop devices will still download the metadata and the first frame of the video, while on mobile devices, browsers more typically avoid this extra bandwidth use.

As a web developer, you may be in a better position than the web browser to decide what bandwidth use may be acceptable to your users. This decision is also an issue because a delayed download of video data will also cause a delay in playback. Maybe web developers do not want to make their users wait for the decoding pipeline to be set up.

Thus, the `@preload` attribute gives you the explicit means to control the download behavior of the web browser on <video> elements.

The `@preload` attribute can take on the values of "none," "metadata," or "auto."

Let's start with the "none" parameter shown in Listing 2-12.

Listing 2-12. A Video Element with @preload "None"

```
<video src="video/HK_Traffic.ogv" poster="img/Traffic.jpg" preload="none" controls></video>
```

You would choose "none" in a situation where you do not expect the user to actually play back the media resource and want to minimize bandwidth use. A typical example is a web page with many video elements—something like a video gallery—where every video element has a `@poster` image and the browser does not have to decode the first video frame to represent the video resource. In the case of a video gallery, the probability that a user chooses to play back all videos is fairly small. Thus, it is a best practice to set the

@preload attribute to "none" in such a situation and avoid bandwidth wasting, but accept a delay when a video is actually selected for playback. You also accept that some metadata is not actually available for the video and cannot be displayed by the browser (e.g., the duration of the video).

Another choice is to preload the metadata, as shown in Listing 2-13.

Listing 2-13. A Video Element with @preload "Metadata"

```
<video src="video/HK_Traffic.mp4" poster="img/Traffic.jpg" preload="metadata" controls>
</video>
```

You will choose "metadata" in a situation where you need the metadata and possibly the first video frame but do not want the browser to start a progressive download. This could be, for example, a video gallery situation, particularly without poster attributes. In this case, you may want to choose "none" if you are delivering your web page to a mobile device or through a low-bandwidth connection but choose "metadata" on high-bandwidth connections. Also, you may want to choose "metadata" if you are returning to a page with a single video that a user has already visited previously, since you might not expect the user to view the video again, but you do want the metadata and first frame to be displayed. The default preload mode is "metadata".

Listing 2-14 shows the final parameter, "auto."

Listing 2-14. A Video Element with @preload "Auto"

```
<video src="video/HK_Traffic.webm" poster="img/Traffic.jpg" preload="auto" controls></video>
```

You will choose "auto" to encourage the browser to actually start downloading the entire resource (i.e., to do a progressive download even if the video resource is not set to @autoplay). The particular browser may not want to do this (e.g., if it is on a mobile device), but you as a web developer signal in this way to the browser that your server will not have an issue with it and would prefer it in this way to optimize the user experience with as little wait time as possible on playback.

Support for @preload is implemented in Firefox and Safari, such that "none" loads nothing and "metadata" and "auto" set up the video element with its metadata and decoding pipeline, as well as the first video frame as poster frame. Chrome and Opera support it, but you cannot use the same video with different preload strategies on different pages or they will freeze. IE doesn't seem to support the attribute yet and ignores it.

As a recommendation, it is, in general, best not to interfere with the browser's default buffering behavior and to avoid using the @preload attribute.

Before diving further into the functionality of the <video> element, we are going to take a couple of pages to introduce its brother, the <audio> element.

The Audio Element

One of the authors, when delivering media seminars, inevitably refers to audio as being the "red-headed child in a family of blondes." By this he means, audio is inevitably overlooked as web designers and developers focus on the shiny new <video> element. This is a huge mistake because, if properly used, audio can actually "seal the deal." Horror movies wouldn't be creepy if there was a scene where the screen is dark and all you hear is shuffling footsteps.

<audio> shares a lot of markup and functionality with the <video> element, but it does not have @poster, @width, and @height attributes, since the native representation of an <audio> element is to not display visually.

At this point, we need to look at the supported audio codecs in HTML5. Table 2-1 displays the table of codecs supported by the main HTML5 media supporting web browsers.

Table 2-1. *Audio Codecs Natively Supported by the Major Browsers*

Browser	WAV	Ogg Vorbis	MP3	M4A/AAC	WebM Opus
Firefox	✓	✓	✓	*	✓
Safari	✓	--	✓	✓	--
Opera	✓	✓	--	--	✓
Google Chrome	✓	✓	✓	✓	✓
IE	--	--	✓	✓	--

* Firefox supports M4A/AAC on Windows and Linux.

You may have noticed that there isn't a single encoding format supported by all web browsers. It can be expected that IE may implement support for WAV, but as WAV is uncompressed, it is not a very efficient option and should be used only for short audio files. At minimum you will need to provide Ogg Vorbis and MP3 files to publish to all browsers.

@src

Listing 2-15 is a simple code example that will embed an audio resource in HTML5.

Listing 2-15. An Audio Element with @src

```
<audio src="audio/Shivervein_Razorpalm.wav"></audio>

<audio src="audio/Shivervein_Razorpalm.ogg"></audio>

<audio src="audio/Shivervein_Razorpalm.mp3"></audio>
```

This is the absolute minimum code needed to play an audio file. Due to the fact that the audio element has no controls, there will be no visual representation of the <audio> element. This is sensible only in two circumstances: either the <audio> is controlled through JavaScript (see Chapter 3) or the <audio> is set to start playback automatically, for which it requires an @autoplay attribute.

@autoplay

To make the audio autostart, you need to add the @autoplay attribute as used in Listing 2-16.

Listing 2-16. An Audio Element with @autoplay

```
<audio src="audio/Shivervein_Razorpalm.mp3" autoplay></audio>
```

The @autoplay attribute is a Boolean attribute and is supported by all browsers, just as it is with the <video> element. Providing it will make the audio begin playing as soon as the browser has downloaded and decoded sufficient audio data. The audio file will play through once from start to end. We recommend that you use this feature sparingly, since it can be highly irritating for users.

Pay attention to the words "sparingly" and "irritating." There has to be a valid reason for its use such as a background audio file. If your reason is that"It's a cool track," then you might want to reconsider.

@loop

To make the audio automatically restart after finishing playback, you use the @loop attribute shown in Listing 2-17.

Listing 2-17. An Audio Element with @autoplay

```
<audio src="audio/Shivervein_Razorpalm.ogg" autoplay loop></audio>
```

The @loop attribute, in conjunction with the @autoplay attribute, provides a means to set continuously playing "background" music or sound on your web page. This is not recommended; it is just mentioned here for completeness.

If you accidentally or deliberately create several such elements, they will all play at the same time and over the top of each other, but not synchronously. In fact, they may expose a massive drift against each other since each <audio> element only follows its own playback timeline. In Chapter 4 we will learn about the @mediagroup attribute that was defined to synchronize such elements. Unfortunately, it is not currently supported by most browsers. So, you have to use JavaScript to synchronize such elements. You would poll for the current playback time of each element and reset all elements to the same playback position at regular intervals. We will learn about the tools to do this in Chapter 3. For audio streams, you could also use the Web Audio API (see Chapter 6).

@controls

You may have noticed our hectoring around the use of the @autoplay and @loop attributes. If you are planning to display an audio resource on your web page for user interaction rather than for background entertainment, you will need to turn on @controls for your <audio> element as shown in Listing 2-18.

Listing 2-18. An Audio Element with @loop

```
<audio src="audio/Shivervein_Razorpalm.wav" controls></audio>
```

One thing you will notice is that the controls (see Figure 2-8) for various browsers use a different design. Their width and height are different and not all of them display the duration of the audio resource. Since the <audio> element has no intrinsic width and height, the controls may be rendered as the browser finds appropriate. This means that Safari uses a width of 200 px; the others all use a width of 300 px. The height ranges from 25 px (Safari, Opera) to 28 px (Firefox) to 30 px (Google Chrome) to 52 px (IE).

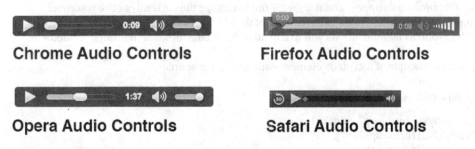

Chrome Audio Controls   **Firefox Audio Controls**

Opera Audio Controls   **Safari Audio Controls**

Figure 2-8. *The audio controls for a number of browsers*

In Chapter 3 we show how you can run your own controls and thus make them consistent across browsers.

@preload

The @preload attribute for <audio> works like the one for <video>. You ordinarily should not have to deal with this attribute. As you can see in the code snippet in Listing 2-19, the @preload attribute accepts three different values: "none," "metadata," or "auto," which are the same values for its <video> cousin.

Listing 2-19. An Audio Element with @preload

```
<audio src="audio/Shivervein_Razorpalm.mp3" controls preload="none"></audio>
```

Web developers may choose "none" in a situation where they do not expect the user to actually play back the media resource and want to minimize bandwidth use. A browser would typically load the setup information of the audio resource, including metadata, such as the duration of the resource. Without the metadata, the duration of the resource cannot be displayed. Thus, choosing no preload only makes sense when dealing with a large number of audio resources. This is typically only useful for web pages that display many audio resources—an archive of podcasts, for example.

Use "metadata" in a situation where you do not expect the user to actually play back the media resource and want to minimize bandwidth use, but not at the cost of missing audio metadata information. This is typically the default behavior of the web browser unless the element is set to autoplay, but can be reinforced by the web developer through this attribute if supported by the browser.

"auto" is typically used in a situation where you expect an audio resource to actually be played back and want to encourage the browser to prebuffer the resource (i.e., to start progressively downloading the complete resource rather than just the setup information). This is typically the case where the <audio> element is the main element on the page, such as a podcast page. The aim of using @preload with "auto" value is to use bandwidth preemptively to create a better user experience with a quicker playback start.

Support for @preload is implemented in most browsers, such that "none" loads nothing and "metadata" and "auto" set up the audio element with its metadata and decoding pipeline.

Now that you are familiar with both the <video> and <audio> elements, we need to examine the <source> element because it has a major role in how both video and audio files will play in the browser.

The Source Element

In the previous chapter you discovered that both the <video> and the <audio> elements, thanks to the browser vendors, do not have a universally supported baseline codec. Therefore, the HTML5 specification has created a means to allow specification of alternative source files through the <source> element. This allows a web developer to integrate all the required links to alternative media resources within the markup without having to test for browsers' support and use JavaScript to change the currently active resource.

Obviously, using individual <video> elements for each of the video types—.mp4, .webm, and .ogg—is simply inefficient. The <source> element allows you to add all of the media files within a single <video> element.

Listing 2-20 shows an example of a <video> element with multiple resources.

Listing 2-20. A Video Element with Different Source Files

```
<video poster="img/BabyVulture.png" controls>
    <source src="video/Vultures.mp4"/>
    <source src="video/Vultures.webm"/>
    <source src="video/Vultures.ogv"/>
</video>
```

For <audio>, shown in Listing 2-21, it looks as follows:

Listing 2-21. An Audio Element with Different Source Files

```
<audio controls>
   <source src="audio/Shivervein_Razorpalm.mp3"/>
   <source src="audio/Shivervein_Razorpalm.ogg"/>
   <source src="audio/Shivervein_Razorpalm.wav"/>
</audio>
```

The <source> element is an empty element. It is not permitted to have any child elements and therefore doesn't have a </source> closing tag. If such a closing tag was used, it would create another <source> element without any attributes, so don't use it. It is, however, possible to add a slash "/" at the end of the <source> element start tag as in <source/>—HTML user agents will parse this—but it is not an HTML5 requirement. If you were using XHTML5, though, you would need to close the empty element in this way to conform with XML requirements.

@src

The list of <source> elements specifies alternative media resources for the <video> or <audio> element, with the @src attribute providing the address of the media resource as a URL (uniform resource locator).

A browser steps through the `<source>` elements in the given order. It will try to load each media resource and the first one that succeeds will be the resource chosen for the <media> element. If none succeeds, the media element load fails, just as it fails when the direct @src attribute's URL of <audio> or <video> cannot be resolved.

For example, the current version of Opera can't play an .mp4 video. In the previous example, it would inspect the .mp4 source and realize, "Nope. Can't use it." Then it will move down the order until it finds one—.webm—that it can use and starts playing it. These file inspections are called **content type sniffing**. They consume valuable time that the browser could use to load a file that it can actually load. This is where the @type attribute comes in.

@type

The <source> element has a @type attribute to specify the media type of the referenced media resource. This attribute is a hint from the web developer and makes it easier for the browser to determine whether it can play the referenced media resource. It will skip over files it is certain it can't load and only test those it has a chance to load.

The @type attributes, shown in Listing 2-22, contain a MIME type with optional codecs parameters.

Listing 2-22. A Video Element with Different Source Files and @type Attributes

```
<video poster="img/BabyVulture.png" controls>
   <source src="video/Vultures.mp4" type='video/mp4'/>
   <source src="video/Vultures.webm" type='video/webm; codecs="vp8, vorbis"'/>
   <source src="video/Vultures.ogv" type='video/ogg; codecs="theora, vorbis"'/>
</video>
```

Note that you need to frame multiple parameters with double quotes and thus you have to put the @type value in single quotes or otherwise escape the double quotes around the @type attribute value. You cannot use single quotes on the codecs parameter, since RFC 4281 (www.ietf.org/rfc/rfc4281.txt) specifies that they have a special meaning. RFC 4281 is the specification that defines the codecs parameter on a MIME type.

41

Embedding audio (see Listing 2-23) with WAV, Ogg Vorbis, and MP3 formats and explicit @type is quite similar.

Listing 2-23. An Audio Element with Different Source Files and @type Attributes

```
<audio controls>
  <source src="audio/Shivervein_Razorpalm.mp3" type="audio/mpeg; codecs=mp3"/>
  <source src="audio/Shivervein_Razorpalm.ogg" type="audio/ogg; codecs=vorbis"/>
  <source src="audio/Shivervein_Razorpalm.wav" type="audio/wav; codecs=1"/>
</audio>
```

The browsers will parse the @type attribute and use it as a hint to determine if they can play the file. MIME types do not always provide a full description of the media resource. For example, if "audio/ogg" is provided, it is unclear whether that would be an Ogg Vorbis, Ogg Flac, Ogg Speex, or an Ogg Opus file. Or if "audio/mpeg" is given, it is unclear whether that would be an MPEG-1 or MPEG-2 audio file Layer 1, 2, or 3 (only Layer 3 is MP3). Also note that codecs=1 for audio/wav is PCM.

Thus, based on the value of the @type attribute, the browser will guess whether it may be able to play the media resource. It can make the following three decisions:

- It does not support the resource type.

- "Maybe": there is a chance that the resource type is supported.

- "Probably": the web browser is confident that it supports the resource type.

A confident decision for "probably" can generally be made only if a codecs parameter is present.

The browser makes a decision for "maybe" based on information it has available as to which codecs it supports. This can be a fixed set of codecs as implemented directly in the browser, or it can be a list of codecs as retrieved from an underlying media framework such as GStreamer, Media Foundation, or QuickTime.

You can use the following code snippet, shown in Listing 2-24, to test your browser for what MIME types it supports:

Listing 2-24. How to Discover Which Video MIME Types Are Supported

```
<p>Video supports the following MIME types:
  <ul>
    <script type="text/javascript">
      var types = new Array();
      types[0] = "video/ogg";
      types[1] = 'video/ogg; codecs="theora, vorbis"';
      types[2] = "video/webm";
      types[3] = 'video/webm; codecs="vp8, vorbis"';
      types[4] = "video/webm";
      types[5] = 'video/webm; codecs="vp9, opus"';
      types[6] = "video/mp4";
      types[7] = 'video/mp4; codecs="avc1.42E01E, mp3"';
      types[8] = "video/mp4";
      types[9] = 'video/mp4; codecs="avc1.42E01E, mp4a.40.2"';
      // create a video element
      var video = document.createElement('video');
      // test types
```

```
    for (i=0; i<types.length; i++) {
      var support = video.canPlayType(types[i]);
      if (support == "") support="no";
      document.write("<li><b>"+types[i]+"</b> : "+support+"</li>");
    }
  </script>
  </ul>
</p>
```

The canPlayType() function is from the JavaScript API, which we will look at in Chapter 3.

The browsers will return "maybe" when given a MIME type without codecs parameters and "probably" when given one with codecs parameters for a format that they support. Otherwise they return the empty string.

As shown in Listing 2-25, you can do the same test for audio.

Listing 2-25. How to Discover Which Audio MIME Types Are Supported

```
<p>Audio supports the following MIME types:
    <ul>
        <script type="text/javascript">
          var types = new Array();
          types[0] = "audio/ogg";
          types[1] = "audio/ogg; codecs=vorbis";
          types[2] = "audio/mpeg";
          types[3] = "audio/mpeg; codecs=mp3";
          types[4] = "audio/wav";
          types[5] = "audio/wav; codecs=1";
          types[6] = "audio/mp4";
          types[7] = "audio/mp4; codecs=mp4a.40.2";
          types[8] = "audio/x-m4b";
          types[9] = "audio/x-m4b; codecs=aac";
          types[10] = "audio/x-m4p";
          types[11] = "audio/x-m4p; codecs=aac";
          types[12] = "audio/aac";
          types[13] = "audio/aac; codecs=aac";
          types[14] = "audio/x-aac";
          types[15] = "audio/x-aac; codecs=aac";
          types[16] = "audio/ogg";
          types[17] = "audio/ogg; codecs=opus";

          // create a audio element
          var audio = document.createElement('audio');
          // test types
          for (i=0; i<types.length; i++) {
            var support = audio.canPlayType(types[i]);
            if (support == "") support="no";
            document.write("<li><b>"+types[i]+"</b> : "+support+"</li>");
          }
        </script>
    </ul>
</p>
```

While all browsers are moving to a so-called sniffing of content types by downloading a small piece of the file to check its type, older browser versions still rely on the MIME types of the files being served correctly. It's best practice to deliver correct MIME types for your files anyway. So, make sure your web server reports the correct MIME types for your files. Usually, there is a mapping between file extensions and MIME types that the web server checks (e.g., for Apache it's the `mime.types` file). In your browser page inspector, check the "content-type" HTTP header that the web browser downloads for a video file to confirm.

Even then, we have to admit we have no control over what screen—Smartphone to the flat-panel TV in your home—will be used to view or listen to your content. In this case you may need to create video files with a variety of resolutions, only one of which gets loaded once the browser figures out what screen is being used. This is where the `@media` attribute plays a huge role in today's Responsive Web Design universe.

The "codecs" parameter in `@type` is optional and even though it helps browsers be more confident around whether they will be able to decode a resource, ultimately that test comes only with trying to load the resource. We therefore recommended that you use only the MIME type without the codecs parameters.

@media

The <source> element only exists to help the browser select the first acceptable media resource from a list. The `@type` attribute helps identify whether the browser supports that media format. The `@media` attribute further provides for associating so-called media queries with a resource.

To preserve your user's sanity, encode your video in an appropriate resolution for the devices you are targeting—it will enable you to both target everything from 4K screen sizes to mobile devices—from the same video element. What you don't do is to adjust the width and height of the video element. You provide copies of the different files called by the media query. You don't want to deliver a huge HD video file to a small mobile screen—it causes the browser to have to download more data than it can display, decode a higher resolution than it can display, and then have to downsample for your actual device. Thus, even a high-quality encoded video will have a poorer rendering on a mobile device than an adequately sized video.

Media queries exist to specify that a specific resource is tailored to a specific (range of) output device(s). For example, a `@media` value of `"min-width: 400px"` specifies that the resource is targeted toward display areas of at least 400 px width.

Many different media queries are possible. Following are just a few examples used on media elements:

- `@media="handheld"` to indicate that the media resource is appropriate for handheld devices.

- `@media="all and (min-device-height:720px)"` to indicate that the media resource is appropriate for screens with 720 lines of pixels or bigger.

- `@media="screen and (min-device-width: 100px)"` to indicate that the media resource is appropriate for screens with 100 lines of pixels or higher.

If you are only concentrating on working with browsers on desktops, laptops, and, in certain instances, tablets, this attribute should not be of much interest.

The Default Player Interfaces

We conclude this discussion with a quick look at the user interfaces the browsers have implemented for audio and video elements. These interface designs are still in flux—YouTube launches a new player interface roughly every six months—and it is likely that web browsers will make improvements and add features to their audio and video players for a while to come.

The default user interface for HTML5 audio and video elements is separated into two different types: the visible controls and the controls hidden in the context menu, usually reached through right-clicking the element. The design of the players is at the discretion of the browsers, which means each player is different.

Visible Controls

We have already encountered the visible controls of the main browsers. In this section we are going to look at them a little more closely in regard to the functionality each browser provides. Controls are mostly identical between audio and video elements.

We start with Firefox's controls shown in Figure 2-9.

Figure 2-9. *The Firefox controls*

Firefox's controls provide the following functionality:

- play/pause toggle

- timeline with direct jump to time offset (seeking)

- timeline displays playback position and buffer progress

- playback time/duration display

- volume slider

- volume on/off button

- full-screen display button

If the video has no audio track, a crossed-out audio volume controller is displayed. The Firefox audio controls have the same functionality except for the full-screen button.

Firefox has made these controls accessible and easily usable through keyboard control.

Firefox's controls also provide the following keyboard access:

- tab: tab onto and off video element.Once on the video element, the following keyboard shortcuts work.

- space bar: toggles between play and pause.

- left/right arrow: winds video forward/back by 15 seconds.

- Command/CTRL+left/right arrow: winds video forward/back by 1/10 of the media duration.

- HOME: jumps to beginning of video.

- End: jumps to end of video.

- up/down arrow: when focused on the volume button, increases/decreases volume.

Full-screen access is not available through a keyboard command.

Macintosh keyboard equivalents are Command for the PC CTRL key and option for the PC Alt key, Function left arrow for the PC Home key, and Function right arrow for the PC End key.

Next up is Safari from Apple. Figure 2-10 shows the Safari player.

Figure 2-10. *The controls on the video elements in Safari*

Safari's controls provide the following functionality:

- 30-second jump back button
- play/pause toggle
- playback time display
- timeline with direct jump to time offset (seeking)
- timeline displays playback position and buffer progress
- playback count-down time display
- volume on/off button with volume slider
- full-screen button

The audio controls have the same functionality as the normal video controls (when displayed at a minimum width of 264 px), except they don't have a full-screen button.

Safari doesn't yet seem to provide keyboard controls for the media elements.

Next, let's take a look at Google Chrome's controls as shown in Figure 2-11.

Figure 2-11. *The controls on the video and audio elements in Google Chrome*

Google Chrome's controls provide the following functionality:

- play/pause toggle
- timeline with direct jump to time offset (seeking)
- timeline displays playback position and buffer progress
- file duration display upon load, playback time display during playback
- volume on/off button
- volume slider
- full-screen button

If the video element has no audio track, the volume button is grayed out. Again, the audio controls are the same as the video controls except they lack the full-screen button.

Google Chrome doesn't yet seem to provide keyboard controls for the media elements.

Next in line is Opera which, as shown in Figure 2-12, closely resembles those from Chrome.

Figure 2-12. *The Opera controls*

Opera's controls provide the following functionality:

- play/pause toggle

- timeline with direct jump to time offset (seeking)

- timeline displays playback position and buffer progress

- file duration display upon load, playback time display during playback

- volume on/off button

- volume slider

- full-screen button

Opera also makes these controls accessible and easily usable through keyboard control. Opera's controls provide the following keyboard access:

- Tab: tab onto play button to transport bar and volume control.

- When on play button: space bar toggles between play and pause.

- When on volume control: space bar toggles between volume on and off.

- When on transport bar: left/right moves to start/end respectively.

- When on transport bar: CTRL-left/right moves 1/10 of the video duration backwards/forwards.

- When on volume control: up/down arrow increases/decreases volume.

Our last browser is Internet Explore 10's controls as shown in Figure 2-13.

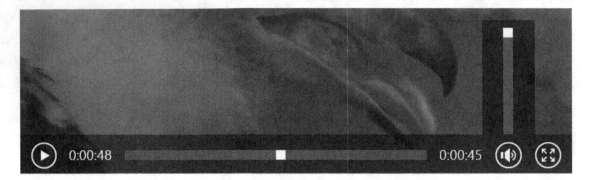

Figure 2-13. The controls on the video and audio elements in IE 10

IE's controls provide the following functionality:

- play/pause toggle
- timeline with direct jump to time offset (seeking)
- timeline displays playback position and buffer progress
- playback time and duration display
- volume slider
- volume on/off button
- full-screen button

IE also makes some of these controls accessible and usable through keyboard control.

- tab: tab onto and away from the video
- space bar: toggles between play and pause
- up/down arrow: increases/decreases volume
- left/right arrow: winds video to the beginning/end

The IE controls are semi-transparent. Firefox's controls are also semi-transparent. All the other browsers have solid-colored controls.

Context Menus

Context menus provide users with shortcuts to common operations. Context menus are visible when the user right-clicks or Control-click's, on a Mac, the video or audio element. Most functionality is the same for audio and video.

Firefox's context menu, Figure 2-14, contains the following items:

- Toggle Play/Pause
- Toggle Mute/Unmute
- Select Play Speed—useful for longer videos
- Toggle Show/Hide controls

- View Video (opens the video by itself in a new tab, similar to View Image).

- Copy Video Location (this is the video URL).

- Save Video As.... Saves the video file locally.

- Save Snapshot As... Saves the current video frame as an image locally.

- Email video... Composes an email with the video URL in the body.

Figure 2-14. *The Firefox context menus*

In the case of Safari, the context menu, shown in Figure 2-15, is a bit different if not minimalist. You have menu items that allow you to Hide the Controls or select a video-only full-screen rendering instead of clicking the Enter Full Screen button on the controller.

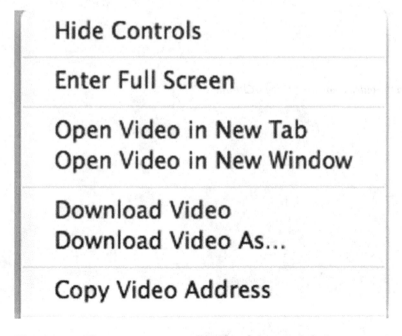

Figure 2-15. *The context menu on the video element in Safari*

Google Chrome's context menu, shown in Figure 2-16, contains the following functionality:

- Toggle Play/Pause
- Toggle Mute/Unmute (when sound is available)
- Toggle Loop on/off
- Toggle Show/Hide controls
- Save Video locally under a name
- Copy Video location
- Open Video in New Tab
- Inspect the <video> element (this feature is for developers who want to inspect the HTML code)

Play
Mute
Loop
✓ Show Controls

Save Video As...
Copy Video URL
Open Video in New Tab

Inspect Element

Figure 2-16. *The context menu on the video element in Google Chrome*

Opera's context menu, shown in Figure 2-17, is pretty similar to the others.

Figure 2-17. *The context menu on the video element in Opera*

The last one is Internet Explorer 10's context menu, shown in Figure 2-18, which offers the usual choices along with an opportunity to Bookmark the page.

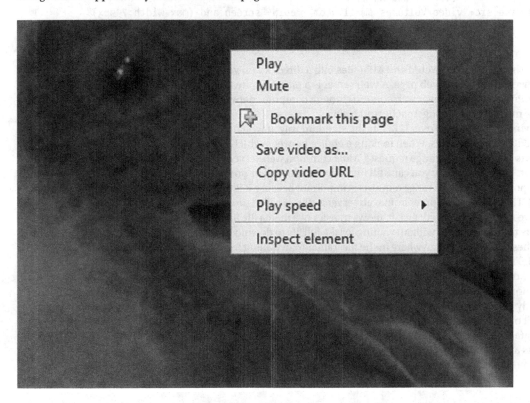

Figure 2-18. *The context menu on the video element in IE*

Publishing

To this point in the chapter we have introduced how to write web pages with HTML5 video elements. In the previous chapter we reviewed how to encode the media files in order to have them supported by HTML5 video capable browsers. Now we close the circle by looking at how to actually publish the videos and their web pages by understanding how these files move from "here"—the server—to "there"—the browser. After this, we have all the tools to make HTML5 web pages with video and audio available.

Here we will merely look at how to publish your set of media files via an ordinary web server. This is the most basic means of publishing.

Remember, you have to create at least one version of your video file in MPEG-4 and one in WebM (or Ogg Theora) to allow you to reach all browsers. For audio files, you will need MP3 and Ogg Vorbis versions. Also, if you are targeting video for a high resolution and a lower resolution, you are best off using different video file versions with different dimensions and use media queries to distinguish between them.

Listing 2-26 shows an example markup for video.

Listing 2-26. A Video Element That Supports Multiple Browsers and Video Element Sizes

```
<video poster="img/BabyVulture.png" controls>
    <source src="video/Vultures.mp4" media="screen and (min-width:800px)"
                type='video/mp4' />
    <source src="video/Vultures-small.mp4" media="screen and (max-width:799px)"
                type='video/mp4' />
    <source src="video/Vultures.webm" media="screen and (min-width:800px)"
                type='video/webm' />
    <source src="video/Vultures-small.webm" media="screen and (max-width:799px)"
                type='video/webm' />
</video>
```

You should copy the WebM and MP4 files into a directory on your web server where it is appropriate for your web application/web page. A web server is a piece of software that can speak HTTP (the HyperText Transfer Protocol) and deliver web content through computer networks. Several open source web servers exist, the most popular being Apache and Nginx.

Serving HTML5 video over HTTP is the standard way in which the HTML5 video element is being supported by web browsers. When making a choice between which server software to choose, make sure it supports HTTP 1.1 byte range requests. Most common web servers, including Apache and Nginx, will support it, but occasionally you can still find one that doesn't or doesn't work properly.

Support for HTTP byte range requests is important because it is the standard way in which browsers receive HTML5 media resources from web servers—this is called progressive download. The importance of byte range requests is twofold: first, it allows transfer of a media file in small chunks, which gives the browser the ability to start playback without waiting for the full file to download. Second, and more important, it allows getting these chunks from anywhere in the file, rather than waiting for all the previous data to have been received. This in particular allows seeking to random locations of the video and starting playback from there.

How does that work? Well, media file decoding is a complicated matter. A media file contains information required to set up the audio and video decoding pipelines (see Chapter 1). This information is typically stored at the beginning of a file. Audio and video data is provided in a multiplexed manner (i.e., a bit of video, then the related bit of audio, then the next bit of video, etc.). To separate between these bits of data, and to get a mapping to playback time, media files often contain an index table. In MP4 files, that index sits at the end of the file. The browser cannot start decoding and playback without receiving this file. So, without byte range requests, we'd have to wait with playback until the complete file was downloaded.

After setting up the metadata and getting the index table, the browser will typically make only one request for the entire media resource and will start playing it back as the data arrives. For a very long file, when download is very far ahead of the current playback position and the user has stopped watching the video, downloading may be paused by the browser. A condition that allows the browser to pause download is that the web server supports byte range requests so the browser may resume downloading when the playback position is again getting closer to the buffered position. This will save bandwidth use, particularly on videos that are longer than a few minutes.

All of the received data will be cached in the browser. When the user seeks and the seek time is not yet buffered, the browser will stop the download and request a byte range that starts at the given time offset the user seeked to.

What we have just described is performed by the browser in the background. It is something the user will never really notice but is important for you to understand.

When setting up your web server to host HTML5 audio and video, you don't have to do anything special. For older browsers, which perform limited content sniffing, you need to ensure that the media resources are served with the correct MIME type. It is possible that your web server may require manually adding some of the following media types to a `mime.types` setup file:

```
audio/ogg     ogg oga
audio/webm    webm
video/ogg     ogv
video/webm    webm
audio/mp4     mp4a
audio/mpeg    mp3
video/mp4     mp4
```

To publish HTML audio and video, you only need to copy the files into a directory structure on your web server and make sure the resource location and hyperlinks are all correct and they work by doing a browser test.

The following text block shows an example layout of a directory structure on a web server (/var/www is the typical root directory of a web site hosted with Apache on a Linux server).

```
/var/www/ - the Web server root directory, exposed e.g. as www.example.net/

/var/www/page.html - the Web page with a video element

/var/www/video/video.webm and
/var/www/video/video.mp4 - the video in two formats

/var/www/thumbs/video.png - the video's thumbnail

/var/www/audio/audio.ogg and
/var/www/audio/audio.mp3 - the compressed audio in two formats
```

What this basically says is that the web page at `www.example.net/page.html` would include a video `<source>` with `video/video.webm` and one with `video/video.mp4`.

To test if your web server supports HTTP 1.1 byte range requests, you can inspect the HTTP header via a browser developer tool or try downloading a video file from the following command line, for example, using a URL loading tool such as curl:

```
$ curl -I  http://www.example.net/video/video.webm
```

You are looking for a response header line that contains "Accept-Ranges: bytes." If that exists, you're fine. If not, you should use a different web server.

Now that you know how to add media, control it, and serve let's take a look at the final piece of the equation—how it is presented to the user through CSS3.

CSS and Video

As is so typical of the evolution of web design and development, things have changed over the years. One of the biggest changes is the shift to Responsive Web Design, which acknowledges that we have no control over the screen/viewport being used to view the content. This has resulted in a move to the use of CSS to control the presentation of a video rather than inline styles whereby the content and its presentation are literally embedded into the body of the HTML document.

Our assumption around CSS is that you have a basic understanding of this technology.

In conjunction with the change to a Responsive universe and the change over to HTML5 there is also an important change in CSS that is underway. A new standard—CSS level 3 or CSS3—is in development which provides many new and improved features including improved layout, shapes, extended media queries, and improvements in rendering text with speech synthesis. Many of these can be applied to HTML5 video and, in this section, we will be taking a brief look at specific examples.

Just to keep things simple, we will be using inline styles to demonstrate techniques rather than using an external style sheet, which is regarded as a best practice.

We start with the basic CSS box model and just add a bit of "jazz" to how the <video> element is presented in the browser. To this point it has simply been treated as content on a page. CSS3 lets you make it more noticeable. In this case we have added a drop shadow and a rounded border, added a bit of padding, and resized the video. Listing 2-27 presents the code.

Listing 2-27. CSS to Make Your Video Look Nicer

```
video{
    width: 80%;
    padding: 15px;
    margin: 0px;
    border: 5px solid black;
    border-radius: 15px;
    box-shadow: 10px 10px 5px gray;
    box-sizing: border-box;
}
```

When viewed in the browser, Figure 2-19 is what the user sees.

The Definitive Guide to HTML 5 Video

The basic code:

Here is an example of CSS3 being used to control the presentation of the video element:

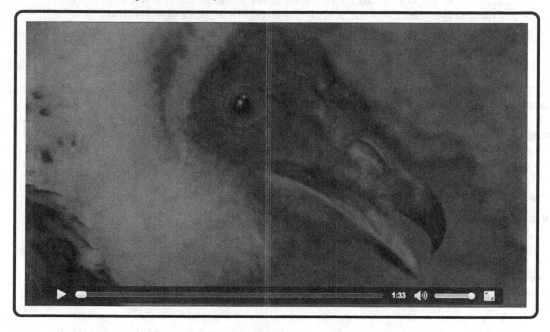

Figure 2-19. *CSS3 styling pulls attention to the video*

It isn't only the styling of the <video> element that can grab the viewer's attention; it is also its positioning on the page that will make it stand out. CSS lays out all elements on a page through its "box model"—that is, all HTML elements are represented by a rectangular box on the page and rendered according to standard rules, all of which can be overruled by CSS properties.

The following are typical CSS properties that are being used to style boxes:

- width and height: as with the @width and @height attributes on HTML elements, you can scale boxes relatively (percentage or em) or absolutely (px).

- padding: space around the content of the box, which shares the background of the content.

- border: the border around the content, including the padding space.

- margin: a transparent space around the outside of the box.

CSS3 introduced many new styling methods, such as border-radius for rounded corners on the box, border-image to use images as borders, border-shadow for drop-shadows, and box-sizing to specify what parts of the box the dimension calculation relates to.

CSS, however, doesn't just do styling. It also takes care of exact positioning of the boxes on the page. This is done first by identifying the box's default display position, then adjusting its position with the "position" and "float" properties

There are three different basic display box types.

- Block boxes (display: block): boxes that are placed on a row by themselves—think of paragraphs of text and how they are placed underneath each other.

- Inline boxes (display: inline): boxes that are placed in the normal flow row by row, usually inside a block box—think of the characters of a sentence of text and how they flow.

- Invisible boxes (display: none): boxes that are not visible on the page (e.g., audio elements without a @controls attribute).

All other display box types are derivatives of these three basic types. Not only that, but you can influence the box type by changing the "display" property on a box.

By default, audio and video have an inline box type. This means they basically behave like a character in a paragraph and move around in the context of neighboring inline box elements and parent block elements.

If we start with the basic code shown in Listing 2-28 we can see this at work in this example with a 50% wide video.

Listing 2-28. A Video Element Is an Inline Element

```
<div class=".container">

    <h2>The basic code:</h2>
    A sentence before the video element.
    <video src ="video/Vultures.mp4"  controls></video>
  A sentence after the video element.
</div>
```

Figure 2-20 shows the result. Note the placement of the sentences above and below the video. This is normal mode.

The Definitive Guide to HTML 5 Video

The basic code:

Here is an example that puts the video in its own (anonymous) block:

A sentence before the video element.

A sentence after the video element.

Figure 2-20. *The video is in its normal inline mode*

To make the video turn up on its own paragraph (line), you can put a <div> or <p> around each of the sentences, which leaves the video in its own anonymous block. You could also put a "display:block" rule on the video element, turning it into a "block" element and forcing the sentence before and after each in their own anonymous block.

Listing 2-29 shows this process with the following markup:

Listing 2-29. Make the Video Stand Out in Its Own Anonymous Block

```
<p>A sentence before the video element.</p>
 <video poster="img/BabyVulture.jpg" controls>
   <source src="video/Vultures.mp4" type='video/mp4'/>
   <source src="video/Vultures.webm" type='video/webm'/>
   <source src="video/Vultures.ogv" type='video/ogg'/>
 </video>
 <p>A sentence after the video element.</p>
```

When you browser test, the content moves to the horizontal content alignment typical of an inline box type as shown in Figure 2-21.

The Definitive Guide to HTML 5 Video

The basic code:

Here is an example that shows that video is an inline element:

A sentence before the video element. 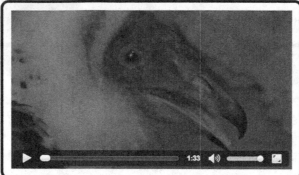 A sentence after the video element.

Figure 2-21. *The video is in its own (anonymous) block*

If we make the video "display:none," it disappears from rendering. We could, instead, make it merely invisible with "visibility:hidden." This will keep the inline video box where it was but make it completely transparent. Note that the video will still preload, so you might want to use @preload="none" to avoid this.

Once the default positioning of the elements on the page has been finished—that is, the browser has placed all the elements in their "normal" display position based on their "display" property—the browser will check on the "position" and "float" properties.

One of the more common techniques is to place the video in a block of text and actually have the text flow around it. This is accomplished using the float property, which can be set to left or right as shown in the code presented in Listing 2-30.

Listing 2-30. Float the Video to the Right Within Its Parent Block

```
video{
    float: right;
    width: 30%;
    padding: 15px;
    margin: 10px;
    border: 5px solid black;
    border-radius: 15px;
    box-shadow: 10px 10px 5px gray;
    box-sizing: border-box;
}
```

The result, shown in Figure 2-22, is text wrapping around a <video> element.

The Definitive Guide to HTML 5 Video

The basic code:

Lorem ipsum dolor sit amet, consectetur adipisicing elit, sed do eiusmod tempor incididunt ut labore et dolore magna aliqua. Ut enim ad minim veniam, quis nostrud exercitation ullamco laboris nisi ut aliquip ex ea commodo consequat. Duis aute irure dolor in reprehenderit in voluptate velit esse cillum dolore eu fugiat nulla pariatur. Excepteur sint occaecat cupidatat non proident, sunt in culpa qui officia deserunt mollit anim id est laborum.

Sed ut perspiciatis unde omnis iste natus error sit voluptatem accusantium doloremque laudantium, totam rem aperiam, eaque ipsa quae ab illo inventore veritatis et quasi architecto beatae vitae dicta sunt explicabo. Nemo enim ipsam voluptatem quia voluptas sit aspernatur aut odit aut fugit, sed quia consequuntur magni dolores eos qui ratione voluptatem sequi nesciunt. Neque porro quisquam est, qui dolorem ipsum quia dolor sit amet, consectetur, adipisci velit, sed quia non numquam eius modi tempora incidunt ut labore et dolore magnam aliquam quaerat voluptatem. Ut enim ad minima veniam, quis nostrum exercitationem ullam corporis suscipit laboriosam, nisi ut aliquid ex ea commodi consequatur? Quis autem vel eum iure reprehenderit qui in ea voluptate velit esse quam nihil molestiae consequatur, vel illum qui dolorem eum fugiat quo voluptas nulla pariatur?

At vero eos et accusamus et iusto odio dignissimos ducimus qui blanditiis praesentium voluptatum deleniti atque corrupti quos dolores et quas molestias excepturi sint occaecati cupiditate non provident, similique sunt in culpa qui officia deserunt mollitia animi, id est laborum et dolorum fuga. Et harum quidem rerum facilis est et expedita distinctio. Nam libero tempore, cum soluta nobis est eligendi optio cumque nihil impedit quo minus id quod maxime placeat facere possimus, omnis voluptas assumenda est, omnis dolor repellendus. Temporibus autem quibusdam et aut officiis debitis aut rerum necessitatibus saepe eveniet ut et voluptates repudiandae sint et molestiae non recusandae. Itaque earum rerum hic tenetur a sapiente delectus, ut aut reiciendis voluptatibus maiores alias consequatur aut perferendis doloribus asperiores repellat

Figure 2-22. *Text wrap using the float:right property*

Now that we understand how CSS can be used to position the `<video>` element, let's take a look at how CSS properties can also change its "look" on the page.

CSS Basic Properties

There are a number of CSS properties that can be applied to HTML5 media elements, but, in the interests of space and time, let's look the following two properties you can apply:

- Opacity: the video is semi-transparent; and

- Gradient: add a color effect to a video.

The opacity property has been around for a long time but has only become standardized across the browsers when it made the official CSS3 lineup. Opacity is defined as any value between 0.0 and 1.0 where 0.0 is when the element is fully transparent and 1.0 where it is fully opaque.

Listing 2-31 presents the code that shows 60% opacity applied to a video and the video moved over the top of an image rendered before it using the "position," "top," and "left" properties.

Listing 2-31. Display a Semi-transparent Video

```
video{
    opacity: 0.6;
    width: 50%;
    padding: 15px;
    margin: 0px;
    border: 5px solid black;
    border-radius: 15px;
    box-shadow: 10px 10px 5px gray;
    box-sizing: border-box;
    position: relative;
```

```
    top: -440px;
    left: 126px;
    background-color: white;
}
...
    <img src="img/BabyVulture.jpg"/>
    <video poster="img/BabyVulture.jpg" controls>
        <source src="video/Vultures.mp4" type='video/mp4'/>
        <source src="video/Vultures.webm" type='video/webm'/>
        <source src="video/Vultures.ogv" type='video/ogg'/>
    </video>
```

As you can see in Figure 2-23 the background image under the video is showing through.

The Definitive Guide to HTML 5 Video

The basic code:

Figure 2-23. *An opacity value of .5 is applied to the video*

Applying a gradient to a video is a pretty interesting challenge. With images, one would put the image into the background and overlay a gradient on top of it. We want to replicate this for video but cannot use CSS to put the video in the background. Thus, we have to render a gradient <div> on top of the video. The CSS3 spec specifies two functions to create gradients: linear-gradient() and radial-gradient().

In our case (see Listing 2-32) we want to apply a linear gradient for the video. To accomplish this we simply created a <div> to hold a gradient that moves from transparent to solid white. Then we overlay the gradient onto the video element using relative positioning.

Listing 2-32. Display a Gradient on Top of the Video

```
<style type= "text/css">
video{
    width: 400px;
        height: 225px;
}
#gradient{
    position: relative;
    width: 400px;
    height: 225px;
    top: -225px;
    background: linear-gradient(rgba(255,255,255,0), white);
    pointer-events: none;
}
</style>
...
    <video src ="video/Vultures.mp4" controls></video>
     <div id="gradient"></div>
```

The key here is the background property. This property requires two values: the start color and the end color. In this case we are moving from a transparent white to an opaque white at the bottom of the gradient. The opacity changes give the effect of the gradient mask over the video. We use the vendor prefixes to ensure the gradient works in all of the browsers. Figure 2-24 shows the end result.

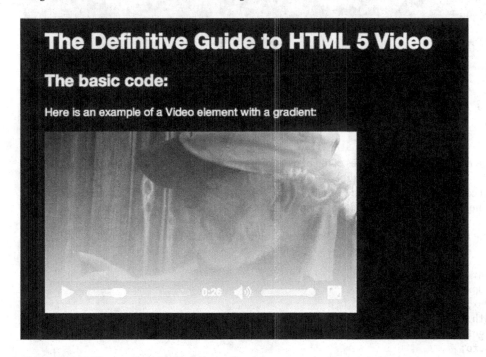

Figure 2-24. *The gradient is placed over the video*

A side effect of this feature is that the video, as you can see, is actually hidden underneath the gradient <div>. The implication here is that the controls are hidden from user interaction. You have to set the CSS pointer-event property on the gradient <div> to "none" to get pointer events redirected to the video element.

You could also set the video to autoplay and remove the @controls attribute instead, but then users cannot interact with the video. Your last resort would be to create your own JavaScript controls. We will teach how to do this in the next chapter.

Playing Background Video

This technique is becoming quite common. You arrive at a site and there is a full-screen video playing under the content on the page. Though there are a number of rather complicated techniques for accomplishing this, it can easily be done. The trick is in the CSS. One of the CSS properties available is z-position. A positive number puts the <div> with the video in front of everything and a negative number pushes it under everything.

Figure 2-25. *Full-screen background video*

As you can see in Figure 2-25, the names of the book authors are displayed over the video playing in the background.

From this you can surmise, as shown in Listing 2-33, that the video was simply "slid" under the content by using the large negative z-index number in the following code block:

Listing 2-33. Using the CSS z-index Property to Position a Video in the Background

```
#video_bkgrnd{
        position: absolute;
        bottom:0px;
        right:0px;
        min-width:100%;
        min-height:100%;
        width:auto;
        height:auto;
        z-index: -1000;
        overflow:hidden;
}
```

```
<video id="video_bkgrnd" poster ="img/BabyVultures.jpg" muted autoplay loop >
  <source src="video/HK_Traffic.mp4" type="video/mp4">
  <source src="video/HK_Traffic.webm" type="video/webm">
  <source src="video/HK_Traffic.ogv" type="video/ogg">
  <p>This browser can't show HTML5 video.</p>
</video>
```

Obviously, having controls and audio for this sort of thing is out of the question, and because we don't have any control over how long the user stays on the page, the video should loop, which is why it has a @loop attribute in Listing 2-33.

Though this technique is in the realm of "cool," it is one you need to use with a high degree of caution.

First, the physical dimensions of the video pretty well shackle it to desktop use. Even then this technique is best-suited to looping videos that are short—around 10–30 seconds—and whose file size is not large. For example, reducing the video's color depth to grayscale or 8-bit (256 colors) will have a significant impact on the final file size. Also, the video needs to be compressed as effectively as possible while still being able to scale across devices and screens. As a rule of thumb, try to keep the file size under 5 mb with 500k being the ideal.

Ideally the video should display a placeholder image to accommodate browsers that do not support HTML5. This placeholder image will also be used a background on mobile devices because most phones and tablets do not support autoplay.

CSS 2D Transforms

A really neat feature of the CSS3 specification is the use of transforms which allow you to reposition the video in its CSS box. The following transform functions are available:

- matrix: describes a linear transformation on the box.

- rotate, rotateX, rotateY: describes how the box is rotated.

- scale, scaleX, scaleY: describes how the x and y axes of the box should be rotated.

- skew, skewX, skewY: describes how the x and y axes should skew based on an angle.

- translate, translateX, translateY: describes the horizontal or vertical repositioning of the box.

In this example we rotate the video -30 degrees. The code in Listing 2-34 makes this happen.

Listing 2-34. Display a -30 Degree Slanted Video

```
video {
 width: 50%;
 transform: rotate(-30deg);
 -webkit-transform: rotate(-30deg);
 position: relative;
 left: 100px;
}

<body>
  <video src="media/HK_Traffic_1.mp4" controls/>
</body>
```

In this example the video is simply rotated 30 degrees to the left using the transform property. We used the –webkit prefix to make this work in Chrome, Safari, and Opera, which are in the process of removing this prefix.

Figure 2-26 shows the end result.

The basic code:

Here is an example of a slanted video element:

Figure 2-26. *The rotate transform applied to the video*

CSS Animations

CSS3 introduces animations that allow you to put objects in motion without writing JavaScript.

Ignoring JavaScript when this specification was being discussed was not without controversy because JavaScript already allows the same effects. However, a key web principle won the day. The principle was one we have stressed throughout this chapter: HTML manages content, CSS handles display, and JavaScript handles interactivity.

Animations are really nothing more than an extension of the CSS transitions. They have a start state and an end state and the object moves from "here" to "there" over a given length of time. You can also add a series of intermediate states to the action through the use of the @keyframes selector.

Listing 2-35 shows the code that moves a video from left to right and back again.

Listing 2-35. The Video Element Moves Twice Between the 0 and the 600 px Mark

```
@keyframes moveIt {
  0% {transform: translateX(0);}
  100% {transform: translateX(600px);}
}
video{
    width: 200px;
    animation-name: moveIt;
    animation-duration: 2s;
    animation-timing-function: ease-out;
    animation-iteration-count: 4;
    animation-fill-mode: forwards;
    animation-direction: alternate;
}
```

We have left out the -webkit prefixes, which are necessary for all browsers except IE and Firefox. Figure 2-27 shows the initial and an intermediate state of the animated video element.

Here is an example of an animated video element:

Here is an example of an animated video element:

Figure 2-27. *Two states of the animated video element*

As you can see from the code, there are actually two pieces to the code. The properties start with a name—moveIt—which makes the link to the @keyframes rule. The @keyframes rule defines the animation stepping points. The video moves across the screen over two seconds and the alternate property simply reverses the animation. You should also pay particular attention to animation-time-function property, which applies easing to the motion.

The @keyframes rule sets the limits on the distance of the motion on the X axis.

We have given merely a small introduction to the use of CSS with the video element. CSS3 in particular has many more features that can be applied to CSS boxes. The visuals that you can develop are almost limitless. In a previous book version we have shown spinning 3D cubes with video running on each side.

Summary

As you have discovered throughout this chapter there is a lot more to working with HTML5 video than simply placing it between the <video></video> tags. We covered

- A thorough review of the <video> element

- A review of the attributes that can be applied to the <video> element

- How to use the attributes for the <audio> element

- A thorough review of how media moves from a server to a web page

- Where CSS fits into the design and development process including the use of CSS transforms, CSS transitions, and CSS animations

That is a lot of stuff to cover, but it is what you need to know to successfully add audio or video to an HTML5 page. In the next chapter we dig into making media interactive through the use of the JavaScript API. We'll see you there.

CHAPTER 3

■ ■ ■

The JavaScript API

With the rise of HTML5 there has been a corresponding rise in the use of JavaScript to extend the functionality of the various elements on a web page. In fact, it is becoming increasingly rare to see an HTML5 page that doesn't include a link to a JavaScript document or library in the header or elsewhere in the document. It is no different when it comes to working with HTML5 video or audio.

JavaScript is the scripting language used in web browsers for client-side programming tasks. JavaScript as used in web browsers is a dialect of the standardized ECMAScript (www.ecma-international.org/publications/standards/Ecma-262.htm) programming language. JavaScript programs can execute all kinds of tasks ranging from the simple to the complex for web pages, ranging from the manipulation of a simple user interface feature to the execution of a complex image analysis program. JavaScript overcomes the limitations of HTML and CSS by providing full flexibility to programmatically change anything in the Document Object Model (DOM).

Since JavaScript support can be turned off in a web browser, it was important to explain what HTML and CSS provide without further scripting. Adding JavaScript to the mix, however, turns these web technologies into a powerful platform for the development of applications and we will see what the media elements can contribute.

In the years before the development of HTML5 and CSS3, JavaScript was used to bring many new features to the Web. Where many people shared common requirements, JavaScript libraries and frameworks such as jQuery, YUI, Dojo, or MooTools were created. These frameworks were used by many web developers to simplify the development of web content. The experience with these libraries, in turn, motivated the introduction of several of the new features of HTML5. As a consequence, we now see many of the functionalities of those early frameworks available natively in HTML5 and new frameworks evolving that make it easier to develop HTML5 web applications.

Since JavaScript executes in the web browser, it uses only the resources of the user's machine rather than having to interact with the web server to make changes to the web page. This is particularly useful for dealing with any kind of user input and makes web pages much more responsive to users since no exchanges over a network will slow down the web page's response. The use of JavaScript is therefore most appropriate where user information is not required to be saved on the server. For example, a game can be written in such a way that the game's logic executes in JavaScript in the web browser and only the achieved high score of the user requires an interaction with the web server. This of course assumes that all the required assets for the game—images, audio, etc.—have been retrieved.

JavaScript interfaces with HTML through the DOM. The DOM is a hierarchical object structure that contains all the elements of a web page as objects with their attribute values and access functions. It represents the hierarchical structure of the HTML document and allows JavaScript to gain access to the HTML objects. WebIDL, the Web interface definition language (www.w3.org/TR/WebIDL/), has been created to allow for the specification of the interfaces that the objects expose to JavaScript and that web browsers implement.

The reason for this is pretty simple. HTML is merely a markup language to put objects on a page. These objects and their attributes are held by the browser and exposed through a programming interface. IDL is really a language to describe these data structures that the browser holds and make them available to JavaScript for manipulation.

WebIDL is particularly purpose-built to

- provide convenience structures that are used often in HTML, such as collections of DOM nodes, token lists, or lists of name-value pairs.

- expose the content attributes of the HTML element and enable the getting and setting of their values.

- explain what JavaScript types HTML element attributes map to and how.

- explain the transformations that have to be made to attribute values upon reading them and before handing them to JavaScript (e.g., the resolution of a uniform resource locator from a relative to an absolute URL).

- list the states that an element may go through and the events that may be executed on them.

- relate to the browsing context of the HTML document.

It is important to understand the difference between the attributes of the HTML5 elements introduced in Chapter 2 and attributes that are exposed for an element in the DOM. The former are called **content attributes**, while the latter are called **IDL attributes.** The easiest way to understand the difference between the two is that the attributes used in the HTML markup are **content attributes** with their values being merely strings. Their same-named brothers available in JavaScript objects are **IDL attributes** and contain values that are of specific JavaScript types. For example, a content attribute with a string value of "1.0" gets exposed to JavaScript as an IDL attribute with a floating point value of 1.0.

To simplify explanation of the JavaScript API of the media elements, we will look at the IDL attributes that were created from content attributes and IDL-only attributes separately. This will provide a better understanding of which attributes come through to JavaScript from HTML and which are created to allow script control and manipulation.

For the purposes of this chapter, we assume that you have a basic understanding of JavaScript and can follow the WebIDL specifications. Reading WebIDL is rather simple and compares to reading the class definitions in many object-oriented programming languages. We will explain the newly introduced interfaces that the HTML5 media elements provide to JavaScript in WebIDL and provide some examples regarding what can be achieved with JavaScript by using these interfaces. We start with content attributes.

Reflected Content Attributes

We have already become acquainted with the content attributes of the HTML5 media elements in Chapter 2. All of them map straight into the IDL interface of the media elements. The HTML specification calls this mapping a "reflection" of the content attributes in IDL attributes. You can see the reflection of the content attributes from Chapter 2 in the media element JavaScript objects.

```
interface HTMLMediaElement : HTMLElement {
    attribute DOMString src;
    attribute DOMString crossOrigin;
    attribute DOMString preload;
    attribute boolean autoplay;
    attribute boolean loop;
    attribute boolean controls;
    attribute boolean defaultMuted;
};
```

```
interface HTMLAudioElement : HTMLMediaElement {};

interface HTMLVideoElement : HTMLMediaElement {
  attribute unsigned long width;
  attribute unsigned long height;
  attribute DOMString poster;
};

interface HTMLSourceElement : HTMLElement {
  attribute DOMString src;
  attribute DOMString type;
  attribute DOMString media;
};
```

If you work your way through the list, every element and attribute presented in Chapter 2 makes an appearance. All these attributes can be read (also called "get") and set in JavaScript. You can see the JavaScript types that the content attributes' values get converted into in the aforementioned code block.

So how does this work on an HTML5 document? The code examples are made available to follow up with at http://html5videoguide.net/. The following code in Listing 3-1 shows an example of how you can set and get some of the content attribute properties through the IDL attributes:

Listing 3-1. Getting a Feeling for the Content Attributes on Media Elements

```
<video controls autoplay>
  <source src="video/HK_Traffic.mp4" type="video/mp4">
  <source src="video/HK_Traffic.webm" type= "video/webm">
</video>

<script type="text/javascript">
  videos = document.getElementsByTagName("video");
  video = videos[0];
  video.controls = false;
  video.width = '400';
  alert(video.autoplay);
</script>
```

We start by adding a video element and then toss in both the controls and autoplay parameters. From there we simply add the source attributes pointing to the videos and we are, for all intents and purposes, good to go. How certain video properties "work," though, is now shifted out of the hands of the HTML and handed over to the JavaScript between the <script></script> tags at the bottom of the code block.

Note how we display the value of the autoplay content attribute through a "getter" API (application programming interface) function and change the values of the width and controls attributes through a "setter," which make the video shrink to 400 pixels wide and the controls disappear.

When you open the page in the browser you can see that "getter" in action. The alert you see (Figure 3-1) shows you the autoplay value—true. Click the OK button and the video shrinks from its width of 1,066 pixels to the 400-pixel width set in the script.

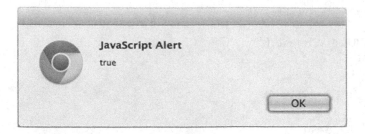

Figure 3-1. *The JavaScript alert telling you that autoplay is true*

Attributes that do not have a value in the HTML source code will be treated as though they have an empty string as their value. This is of particular interest for the src attribute, since it is associated with the video element. However, the media's source URL may actually be specified in a <source> element, as in the previous example. In this case, getting the value of the video's src content attribute will return an empty string. This is where the additional IDL attributes become important.

Further IDL Attributes

IDL attributes—also called DOM attributes—reflect the current state of a media element. We will look at these state-related additional IDL attributes that go beyond the reflected content attributes in this section. They are mostly read-only attributes. Only a few can be set which allow changing the playback of the media element. These are of particular importance to a web developer. Note that there are events being raised as part of changing these state-related IDL attributes. We will describe events as they become relevant and list them comprehensively in the section "States of the Media Element" in this chapter.

The following code block shows a list of these state-related IDL attributes for audio and video elements (the <source> element has no additional IDL attributes to the reflected content attributes—its functionality is contributed to the HTMLMediaElement). The state constants have been omitted from this list and will be described as we go through the IDL attributes. There are quite a few IDL attributes to go through, so we will look at them in subsections of three groups: those conveying general state, those conveying playback-related state, and those conveying error states. Following is the code:

```
interface HTMLMediaElement : HTMLElement {
    // error state
    readonly attribute MediaError error;

    // network state
    readonly attribute DOMString currentSrc;
    readonly attribute unsigned short networkState;
    readonly attribute TimeRanges buffered;

    // ready state
    readonly attribute unsigned short readyState;
    readonly attribute boolean seeking;
```

```
// playback state
        attribute double currentTime;
readonly attribute double duration;
readonly attribute boolean paused;
        attribute double defaultPlaybackRate;
        attribute double playbackRate;
readonly attribute TimeRanges played;
readonly attribute TimeRanges seekable;
readonly attribute boolean ended;

// controls
        attribute double volume;
        attribute boolean defaultMuted;
};

interface HTMLAudioElement : HTMLMediaElement {};

interface HTMLVideoElement : HTMLMediaElement {
    readonly attribute unsigned long videoWidth;
    readonly attribute unsigned long videoHeight;
};
```

■ **Note**   There used to be IDL attributes called startTime, initialTime, and startOffsetTime, all of which were meant to help indicate that a file didn't start at time 0, but at a non-zero time. This functionality has now been moved to a control method called getStartDate(), which we will describe in the section "Control Methods in the API," when we discuss control methods on media elements. If a browser doesn't yet implement the getStartDate() method, you can also get startTime from the first range stored in the @seekable time ranges.

General Features of Media Resources

The following IDL attributes represent general features of a media resource:

- currentSrc
- duration
- volume
- defaultMuted
- videoWidth
- videoHeight

@currentSrc

The resource location of the media element can be specified through @src content attributes either directly on the <audio> or <video> element, or on the selected <source> element. These are part of the HTML markup to give the browser a choice of the best possible resource for its particular situation. The location of the resource that the browser actually selected for use is stored in the @currentSrc IDL attribute and can be read by JavaScript. To dynamically change the resource location of the media element, you can always set the @src content attribute of the media element using JavaScript and call the load() method to reload a new media resource URL. This tells the browser to definitely attempt to load that particular resource.

The process of how a media resource is selected is somewhat complicated. It involves queuing tasks, firing events, setting network states, ready states, and, potentially, error states. This resource selection algorithm is invoked as the media element is loaded and asynchronously executes thereafter. It will also initiate the resource fetch algorithm, which actually downloads the media data and decodes it.

We will look at the different aspects of the resource selection algorithm through the different IDL attributes as we discuss them. Here, we focus on how the media resource location is identified and @currentSrc is set.

@currentSrc is initially an empty string which you can see in Figure 3-2. You cannot rely on it being available to JavaScript before the resource selection algorithm has finished and the browser has started fetching media data. Media fetching is signified by the browser through firing of a progress event. This, however, will not work with an already buffered video resource since, in this case, no progress event is fired. Thus, the event that will indicate that a media resource is now usable is the loadedmetadata event, which works for both newly fetched resources and already buffered resources. In summary, you need to listen for the loadedmetadata event being fired before accessing @currentSrc.

currentSrc on load: .

currentSrc after progress: http://html5videoguide.net/NEW/CH3/video/HK_Traffic.webm.

currentSrc after loadedmetadata: http://html5videoguide.net/NEW/CH3/video/HK_Traffic.webm.

Figure 3-2. *Retrieving the @currentSrc value*

In JavaScript, there are three means for setting up an event listener. The first two follow the traditional model (www.quirksmode.org/js/events_tradmod.html), the third is the W3C's modern and recommended model (www.quirksmode.org/js/events_advanced.html).

The first event listener method uses an event attribute that is created by adding the prefix "on" to the event name. For example,

```
function execute() {
  // do something
}
<video onprogress="execute()" src="video.mp4"></video>
```

The second is to use the event IDL attribute in JavaScript. For example,

```
video.onprogress = execute;
```

The third method follows the W3C's DOM events model (www.w3.org/TR/2000/REC-DOM-Level-2-Events-20001113/events.html) for registering events by explicitly attaching an EventListener to the video.

```
video.addEventListener("progress", execute, false);
```

We'll be using the third method throughout this book.

The following code, seen in Listing 3-2, shows an example of how to retrieve the @currentSrc attribute during page load time, after a progress event and after a loadedmetadata event.

Listing 3-2. Tracking @currentSrc

```
<video controls autoplay width="400">
  <source src="video/HK_Traffic.mp4" type= "video/mp4" >
  <source src="video/HK_Traffic.webm" type="video/webm">
</video>

<p>CurrentSrc on start: <span id="first"></span>.</p>
<p>CurrentSrc after progress: <span id="progress"></span>.</p>
<p>CurrentSrc after loadedmetadata: <span id="loadedmetadata"></span>.</p>

<script type="text/javascript">
  var video = document.getElementsByTagName("video")[0];
  var span1 = document.getElementById("first");
  var span2 = document.getElementById("progress");
  var span3 = document.getElementById("loadedmetadata");

  span1.innerHTML = video.currentSrc;

  function span2Update(evt) {
    span2.innerHTML = video.currentSrc;
  }

  function span3Update(evt) {
    span3.innerHTML = video.currentSrc;
  }

  video.addEventListener("progress", span2Update, false);
  video.addEventListener("loadedmetadata", span3Update, false);
</script>
```

Essentially, JavaScript is identifying the elements in the HTML and, as shown in Figure 3-2, is printing the state of the @currentSrc attribute to the <span> elements during document load, after a progress event and after a loadedmetadata event.

There are a couple of differences in how the browsers handle this IDL. Internet Explorer (IE) will display a loaded resource on start, while the others don't. This is because IE has already parsed the DOM by the time it executes that line of JavaScript, while the others haven't. This merely shows that you cannot rely on reading the @currentSrc attribute before the loadedmetadata event has fired.

@duration

When a media resource's metadata is loaded and before any media data is played back, you can get the duration of the audio or video file. The read-only @duration IDL attribute returns the time of the end of the media resource in seconds. During loading time, @duration will return the NaN value (Not-a-Number). If it is a live or an unbound stream, the duration is *infinity*, unless the stream ends, at which time the duration changes to the duration given through the last samples in the stream.

Every update of the @duration of the media resource causes a durationchange event to be fired, so you can always retrieve the exact @duration value that the browser is working with. A durationchange event is also fired when a different resource is loaded by changing @src.

Listing 3-3 shows an example of how to retrieve the @duration attribute during page load time, after a loadedmetadata event, a durationchange event, and an ended event.

Listing 3-3. Getting the Resource Duration at Different Stages of the Resource Loading Process

```
<video controls autoplay width="400">
  <source src="video/HK_Traffic.mp4" type= "video/mp4" >
  <source src="vidoe/HK_Traffic.webm" type="video/webm">
</video>

<p>duration on start: <span id="duration_first"></span>.</p>
<p>duration after loadedmetadata: <span id="duration_loadedmetadata"></span>.</p>
<p>duration after durationchange: <span id="duration_durationchange"></span>.</p>
<p>duration after ended: <span id="duration_ended"></span>.</p>

<script type="text/javascript">
  var video = document.getElementsByTagName("video")[0];
  var span1 = document.getElementById("duration_first");
  var span2 = document.getElementById("duration_loadedmetadata");
  var span3 = document.getElementById("duration_durationchange");
  var span4 = document.getElementById("duration_ended");

  span1.innerHTML = video.duration;

  function span2Update(evt) {  span2.innerHTML = video.duration; }
  function span3Update(evt) {  span3.innerHTML = video.duration; }
  function span4Update(evt) {  span4.innerHTML = video.duration; }

  video.addEventListener("loadedmetadata", span2Update, false);
  video.addEventListener("durationchange", span3Update, false);
  video.addEventListener("ended", span4Update, false);
</script>
```

The browsers such as Chrome (Figure 3-3) will show rather long numbers. Safari, for example will display a value of 25.343979 while Firefox and Opera return 25.357.

duration on load: NaN.

duration after loadedmetadata: 25.343979.

duration after durationchange: 25.343979.

duration after ended: 25.343979.

Figure 3-3. *Getting the duration value for a media element*

■ **Note**   Transcoded versions can be slightly different in duration (e.g., because some codecs can only encode audio samples in chunks of a fixed size). In this case, our input QuickTime file was 25.291933s long, the transcoded MP4 file is 25.343978s long, and the transcoded WebM file is 25.357000s (using ffprobe). It seems likely that Safari, Chrome, and ffprobe all use slightly different approaches and resolutions to calculate the duration of the MP4 file—possibly because of a difference in counting leading silence as part of the duration. The lesson to be learned here is that time is a matter of uncertain accuracy in video. If you have to check on playback positions or duration, treat them as inaccurate floating point numbers and check for ranges rather than equality.

@volume

When reading the @volume IDL attribute of a media resource, the playback volume of the audio track is returned in the range 0.0 (silent) to 1.0 (loudest). On initial load of the media resource, its @volume is set to the loudest setting 1.0. After use of the media resource and change of its volume setting—through either user or script interaction—the @volume value may have changed. The web browser may remember this setting for a later reload of the resource to allow a user to return to the volume adjustments made earlier.

The @volume IDL attribute can be set through JavaScript to change the volume of the media resource. A value between 0.0 and 1.0 inclusive is allowed—anything else will raise an IndexSizeError exception. The playback volume will be adjusted correspondingly as soon as possible after setting the attribute. Note that the range may not be linear but is determined by the web browser. Further, the loudest setting may be lower than the system's loudest possible setting, since the user's computer's volume setting will control all audio playback on his or her system.

Whenever the volume of the media resource is changed—either through user interaction in the video or audio controls or through JavaScript—a volumechanged event is fired.

The code shown in Listing 3-4 is an example of how to get and set the @volume attribute using an audio element when the timeupdate event is fired.

Listing 3-4. Reading and Changing the Volume of an Audio File During Playback

```
<audio controls autoplay>
    <source src="audio/Shivervein.mp3" type="audio/mp4">
    <source src="audio/Shivervein.ogg" type="audio/ogg">
</audio>

<p>volume on start: <span id="volume_first"></span>.</p>
<p>volume after volumechange: <span id="volumechange"></span>.</p>
<p>volume after timeupdate: <span id="timeupdate"></span>.</p>

<script type="text/javascript">
  var audio = document.getElementsByTagName("audio")[0];
  var span1 = document.getElementById("volume_first");
  var span2 = document.getElementById("volumechange");
  var span3 = document.getElementById("timeupdate");

  span1.innerHTML = audio.volume;

  function span2Update(evt) { span2.innerHTML = audio.volume; }
  function span3Update(evt) {
    if (audio.volume > 0.1) {
      audio.volume = audio.volume - 0.05;
    } else {
      audio.volume = 1.0;
    }
    span3.innerHTML = audio.volume;
  }

  audio.addEventListener("volumechange", span2Update, false);
  audio.addEventListener("timeupdate", span3Update, false);
</script>
```

We reduce the volume by 0.05—`audio.volume = audio.volume - 0.05;`—until we reach a volume of less than 0.1. Then we reset the value to 1.0—`audio.volume = 1.0;`—and start pulling it down again, resulting in a sawtooth of volume state over the duration of the resource. The result is a volume level (see Figure 3-4), which constantly changes as the file plays. This example is a bit disorienting if you try it, but it is a great example of using the @volume IDL attribute.

volume on load: 1.

volume after volumechange: 0.29999999999999966.

volume after timeupdate: 0.29999999999999966.

Figure 3-4. Retrieving and setting the volume value

■ **Note**   The frequency at which `timeupdate` is being called is different between the browsers and as such they all arrive at different volumes at the end of playback.

@defaultMuted

While the @muted IDL attribute allows JavaScript to mute and unmute a media resource, the @defaultMuted attribute reports to JavaScript about the presence of an @muted content attribute in the original HTML markup. Thus, it will report "true" if an @muted attribute was used and "false" otherwise. This allows the JavaScript developer to return @muted to its original state after some muting and unmuting action of the user and of JavaScript.

The code example, Listing 3-5, shows how to get the @defaultMuted attribute and how changing the @muted attribute doesn't change the @defaultMuted attribute. In this example we have a video and an audio element. For the first 5 seconds, the video element is muted and the audio element is playing, then we change the muted state of both.

Listing 3-5. Reading defaultMuted and muted Attributes

```
<video controls autoplay muted width="400">
    <source src="video/HK_Traffic.mp4" type="video/mp4"/>
    <source src="video/HK_Traffic.webm" type="video/webm"/>
</video>

<audio controls autoplay>
    <source src="audio/Shivervein.mp3" type="audio/mp4"/>
    <source src="audio/Shivervein.ogg" type="audio/ogg"/>
</audio>

<p>defaultMuted/muted for video: <span id="muted_v_first"></span>.</p>
<p>defaultMuted/muted for audio: <span id="muted_a_first"></span>.</p>
```

```
<script type="text/javascript">
var video = document.getElementsByTagName("video")[0];
var audio = document.getElementsByTagName("audio")[0];
var span1 = document.getElementById("muted_v_first");
var span2 = document.getElementById("muted_a_first");

function spanUpdate(evt) {
    span1.innerHTML = video.defaultMuted + "/" + video.muted;
    span2.innerHTML = audio.defaultMuted + "/" + audio.muted;
}

function mutedChange(evt) {
    if (video.currentTime > 5) {
        video.muted = !video.muted;
        audio.muted = !audio.muted;
        audio.removeEventListener("timeupdate", mutedChange, false);
    }
}
audio.addEventListener("timeupdate", mutedChange, false);
audio.addEventListener("loadedmetadata", spanUpdate, false);
audio.addEventListener("volumechange", spanUpdate, false);
</script>
```

Figure 3-5 shows the key to this code. The screenshot has been taken at 6 seconds in and shows how, even after changing the muted state of the video and the audio element, JavaScript still reports the video element as being @defaultMuted="true" and the audio element @defaultMuted="false".

defaultMuted/muted for video: true/false.

defaultMuted/muted for audio: false/true.

Figure 3-5. *Retrieving the defaultMuted value and setting the muted value*

@videoWidth, @videoHeight

For video resources, there are the read-only IDL attributes, @videoWidth and @videoHeight, which return the actual width and height of the video, or zero if the dimensions are not known as is the case during video load time. The dimensions are calculated in CSS pixels including information about the resource's dimensions, aspect ratio, resolution, etc., as defined by the resource's file format.

It is very important that you understand the difference between the @width and @height content attributes and these IDL attributes. They do not mean the same thing.

With the @width and @height content attributes, you change the width and height of the video in CSS pixels or in percentages. In contrast, the read-only @videoWidth and @videoHeight IDL attributes refer to the width and height of the video itself as it comes from the decoding pipeline. They represent nothing more than the original dimensions of the video. Changing the @width and @height content attribute values has no effect on the value of the @videoWidth and @videoHeight attributes. Specifying the @width and @height attributes will therefore have the effect of scaling the video from its original @videoWidth and @videoHeight to fit inside the specified dimensions while also maintaining aspect ratio of the original dimensions.

Listing 3-6 shows an example of how to get the @videoWidth and @videoHeight attributes and how their values compare to the @width and @height values.

Listing 3-6. Obtaining videoWidth and videoHeight in Contrast to Width and Height Attributes

```
<video controls width= "400">
    <source src="video/HK_Traffic.mp4" type="video/mp4"/>
    <source src="video/HK_Traffic.webm" type="video/webm"/>
</video>

<p>Dimensions on start: <span id="dimensions_first"></span>.</p>
<p>Dimensions after loadedmetadata: <span id="dimensions_loadedmetadata"></span>.</p>

<script type="text/javascript">
    var video = document.getElementsByTagName("video")[0];
    var span1 = document.getElementById("dimensions_first");
    var span2 = document.getElementById("dimensions_loadedmetadata");

    span1.innerHTML = video.videoWidth + "x" + video.videoHeight + " / "
                                    + video.width + "x" + video.height;
    function span2Update(evt) {
        span2.innerHTML = video.videoWidth + "x" + video.videoHeight + " / "
                                    + video.width + "x" + video.height;
    }

    video.addEventListener("loadedmetadata", span2Update, false);
</script>
```

When you run the code you will see the result shown in Figure 3-6. The important things to note are the dimensions shown. The start dimension is 0 simply because the video is loading. At that time, the content attribute values are already known and therefore @width is "400" and @height is 0, since height hasn't been set on the <video> element. The last line shows the original dimensions of the video, which are now available after having loaded the video's metadata. Incidentally, to get to the actually displayed width and height, you have to use video.clientWidth and video.clientHeight—these are the width and height values of the CSS box model after layout.

Dimensions on load: 0x0 / 400x0.

Dimensions after loadedmetadata: 1066x600 / 400x0.

Figure 3-6. Retrieving the videoWidth *and* videoHeight/*width and height*

Playback-Related Attributes of Media Resources

To this point in the chapter we have concentrated on understanding the generic IDL attributes of the media elements: currentSrc, duration, volume, muted state, original width and height. In this section we will be concentrating on the IDL attributes commonly used to control the playback of a media resource.

The following IDL attributes all relate to playback position and control.

- currentTime
- seeking
- paused
- ended
- defaultPlaybackRate
- playbackRate

@currentTime

This IDL attribute is the basis for any seeking you may do within a video or audio file.

The @currentTime IDL attribute returns the current playback position of the media resource in seconds. Under normal circumstances, the media resource starts at 0, in which case the @currentTime during uninterrupted playback will contain the time passed since starting playback of the media resource.

It is possible to seek to a time offset during video load by setting @currentTime and then @currentTime will immediately start at that offset. It is also possible to use media fragment URIs (uniform resource identifier) (see Chapter 4) for loading media elements and then @currentTime will start at that offset. For example, @src="video.webm#t=10,15" will load the video.webm file and directly seek to 10 seconds time offset, so @currentTime=10 for this video.

The @currentTime can also be set by JavaScript, which will initiate a seek by the web browser to a new playback position. Depending on whether the resource is seekable and the position is both available and reachable, either the @currentTime is successfully changed or an exception is raised.

■ **Tip**   Seeking should only be undertaken when the media element's metadata has been loaded. It is best to wait until a loadedmetadata event before trying to change the @currentTime value, since some browsers will otherwise ignore your seek.

A timeupdate event will be fired upon a successful seek. You have most likely experienced this when you drag a video's seek bar deeper into the video and had to wait for the video to display the video from that point.

A web browser will interrupt any current seeking activities if you start a new seeking action. If you seek to a time where the data is not available yet, current playback (if any) will be stopped and you will have to wait until that data is available. A waiting event will be fired.

If you seek past the end of the media resource, you will be taken to the end. If you seek to a time before the @startTime of the media resource, you will be taken to the @startTime. If you seek to a time that is not seekable (i.e., it is not inside one of the time ranges in the @seekable attribute), the web browser will position the seek to the nearest seekable position. If your seek position is exactly between two seekable positions, you will be positioned at the nearest seekable position that's closest to the current playback position. Unless the media resource is a live streaming resource, all positions in your media resource are typically seekable.

@currentTime provides a means to seek to a precise position. Some browsers are sample accurate in their seeking down to the individual audio sample!

It is important to understand that such precise seeking can be resource intensive. If the seek position falls between two encoded keyframes, the decoder needs to go back to the previous keyframe, which can be a few seconds back. Then it has to decode all the frames from that position to the seek position before being able to display the accurate video frame and audio sample. The WHATWG HTML specification has therefore added a fastSeek() method which takes a seek time as input, but will only seek to the closest keyframe. Thus, the seek position provided to fastSeek() is merely an approximate position, which is often sufficient.

In Listing 3-7, we demonstrate how to get and set the @currentTime attribute. After having played one-third of the resource, we jump forward by a third, and then the next timeupdate event shows the point in the video to where we jumped.

Listing 3-7. Retrieving and Setting the currentTime

```
<video controls width= "400">
    <source src="video/Waterfall.mp4" type="video/mp4"/>
    <source src="video/Waterfal.webm" type="video/webm"/>
</video>

<p>CurrentTime on start: <span id="currentTime_first"></span>.</p>
<p>CurrentTime after timeupdate: <span id="currentTime_timeupdate"></span>.</p>
<p>CurrentTime after ended: <span id="currentTime_ended"></span>.</p>

<script type="text/javascript">
    var video = document.getElementsByTagName("video")[0];
    var span1 = document.getElementById("currentTime_first");
    var span2 = document.getElementById("currentTime_timeupdate");
    var span3 = document.getElementById("currentTime_ended");
```

```
span1.innerHTML = video.currentTime;
function span2Update(evt) {
    span2.innerHTML = video.currentTime;
    video.removeEventListener("timeupdate", span2Update, false);
}
function span3Update(evt) {   span3.innerHTML = video.currentTime; }
function timeupdatecallback(evt) {
    if (video.currentTime > video.duration/3) {
        video.currentTime = 2*video.duration/3;
        video.removeEventListener("timeupdate", timeupdatecallback, false);
        video.addEventListener("timeupdate", span2Update, false);
    }
}

video.addEventListener("timeupdate", timeupdatecallback, false);
video.addEventListener("ended", span3Update, false);
</script>
```

The `timeupdatecallback()` function is the key here. The video is roughly 21 seconds in length so the first line of the function determines if the `currenttime` is greater than 7 seconds (a third of the duration). If it is, the playhead is scooted to the 14-second mark (the two-thirds mark)—`video.currentTime = 2*video.duration/3;`—and that value is then shown (see Figure 3-7) in the `currentTime after timeupdate` field. Finally, we also show the currentTime after the ended event is fired.

CurrentTime on load: 0.

CurrentTime after timeupdate: 14.520889282226562.

CurrentTime after ended: 21.781333923339844.

Figure 3-7. Retrieving and setting the currentTime value in Safari

Listen to the *seeked* event to determine when the browser has finished seeking. When you set @currentTime to a specific value, don't expect that value to also be the one that @currentTime is set to after the seek—as mentioned before, everything to do with time is best handled as time ranges.

■ **Note** When you compress a video you may have noticed that you can set the distance between keyframes or leave that choice to the software. The frames between the keyframes are called difference or delta frames and contain only the information that has changed for that frame since the keyframe. These frames have a major impact on any seeking you may do because the browser can't display a delta frame and thus has to decode all the frames from the last keyframe. If you know that there will be lots of exact seeking necessary on your media file, you may want to decrease the distance between keyframes when encoding your media resource, even if this means increasing file size.

@seeking

The read-only *@seeking* IDL attribute is set by the web browser to "true" during times of seeking and is "false" at all other times.

Listing 3-8 shows how to get the value of the @seeking attribute. Since seeking times are typically short, we have to catch the @seeking attribute value as soon after starting to seek as possible. Thus, we print it straight after changing @currentTime. Figure 3-8 shows the results in Safari.

Listing 3-8. Tracking the Value of the @seeking Attribute

```
<video controls autoplay width="400">
    <source src="video/Waterfall.mp4"  type="video/mp4"/>
    <source src="video/Waterfall.webm" type="video/webm"/>
</video>

<p>seeking on start: <span id="seeking_first"></span>.</p>
<p>seeking after timeupdate: <span id="seeking_timeupdate"></span>.</p>
<p>seeking after ended: <span id="seeking_ended"></span>.</p>

<script type="text/javascript">
    var video = document.getElementsByTagName("video")[0];
    var span1 = document.getElementById("seeking_first");
    var span2 = document.getElementById("seeking_timeupdate");
    var span3 = document.getElementById("seeking_ended");

    span1.innerHTML = video.seeking;
    function span2Update(evt) {
        if (video.currentTime > video.duration/3) {
            video.currentTime = 2*video.duration/3;
            video.removeEventListener("timeupdate", span2Update, false);
            span2.innerHTML = video.seeking;
        }
    }
```

```
    function span3Update(evt) {
        span3.innerHTML = video.seeking;
    }

    video.addEventListener("timeupdate", span2Update, false);
    video.addEventListener("ended", span3Update, false);
</script>
```

You can see in Figure 3-8 that @seeking is "true" just after seeking. All browsers exhibit the same behavior for this example.

seeking on load: false.

seeking after timeupdate: true.

seeking after ended: false.

Figure 3-8. *Retrieving the seeking attribute value Firefox*

This IDL attribute doesn't really have a lot of real-world use. It's basically true while the video is moving the playback head to a new location and then while it is trying to get the media data buffered for continuing playback. You've seen this situation in YouTube: it's when the spinner is sitting there and buffering data after you've jumped to a new location. Thus this IDL attribute is mostly useful only to JavaScript developers who need fine-grained control over every state of the video player: e.g. "I'm waiting for the seeked event to be raised, but it's not coming" or "Is the video still seeking or has a network error occurred?" Normally, you would just wait for the seeked event.

@paused

The read-only @paused IDL attribute is set by the web browser to "true" if the media playback is paused. Pausing can happen either through user interaction on the interface or through JavaScript. Initially, @paused is "true" and is only set to "false" when the media resource is supposed to start playing. Sort of …

You cannot assume that the video is playing when @paused is "false." Even when *@paused* is "false," it is possible the media resource is currently in a state of buffering, is in an error state, or has reached the end and is waiting for more media data to be appended. Since there is no explicit *@playing* IDL attribute, you need to use the @paused value and other hints to determine if the web browser really is currently playing back a media resource. The combined hints are

- @paused is "false,"

- @ended is "false,"

- the readyState is HAVE_FUTURE_DATA or HAVE_ENOUGH_DATA, and

- @error is null.

There are also events that can help you track that playback continues working—the playing event is fired when playback starts—and as long as no waiting or ended or error event is fired and @paused is "false," you can safely assume that you are still playing.

When the @paused IDL attribute changes value, a timeupdate event is fired.

The code block in Listing 3-9 is an example of how to get the value of the @paused attribute and to deduce an assumption for a playing status. Halfway through the media resource, we briefly paused the video to catch the states and then start playback again. Figure 3-9 shows the results in Chrome.

Listing 3-9. Obtaining an @paused Attribute Value

```
<video controls autoplay width= "400">
    <source src="video/Waterfall.mp4" type="video/mp4"/>
    <source src="video/Waterfall.webm" type="video/webm"/>
</video>

<p>Paused on start: <span id="paused_first"></span>.</p>
<p>Paused after pause(): <span id="paused_timeupdate"></span>.</p>
<p>Paused after play(): <span id="paused_playing"></span>.</p>
<p>Paused after ended: <span id="paused_ended"></span>.</p>

<script type="text/javascript">
    var video = document.getElementsByTagName("video")[0];
    var span1 = document.getElementById("paused_first");
    var span2 = document.getElementById("paused_timeupdate");
    var span3 = document.getElementById("paused_playing");
    var span4 = document.getElementById("paused_ended");

    function playing() {
        return (!video.paused && !video.ended && video.error==null
            && (video.readyState==video.HAVE_FUTURE_DATA ||
                video.readyState==video.HAVE_ENOUGH_DATA));
    }
    span1.innerHTML = video.paused + " (playing: " + playing() + ")";
```

```
function span2Update(evt) {
    if (video.currentTime > video.duration/2) {
        video.pause();
        video.removeEventListener("timeupdate", span2Update, false);
        span2.innerHTML = video.paused + " (playing: " + playing() + ")";
        video.play();
        span3.innerHTML = video.paused + " (playing: " + playing() + ")";
    }
}
}
function span4Update(evt) {
    span4.innerHTML = video.paused + " (playing: " + playing() + ")";
}

video.addEventListener("timeupdate", span2Update, false);
video.addEventListener("ended", span4Update, false);
</script>
```

Paused on load: true (playing: false).

Paused after pause(): true (playing: false).

Paused after play(): false (playing: true).

Paused after ended: true (playing: false).

Figure 3-9. Retrieving the paused attribute value and also a playing status in Chrome

We start by displaying the paused state at the beginning while the video element is still being prepared: the video is paused and not playing because it doesn't yet have enough data to play.

Next, the span2Update() function is called until video's currentTime is beyond the halfway mark. At that point, we pause the video and check the playing state again (it is of course not playing when it's paused). Then we start playing once which means we are no longer paused and are indeed playing with sufficiently buffered data. Once we arrive at the end, the video is paused again and thus not playing.

All browsers (Figure 3-9) behave the same with the state of @paused; IE9 additionally rewinds to the beginning of the resource and pauses the video there.

@ended

It is always nice to be able to know when a video has ended if you want to have an event occur at that point, such as a rewind to the start. The read-only @ended IDL attribute is set by the web browser to "true" if the media playback has ended and the direction of playback is forward (see @playbackRate), otherwise @ended is "false."

■ **Note**   Be aware that "true" doesn't always mean "true." For example, when the @loop content attribute is set to "true" and the current playback position reaches the end of the media resource and the playback direction is forward, then @ended will not be set to "true." Instead the web browser will seek to the beginning of the media resource and continue playback. The browser will not even raise an ended event in this case.

When @ended is set to "true," the web browser will fire both a timeupdate event and an ended event.

Interestingly, when the playback direction is backward and the playback position reaches the beginning of the media resource, the value of the @loop content attribute is irrelevant and playback will stop. Only a timeupdate event will be fired. Since Safari is the only browser that implements a backward play direction, this is a rather academic situation.

Listing 3-10 shows how to get the @ended attribute.

Listing 3-10. Values of the ended IDL attribute at Media Start and End

```
<video controls width= "400" autoplay>
    <source src="video/Waterfall.mp4" type="video/mp4"/>
    <source src="video/Waterfall.webm" type="video/webm"/>
</video>
<p>Ended on start: <span id="ended_first"></span>.</p>
<p>Ended after ended: <span id="ended_ended"></span>.</p>
<script type="text/javascript">
    var video = document.getElementsByTagName("video")[0];
    var span1 = document.getElementById("ended_first");
    var span2 = document.getElementById("ended_ended");
    span1.innerHTML = video.ended;
    function span2Update(evt) { span2.innerHTML = video.ended; }
    video.addEventListener("ended", span2Update, false);
</script>
```

The magic happens in the last two lines of the script and the results are shown in Figure 3-10.

Ended on load: false.

Ended after ended: true.

Figure 3-10. Retrieving the ended attribute value in Opera

@defaultPlaybackRate, @playbackRate

The @playbackRate IDL attribute returns the speed at which the media resource is playing. It can be set to change the playback speed. The value for normal speed is 1.0. Anything larger than 1.0 is faster than normal. Anything smaller is slow motion. Zero pauses the video. Negative values reverse the playback direction. Similar to fast playback, values smaller than -1.0 are fast backward playback and values between -1.0 and 0 are slow backward motion.

All browsers implement @playbackRate, but only Safari implements backward or reverse playback.

The @defaultPlaybackRate IDL attribute sets the default playback speed for the media engine. It is initially 1.0, but can be changed by script to a different default playback speed. You have to call the load() function again after you change the @defaultPlaybackRate for it to have effect. During loading, @playbackRate is set to the value of the @defaultPlaybackRate. Changing the @defaultPlaybackRate without reloading the resource has no effect.

When a user clicks the "play" button in the web browser controls the @playbackRate IDL attribute's value is reset to the value of the @defaultPlaybackRate before starting playback.

You will likely use @playbackRate if you want faster/slower playback, but the @defaultPlaybackRate is not as useful. One use case is to enable blind users to set a higher default playback speed than 1.0, since they are highly trained to consume audio at high playback speeds. Note, however, that Safari does not support @defaultPlaybackRate and that the audio isn't really decoded properly during fast forward/backward playback. Typically, browsers skip packets between the different playback positions, so the audio will have artifacts. Until this is fixed, the use of @defaultPlaybackRate is of limited value.

When the @defaultPlaybackRate or the @playbackRate attribute values are changed, a rateChange event is fired.

___

■ **Note**   If you are playing back at a high @playbackRate, the download and decoding of the media resource may not be able to keep up and you may get stalled as buffering takes place.

___

In the code example in Listing 3-11, we show how to make use of both the @defaultPlaybackRate and @playbackRate attributes.

Listing 3-11. Playback Rate Changes

```
<video controls autoplay width= "400">
    <source src="video/Waterfall.mp4" type="video/mp4"/>
    <source src="video/Waterfall.webm" type="video/webm"/>
</video>

<p>Default/PlaybackRate on start:<span id="defaultPlaybackRate_first"></span>.</p>
<p>Default/PlaybackRate as set: <span id="defaultPlaybackRate_set"></span>.</p>
<p>Default/PlaybackRate after timeupdate:<span id="defaultPlaybackRate_timeupdate"></span>.</p>

<script type="text/javascript">
    var video = document.getElementsByTagName("video")[0];
    var span1 = document.getElementById("defaultPlaybackRate_first");
    var span2 = document.getElementById("defaultPlaybackRate_set");
    var span3 = document.getElementById("defaultPlaybackRate_timeupdate");

    video.defaultPlaybackRate = 0.5;
    video.load();
    span1.innerHTML = video.defaultPlaybackRate + ", " + video.playbackRate;
    function span2Update(evt) {
        span2.innerHTML = video.defaultPlaybackRate + ", " + video.playbackRate;
    }
    function span3Update(evt) {
        if (video.currentTime > video.duration/4) {
            video.playbackRate = 2;
            video.playbackRate = -2;
            span3.innerHTML = video.defaultPlaybackRate + ", " + video.playbackRate;
            video.removeEventListener("timeupdate", span2Update, false);
        }
    }
    video.addEventListener("loadedmetadata", span2Update, false);
    video.addEventListener("timeupdate", span3Update, false);
</script>
```

First we set the default to 0.5, and then we reload the resource to make it play in slow motion. When a quarter of the video is played back, we change the playback rate to 2, and then to -2 as shown in Figure 3-11. This makes those browsers that don't' support a backward playing direction at least play back at twice the speed, since they will igore the negative value.

Default/PlaybackRate on load:0.5, 0.5.

Default/PlaybackRate as set: 0.5, 1.

Default/PlaybackRate after timeupdate:0.5, -2.

Figure 3-11. *Retrieving the playback attribute values in Safari*

Note that Safari does set the @playbackRate from the @defaultPlaybackRate, but once loadedmetadata is reached, it is reset to 1, thus not effectively used. You really want to see this example at work in Safari—it is very impressive to see reverse playback at work!

The fact that only Safari implemented support for this attribute may be related to the codec and media frameworks in use—possibly the media frameworks in use in Chrome, Opera, IE, and Firefox require new functionality to play the codecs backward. Since the feature is a bit of a gimmick, it's unlikely that this feature will become widely available.

States of the Media Element

We have all experienced this: a video that takes forever to start playing because it is buffering. Wouldn't it be neat if you could inform your users of the issue and, for example, when the buffering is finished, you could indicate the media can now be played? This is where the media element states can play a large role in your work.

The IDL attributes, which represent web browser managed states of a media element, explained in this section, are

- networkState
- readyState
- error
- buffered TimeRanges
- played TimeRanges
- seekable TimeRanges

@networkState

The @networkState IDL attribute represents the current state of network activity of the media element. The available states are

- ***NETWORK_EMPTY* (0):**

    No @currentSrc has been identified—this may be because the element has not yet been initialized, or because the resource selection hasn't found an @src attribute or <source> elements and is waiting for a load() function call to set it.

- ***NETWORK_IDLE* (1):**

    A @currentSrc has been identified and resource fetching is possible, but the web browser has currently suspended network activity while waiting for user activity. This typically happens after the web browser has downloaded the media element metadata on a resource that is not set to @autoplay. It also happens when the media resource has been partially downloaded and network buffering is suspended for some reason such as a connection interruption, media resource file corruption, a user abort, or for the simple fact that the browser has pre-buffered more than enough media data ahead of the playback position so is waiting for the playback to catch up. Finally it also occurs when a resource is completely downloaded. A suspend event is fired as the web browser enters the NETWORK_IDLE state.

- ***NETWORK_LOADING* (2):**

    The web browser is trying to download media resource data. The first time this happens on a media resource, as part of the resource selection, the loadstart event is fired. If the @networkState changes at a later stage back to NETWORK_LOADING and the web browser is fetching media data, a progress event is fired periodically. If media data is unexpectedly not arriving from the network while trying to load, a stalled event is fired.

- ***NETWORK_NO_SOURCE* (3):**

    The resource selection has identified a @currentSrc, but the resource has failed to load or the URL couldn't be resolved or there is no resource provided (i.e., no @src or valid <source> children).

The code in Listing 3-12 provides an example of how the different @networkState values are reached. The states are displayed before load, after loading the resource metadata, after a progress event, and after changing the video's @src half way through the video to a nonexistent resource.

Listing 3-12. Tracking networkState Through the Playback of a Resource

```
<video controls autoplay width= "400">
    <source src="video/Waterfall.mp4" type="video/mp4"/>
    <source src="video/Waterfall.webm" type="video/webm"/>
</video>

<p>NetworkState on start: <span id="networkState_first"></span>.</p>
<p>NetworkState after loadedmetadata: <span id="networkState_loadedmetadata"></span>.</p>
<p>NetworkState after progress: <span id="networkState_progress"></span>.</p>
<p>NetworkState after timeupdate: <span id="networkState_timeupdate"></span>.</p>

<script type="text/javascript">
    var video = document.getElementsByTagName("video")[0];
    var span1 = document.getElementById("networkState_first");
    var span2 = document.getElementById("networkState_loadedmetadata");
    var span3 = document.getElementById("networkState_progress");
    var span4 = document.getElementById("networkState_timeupdate");

    span1.innerHTML = video.networkState;
    function span2Update(evt) {
        span2.innerHTML = video.networkState;
    }
    function span3Update(evt) {
        span3.innerHTML = video.networkState;
    }
    function span4Update(evt) {
        if (video.currentTime > video.duration/2) {
            video.src = "notavail.mp4";
            video.load();
            span4.innerHTML = video.networkState;
        }
    }
    video.addEventListener("loadedmetadata", span2Update, false);
    video.addEventListener("progress", span3Update, false);
    video.addEventListener("timeupdate", span4Update, false);
</script>
```

Though the code works, the web browsers slightly differ in their implementations of the code, though consistency has improved a lot in recent browser versions. At the start (see Figure 3-12), we can find the browsers all in the @networkState NETWORK_NO_SOURCE (3) state.

NetworkState on start: 3.

NetworkState after loadedmetadata: 1.

NetworkState after progress: 1.

NetworkState after timeupdate: 3.

Figure 3-12. *Retrieving the networkState attribute values in Firefox*

After the metadata is loaded, @networkState first goes to NETWORK_LOADING (2) and then transitions to NETWORK_IDLE (1) once enough data is buffered.

After a progress event, browsers can be found in the NETWORK_LOADING (2) and then transition to the NETWORK_IDLE (1) state again.

After trying to load a nonexistent media resource, all browsers, with the exception of Firefox, report to be in NETWORK_LOADING (2) state. Firefox correctly reports a NETWORK_NO_SOURCE (3) state.

■ **Note**   Clearly, tracking of states is not a good idea, since often you're just watching a process in transition. We therefore recommend watching events and making use of callbacks instead.

@readyState

The @readyState IDL attribute represents the current state of the media element in relation to its playback position. The available states are the following:

- ***HAVE_NOTHING* (0):**

  No information regarding the video resource is available, including its playback position. This is typically the case before a media resource starts downloading. Media elements whose @networkState attribute is set to NETWORK_EMPTY are always in the HAVE_NOTHING @readyState.

- ***HAVE_METADATA (1):***

  The setup information of the media resource has been received, such that the decoding pipeline is set up, the width and height of a video resource are known, and the duration of the resource(if it can be determined) is available. Seeking and decoding are now possible, even though no actual media data is available yet for the current playback position. As the HAVE_METADATA state is reached, a loadedmetadata event is fired.

- ***HAVE_CURRENT_DATA (2):***

  Decoded media data for the current playback position is available, but either there is not enough date to start playing back continuously or the end of the playback direction has been reached. If this state is reached for the first time, a loadeddata event is fired. Note that this state may not be taken, but rather a HAVE_FUTURE_DATA or HAVE_ENOUGH_DATA state may be directly achieved after HAVE_METADATA, in which case the loadeddata event is fired upon reaching them for the first time. This state will also be reached when waiting for enough data to download for playback (e.g. after a seek or after the buffered data ran out); in this case, a waiting and a timeupdate event are fired.

- ***HAVE_FUTURE_DATA (3):***

  Decoded media data for the current playback position and the next position is available (e.g., the current video frame and the one following it). If this state is reached for the first time, a canplay event is fired. If the element is not paused and not seeking and HAVE_FUTURE_DATA is reached, a playing event is fired. If the browser actually starts playback at this stage, it may still need to stop soon afterward to buffer more data.

- ***HAVE_ENOUGH_DATA (4):***

  Enough decoded media data is available for the current and next playback positions and the network download rate is fast enough that the web browser estimates that data will be fetched and decoded at the @defaultPlaybackRate sufficiently to allow continuous playback to the end of the media resource without having to stop for further buffering. If this state is reached without going through HAVE_FUTURE_DATA, a canplay event is fired. If the element is not paused and not seeking and this state is reached without going through HAVE_FUTURE_DATA, a playing event is fired. If the HAVE_ENOUGH_DATA state is reached for the first time, a canplaythrough event is fired.

Listing 3-13 shows how the different @readyState values can be reached. We check the state at specific events: after starting to load the video, after the metadata is loaded, after a timeupdate event, and after a progress event.

Listing 3-13. Getting the readyState Values for a Media Rlement

```
<video controls width= "400">
        <source src="video/Waterfall.mp4" type="video/mp4"/>
        <source src="video/Waterfall.webm" type="video/webm"/>
    </video>

    <p>ReadyState on load: <span id="readyState_first"></span>.</p>
    <p>ReadyState after loadedmetadata: <span id="readyState_loadedmetadata"></span>.</p>
    <p>ReadyState after progress: <span id="readyState_progress"></span>.</p>
    <p>ReadyState after timeupdate: <span id="readyState_timeupdate"></span>.</p>

    <script type="text/javascript">
        var video = document.getElementsByTagName("video")[0];
        var span1 = document.getElementById("readyState_first");
        var span2 = document.getElementById("readyState_loadedmetadata");
        var span3 = document.getElementById("readyState_progress");
        var span4 = document.getElementById("readyState_timeupdate");

        span1.innerHTML = video.readyState;
        function span2Update(evt) {
            span2.innerHTML = video.readyState;
        }
        function span3Update(evt) {
            span3.innerHTML = video.readyState;
        }
        span4 = document.getElementById("readyState_timeupdate");
        function span4Update(evt) {
            span4.innerHTML = video.readyState;
        }
        video.addEventListener("loadedmetadata", span2Update, false);
        video.addEventListener("progress", span3Update, false);
        video.addEventListener("timeupdate", span4Update, false);
    </script>
```

Figure 3-13 shows the results in Chrome and Firefox.

ReadyState on load: 0.

ReadyState after loadedmetadata: 2.

ReadyState after progress: 4.

ReadyState after timeupdate: 2.

ReadyState on load: 0.

ReadyState after loadedmetadata: 1.

ReadyState after progress: 4.

ReadyState after timeupdate: 4.

Figure 3-13. *Retrieving the readyState attribute values in Firefox (L) and Chrome (R)*

At the start, all browsers are in a HAVE_NOTHING (0) state. After the video element has been initialized, Opera, Chrome, and Safari go into the HAVE_METADATA (1) state (Chrome is shown, representing this group), while Firefox and IE9 show HAVE_CURRENT_DATA (2) (Firefox is shown, representing this group). Thus, you can rely on metadata being available with a @readyState being at minimum 1.

As we press the play button and the video starts playing, the timeupdate event provides us with HAVE_ENOUGH_DATA (4) ready state on all browsers except for IE9, which shows HAVE_CURRENT_DATA (2).

As we reach a progress event, all browsers except for IE9 shows HAVE_ENOUGH_DATA(4) and IE9 sticks with HAVE_CURRENT_DATA (2). Thus, you can rely on being able to play with a @readyState being at minimum 2.

@error

The @error IDL attribute represents the latest error state of the media element as a MediaError object.

The MediaError object has the following structure:

```
interface MediaError {
  const unsigned short MEDIA_ERR_ABORTED = 1;
  const unsigned short MEDIA_ERR_NETWORK = 2;
  const unsigned short MEDIA_ERR_DECODE = 3;
  const unsigned short MEDIA_ERR_SRC_NOT_SUPPORTED = 4;
  readonly attribute unsigned short code;
};
```

If there is no error, @error will be null, otherwise @error.code will have the error state. The available errors are as follows:

- ***MEDIA_ERR_ABORTED* (1):**

    This error is raised when the fetching process for the media resource is aborted by the user (e.g., when browsing to another web page). The @networkState will be either NETWORK_EMPTY or NETWORK_IDLE, depending on when the download was aborted. An abort event is fired.

- ***MEDIA_ERR_NETWORK* (2):**

    This error is raised when any kind of network error caused the web browser to stop fetching the media resource after the resource was established to be usable (e.g., when the network connection is interrupted). The @networkState will be either NETWORK_EMPTY or NETWORK_IDLE, depending on when the download was aborted. An error event is fired.

- ***MEDIA_ERR_DECODE* (3):**

    This error is raised when decoding of a retrieved media resource failed and video playback had to be aborted (e.g., because the media data was corrupted or the media resource used a feature that the browser does not support). The @networkState will be either NETWORK_EMPTY or NETWORK_IDLE, depending on when the download was aborted. An error event is fired.

- ***MEDIA_ERR_SRC_NOT_SUPPORTED* (4):**

    This error is raised when the media resource in the @src attribute failed to load or the URL could not be resolved. The media resource may not load if the server or the network failed or because the format is not supported. The @networkState will be either NETWORK_EMPTY or NETWORK_IDLE, depending on when the download was aborted. An error event is fired.

The code in Listing 3-14 shows an example of how to catch an @error value. The error is triggered at the quarter duration mark of the video by trying to load a nonexistent media resource.

Listing 3-14. Getting Error States for a Media Element

```
<video controls autolpay width="400">
    <source src="video/Waterfall.mp4" type="video/mp4"/>
    <source src="video/Waterfall.webm" type="video/webm"/>
</video>

<p>Error on start: <span id="error_first"></span>.</p>
<p>Error after timeupdate: <span id="error_timeupdate"></span>.</p>
<p>Error after error: <span id="error_error"></span>.</p>

<script type="text/javascript">
    var video = document.getElementsByTagName("video")[0];
    var span1 = document.getElementById("error_first");
    var span2 = document.getElementById("error_timeupdate");
    var span3 = document.getElementById("error_error");
```

```
    span1.innerHTML = (video.error ? video.error.code : "none");
    function span2Update(evt) {
        if (video.currentTime > video.duration/4) {
            video.src = "notavail.mp4";
            video.load();
            span2.innerHTML = (video.error ? video.error.code : "none");
        }
    }
    function span3Update(evt) {
        span3.innerHTML = (video.error ? video.error.code : "none");
    }

    video.addEventListener("timeupdate", span2Update, false);
    video.addEventListener("error", span3Update, false);
</script>
```

We are forcing the browser to try to load a nonexistent media file, which leads to the browsers throwing an error and @error.code resulting in MEDIA_ERR_SRC_NOT_SUPPORTED. Figure 3-14 shows the error screen on Chrome. Compare this to the more informative error screen of Firefox in Figure 3-12 for the same error.

Error on start: none.

Error after timeupdate: none.

Error after error: 4.

Figure 3-14. Retrieving the error attribute values in Chrome

@buffered

The @buffered IDL attribute retains the ranges of the media resource that the web browser has buffered. The value is stored in a normalized TimeRanges object, which represents a list of ranges (intervals or periods) of time.

The TimeRanges object syntax would be as follows:

```
interface TimeRanges {
  readonly attribute unsigned long length;
  float start(unsigned long index);
  float end(unsigned long index);
};
```

The IDL attributes of the TimeRanges object have the following meaning:

- @length: contains the number of ranges in the object, counting from 0 to @length - 1.

- start(i): returns the start time for range number i in seconds from the start of the timeline,

- end(i): returns the end time for range number i in seconds from the start of the timeline.

■ **Note**   start(i) and end(i) raise INDEX_SIZE_ERR exceptions if called with an index greater than or equal to @length.

A *normalized* TimeRanges object is one that consists only of ranges that

- aren't empty: *start(i) < end(i)* for all *i*

- are ordered, don't overlap, and don't touch: *start(i) > end(j)* for all *j<i*

- If adjacent ranges would need to be created, they are instead folded into one bigger range.

The timeline of the @buffered IDL attribute is the timeline of the media resource.

For a media resource that plays from start to end, the @buffered IDL attribute contains a single time range which begins at the @startTime of the media resource and grows as more media data is downloaded until all of the media data has been received. For a large resource where seeking is undertaken to later points in the resource, the web browser will instead store multiple byte ranges of the areas that were seeked to, thus creating multiple time ranges.

■ **Note**   Web browsers are free to discard previously buffered data; thus time ranges that may be available earlier are not guaranteed to be still available at a later time.

In the code example in Listing 3-15, the browser retrieves the @buffered value at different playback states and displays the ranges. Since we autoplay, browsers will first need to buffer the beginning. Then we seek to the halfway mark and continue updating the buffered ranges.

Listing 3-15. Check the Buffered Ranges of a Long File After Seeking

```
<video controls autoplay width= "400">
    <source src="video/ElephantDreams.mp4" type="video/mp4"/>
    <source src="video/ElephantDreams.webm" type="video/webm"/>
</video>

<p>Buffered ranges on load: <span id="buffered_first"></span></p>
<p>Buffered ranges after loadedmetadata: <span id="buffered_loadedmetadata"></span></p>
<p>Buffered ranges after seeking: <span id="buffered_seeking"></span></p>
<p>Buffered ranges after timeupdate: <span id="buffered_timeupdate"></span></p>

<script type="text/javascript">
    function printTimeRanges(tr) {
        if (tr.length == 0) return "none";
        s = tr.length + ": ";
        for (i=0; i<tr.length; i++) {
            s += tr.start(i) + " - " + tr.end(i) + "; ";
        }
        return s;
    }
    var video = document.getElementsByTagName("video")[0];
    var span1 = document.getElementById("buffered_first");
    var span2 = document.getElementById("buffered_loadedmetadata");
    var span3 = document.getElementById("buffered_seeking");
    var span4 = document.getElementById("buffered_timeupdate");

    span1.innerHTML = printTimeRanges(video.buffered);
    function span2Update(evt) {
        span2.innerHTML = printTimeRanges(video.buffered);
        video.currentTime = video.duration/2;
        video.play();
        span3.innerHTML = printTimeRanges(video.buffered);
    }
    function span4Update(evt) {
        span4.innerHTML = printTimeRanges(video.buffered);
    }

    video.addEventListener("loadedmetadata", span2Update, false);
    video.addEventListener("timeupdate", span4Update, false);
</script>
```

In this test we need a rather long video file so the browser won't buffer it all. We are therefore making use of the Creative Commons Attribution Licensed "Elephants Dream" short film from the Blender Foundation. We thank the Blender Foundation for making this short film available under such a free license.

If you test this in a browser (see Figure 3-15), you will discover that the browsers all provide the attribute and update its content.

Buffered ranges on load: none

Buffered ranges after loadedmetadata: 1: 0 - 0.75;

Buffered ranges after seeking: 1: 0 - 0.75;

Buffered ranges after timeupdate: 5: 43.319 - 43.833; 48.831 - 292.625; 299.404 - 300.208; 322.937 - 323.958; 326.831 - 653.75;

Figure 3-15. *Retrieving the buffering attribute values in Firefox*

The attribute also exposes some of the buffering strategy—Firefox first buffers the beginning of the video, then the end (probably when we're using video.duration, and it checks on the data being accurate), and then starts buffering from the halfway mark, which is from about 326 seconds onward. Some of the other browsers don't actually buffer the beginning because they immediately get to the seek point. None of the other browsers buffer a range at the end.

@played

The @played IDL attribute retains the ranges of the media resource that the web browser has played. The value is stored in a normalized TimeRanges object (see @buffered attribute). The timeline of the @played IDL attribute is the timeline of the media resource.

Typically, the @played IDL attribute contains a single time range, which starts at 0 and grows as more media data is downloaded and played until all the media data has been received. However, for a large resource where seeking is undertaken to diverse points in the resource, the web browser may store multiple time ranges.

The code example in Listing 3-16 retrieves the @played value at different playback states and displays the ranges in basically the same way as the previous @buffered example.

Listing 3-16. Check the Played Ranges of a Long File After Seeking

```
<video controls autoplay width="400">
    <source src="video/Waterfall.mp4" type="video/mp4"/>
    <source src="video/Waterfall.webm" type="video/webm"/>
</video>

<p>Played ranges on load: <span id="played_first"></span>.</p>
<p>Played ranges after loadedmetadata:<span id="played_loadedmetadata"></span></p>
<p>Played ranges after seeking: <span id="played_seeking"></span></p>
<p>Played ranges after timeupdate: <span id="played_timeupdate"></span></p>
```

```
<script type="text/javascript">
    function printTimeRanges(tr) {
        if (tr.length == 0) return "none";
        s = tr.length + ": ";
        for (i=0; i<tr.length; i++) {
            s += tr.start(i) + " - " + tr.end(i) + "; ";
        }
        return s;
    }
    var video = document.getElementsByTagName("video")[0];
    var span1 = document.getElementById("played_first");
    var span2 = document.getElementById("played_loadedmetadata");
    var span3 = document.getElementById("played_seeking");
    var span4 = document.getElementById("played_timeupdate");

    span1.innerHTML = printTimeRanges(video.played);
    function span2Update(evt) {
        span2.innerHTML = printTimeRanges(video.played);
        video.currentTime = video.duration/2;
        video.play();
        span3.innerHTML = printTimeRanges(video.played);
    }
    function span4Update(evt) {
        span4.innerHTML = printTimeRanges(video.played);
    }

    video.addEventListener("loadedmetadata", span2Update, false);
    video.addEventListener("timeupdate", span4Update, false);
</script>
```

Note that if the user seeks to different time ranges and plays them back, several time ranges (see Figure 3-16) will be reported in the @played attribute. We'll leave this as an exercise to the user.

Played ranges on load: none.

Played ranges after loadedmetadata:none

Played ranges after seeking: none

Played ranges after timeupdate: 2: 326.89599609375 - 339.506591796875; 406.952163265306 - 418.9993896484375;

Figure 3-16. *Retrieving the played attribute values in Safari*

@seekable

The @seekable IDL attribute retains the ranges of the media resource to which the web browser can seek. The value is stored in a normalized TimeRanges object (see @buffered attribute). The timeline of the @seekable IDL attribute is the timeline of the media resource.

Typically, the @seekable IDL attribute contains a single time range which starts at 0 and ends at the media resource @duration. If the duration is not available from the start, such as an infinite stream, the time range may continuously change and just keep a certain window available.

The code in Listing 3-17 retrieves the @seekable value during load and after metadata load. It then displays the ranges in much the same way as the earlier @buffered example.

Listing 3-17. Getting the Seekable Ranges for a Media Element

```
<video controls autoplay width="400">
    <source src="video/ElephantDreams.mp4" type="video/mp4"/>
    <source src="video/ElephantDreams.webm" type="video/webm"/>
</video>

<p>Seekable on start: <span id="seekable_first"></span></p>
<p>Seekable after loadedmetadata:<span id="seekable_loadedmetadata"></span></p>

<script type="text/javascript">
    function printTimeRanges(tr) {
        if (tr.length == 0) return "none";
        s = tr.length + ": ";
        for (i=0; i<tr.length; i++) {
            s += tr.start(i) + " - " + tr.end(i) + "; ";
        }
        return s;
    }
    var video = document.getElementsByTagName("video")[0];
    var span1 = document.getElementById("seekable_first");
    var span2 = document.getElementById("seekable_loadedmetadata");

    span1.innerHTML = printTimeRanges(video.seekable);
    function span2Update(evt) {
        span2.innerHTML = printTimeRanges(video.seekable);
    }

    video.addEventListener("loadedmetadata", span2Update, false);
</script>
```

Seekable on start: none

Seekable after loadedmetadata:1: 0 - 653.75;

Figure 3-17. *Retrieving the seekable attribute values in Firefox*

The browsers have all implemented support for the @seekable IDL attribute. The major difference is the number of decimal places they provide, which is the same problem for @duration.

Control Methods in the API

Methods are the verbs of an object—the things an object can do. They are easily spotted because they usually end in parenthesis ( ), which is the punctuation that actually runs the method in question. In the case of video and audio, methods are how you control the media element. This section explains the following JavaScript control methods defined on media elements:

- load()
- play()
- pause()
- canPlayType()
- getStartDate()

load()

The load() control method, when exectued on a media element, causes all activity on a media resource to be suspended (including resource selection and loading, seeking, and playback), all network activity to be seized, the element to be reset (including removal of pending callbacks and events), and the resource selection and loading process to be restarted. If the browser was in the middle of fetching a media resource, an abort event is fired.

In a typical scenario for a successful load(), the following sequence of steps will roughly occur:

- **Initialization:**
  - @networkState is set to NETWORK_EMPTY
  - an emptied event is fired

- @readyState is set to HAVE_NOTHING
- @paused is set to "true"
- @seeking is set to "false"
- @ended is set to "false"
- @currentTime is set to 0 and a timeupdate event is fired
- @duration is set to NaN
- @error is set to null
- @buffered, @played, and @seekable are set to empty
- @playbackRate is set to the value of @defaultPlaybackRate
- @autoplaying is set to "true"

- **Resource selection:**
  - @networkState is set to NETWORK_NO_SOURCE
  - @currentSrc is set from the given @src value or the <source> elements
  - @networkState is set to NETWORK_LOADING
  - the loadstart event is fired

- **Resource fetching:**
  - begin downloading the media resource identified in the @currentSrc attribute
  - progress event is fired roughly every 350 ms or for every byte received (whichever is less frequent)
  - @preload and @autoplay values help determine how much to download
  - if/when the browser suspends download, a suspend event is fired
  - when the resource's metadata has been downloaded:
  - @audioTracks and @videoTracks are filled
  - @duration is determined
  - the durationchange event is fired
  - @videoWidth and @videoHeight are determined (if video element) and a resize event is fired
  - @seekable is determined
  - @readyState is set to HAVE_METADATA
  - the loadedmetadata event is fired
  - seek to the appropriate start time given in the media resource or the @currentSrc URI
  - @currentTime is set to this start time
  - the timeupdate event is fired

- potentially more media data is downloaded (and decoded):
- @readyState changes to HAVE_CURRENT_DATA or higher
- the loadeddata event is fired
- the canplay event is fired for any @readyState higher than HAVE_FUTURE_DATA
- @buffered is updated
- @networkState is set to NETWORK_IDLE and buffering stops
- **Playback start, if @autoplay is "true":**
  - download more data until @readyState is HAVE_FUTURE_DATA or higher (preferably HAVE_ENOUGH_DATA so playback doesn't get stalled)
  - the canplaythrough event is fired
  - @paused is set to "false"
  - the play event is fired
  - the playing event is fired
  - playback is started

Note that many error situations and network state situations are also dealt with through the loading process. For example, if the network download stalls and the web browser hasn't received data for more than about 3 seconds, a stalled event will be fired.

Several previous examples in this chapter have made use of the load() control method; thus, we will not include another example here.

play( )

The play() control method executed on a media element sets the @paused IDL attribute to "false" and starts playback of the media resource, downloading and buffering media data as required.

In a typical scenario for a successful play(), the following typical sequence of steps will occur:

- if @networkState is NETWORK_EMPTY—that is, no @currentSrc has been determined yet (e.g., because the @src of the element was empty as the element was set up, but now the attribute was set through JavaScript and the resource can be fetched)— "resource selection" and "resource fetching," as described for load(), are executed
- if @ended is "true" and the playback direction is forward, the web browser seeks to the beginning
- @currentTime is set to 0
- timeupdate event is fired
- "start playback" as described for load() is executed

We'll look at the use of play() together with pause() in the next example.

pause( )

The pause() control method executed on a media element sets the @paused IDL attribute to "true" and stops playback of the media resource.

In a typical scenario for a successful pause(), the following sequence of steps will happen to pause a media resource:

- if @networkState is NETWORK_EMPTY (i.e., no @currentSrc has been determined yet), "resource selection" and "resource fetching" as described for load(), are executed. @currentSrc may not have been determined yet because the @src of the element was empty as the element was set up, but now the attribute was set through JavaScript and the resource can be fetched

- pause playback

  - @paused is set to "true"

  - timeupdate event is fired

  - pause event is fired

  - downloading of more media data is potentially suspended and a suspend event is fired if the browser is far ahead of the current playback position

The code example in Listing 3-18 makes use of both play() and pause(). At first, no media resource is specified for a video element—then we set the @src attribute depending on what format a browser supports and call play(). Later we call pause() halfway through playing. Figure 4-17 shows the results in the browsers.

Listing 3-18. Using the play() and pause() Control Methods for a Media Element

```
<video controls width="400">
</video>

<p>CurrentSrc on start: <span id="currentSrc_first"></span>.</p>
<p>CurrentSrc after loadedmetadata: <span id="currentSrc_loadedmetadata"></span>.</p>
<p>CurrentTime on pause: <span id="currentTime_pause"></span>.</p>

<script type="text/javascript">
    var video = document.getElementsByTagName("video")[0];
    var source = document.getElementsByTagName("source");
    var span1 = document.getElementById("currentSrc_first");
    var span2 = document.getElementById("currentSrc_loadedmetadata");
    var span3 = document.getElementById("currentTime_pause");

    span1.innerHTML = video.currentSrc;
    if (video.canPlayType("video/webm") != "") {
        video.src = "video/HK_Traffic.webm";
    } else if (video.canPlayType("video/mp4") != "") {
        video.src = "video/HK_Traffic.mp4";
    }
    video.play();

    function span2Update(evt) { span2.innerHTML = video.currentSrc; }
    function callpause(evt) {
        if (video.currentTime > video.duration/2) {
            video.pause();
        }
    }
    function span3Update(evt) {  span3.innerHTML = video.currentTime;  }
```

```
    video.addEventListener("loadedmetadata", span2Update, false);
    video.addEventListener("timeupdate", callpause, false);
    video.addEventListener("pause", span3Update, false);
</script>
```

When running this code (see Figure 3-18), you will see that at first, no video URL is available, but it is then set and loaded and playback starts. Removing the video.play() command, you would need to start playback by clicking the play button in the video controls—it has the same effect. Pausing happens at the halfway point, see the callpause() function.

CurrentSrc on start: .

CurrentSrc after loadedmetadata: http://html5videoguide.net/NEW/CH3/video/HK_Traffic.webm.

CurrentTime on pause: 12.752197.

Figure 3-18. *Using the play( ) and pause( ) control methods in Chrome*

canPlayType( )

This method is particularly useful in situations where you wonder if the browser can actually play the media file. The canPlayType (in DOMString type) control method for a media element takes a string as a parameter which is a MIME type and returns whether the web browser is confident that it can play back that media type.

Possible return values are:

- the empty string " ": The web browser is confident it cannot decode and render this type of media resource in a media element

- "maybe": The web browser is not sure if it can or cannot render this type of media resource in a media element

- "probably": the web browser is confident that it can decode and render this type of media resource in a media element; since this implies knowledge about whether the codecs in a container format are supported by the web browser, they are encouraged to only return "probably" for a MIME type that includes the codecs parameter

The previous code block made use of the canPlayType() control method.

```
if (video.canPlayType("video/webm") != "") {
        video.src = "video/HK_Traffic.webm";
} else if (video.canPlayType("video/mp4") != "") {
        video.src = "video/HK_Traffic.mp4";
}
```

As you can see, it simply checks to see if the browser is able to play the various formats for the HK_Traffic video.

getStartDate()

Some media resources are associated with a real-world clock-time and date. Think, for example, of live streaming video. For such resources, the playback time of 0 is associated with a JavaScript Date object, which stores a date and a time—the so-called timeline offset. This date establishes a media timeline that begins at this start date as the earliest defined position and ends at the latest defined position.

For example, in a live stream, the start date could be the time at which the user connects to the stream and the end of the timeline would be the ever-changing current playback time.

Another example is the recording of a live stream, which has a timeline defined by its start date and end date.

In the end, the start date is nothing more than a label attached to the 0 time of the video controls, which can be exposed to the user for informative purposes.

Most browsers haven't actually implemented this method, so don't rely on it being available.

There is also a new method available in some browsers: fastSeek(double time). This method allows seeking to keyframes in a video rather than to exact time offsets. We mentioned this method in the context of @currentTime as a replacement for seeking by @currentTime. We are aware that at least Firefox supports this method.

Events

The browser raises media events during handling of a media resource whenever its state changes. It allows a web developer to react to this state change. We have already used some of these events extensively in this chapter. For example, you will use the loadedmetadata event whenever you want to read properties of the media resource (such as its duration or width and height) because you have to wait until these properties are available.

Rather than demonstrating the use of each possible event, we summarize them in the following table. As you go through, you may recognize some of them from earlier code samples in this chapter. This is just an overview table to find everything in one place.

Table 3-1. *Overview of the Media Element related Events*

Event	Is dispatched when...	Preconditions
loadstart	The web browser begins looking for media data, as part of the resource selection upon media element load, or load(), play(), or pause().	@networkState is NETWORK_LOADING for the first time.
progress	The web browser is fetching media data.	@networkState is NETWORK_LOADING.
suspend	The web browser has paused fetching media data but does not have the entire media resource downloaded yet.	@networkState is NETWORK_IDLE.
abort	The web browser was stopped from fetching the media data before it is completely downloaded, but not due to an error—rather, due to a user action, such as browsing away.	@error is MEDIA_ERR_ABORTED. @networkState is either NETWORK_EMPTY or NETWORK_IDLE, depending on when the download was aborted.
error	An error occurred while fetching the media data.	@error is MEDIA_ERR_NETWORK or higher. @networkState is either NETWORK_EMPTY or NETWORK_IDLE, depending on when the download was aborted.
emptied	A media element has just lost the network connection to a media resource, either because of a fatal error during load that's about to be reported or because the load() method was invoked while the resource selection algorithm was already running.	@networkState is NETWORK_EMPTY for the first time and all the IDL attributes are in their initial states.
stalled	The web browser tries to fetch media data, but data has not arrived for more than 3 seconds.	@networkState is NETWORK_LOADING.
loadedmetadata	The web browser has just set up the decoding pipeline for the media resource and determined the @duration and dimensions.	@readyState is HAVE_CURRENT_DATA or greater for the first time.
loadeddata	The web browser can render the media data at the current playback position for the first time.	@readyState is HAVE_CURRENT_DATA or greater for the first time.
canplay	The web browser can start or resume playback of the media resource, but without being certain of being able to play through at the given playback rate without a need for further buffering.	@readyState newly increased to HAVE_FUTURE_DATA or greater.

(continued)

Table 3-1. (*continued*)

Event	Is dispatched when...	Preconditions
canplaythrough	The web browser is now certain that with the given media data, the rate at which the network delivers further media data, and the given playback rate, the media resource can play through without further buffering.	@readyState is newly equal to HAVE_ENOUGH_DATA.
playing	Playback has started.	@readyState is newly equal to or greater than HAVE_FUTURE_DATA, @paused is "false," @seeking is "false," or the current playback position is contained in one of the ranges in @buffered.
waiting	Playback has stopped because the next media data is not available from the network yet, but the web browser expects that frame to become available in due course (i.e., less than 3 seconds). This can be after a seek, or when the network is unexpectedly slow.	@readyState is newly equal to or less than HAVE_CURRENT_DATA, and @paused is "false." Either @seeking is "true" or the current playback position is not contained in any of the ranges in @buffered.
seeking	The web browser is seeking and the seek operation is taking long enough that the web browser has time to fire the event.	@seeking is "true" and @readyState is less than HAVE_FUTURE_DATA.
seeked	The web browser is finished seeking.	@seeking has changed to "false."
ended	Playback has stopped because the end of the media resource was reached.	@ended is newly "true" and @currentTime is equal to @startTime plus @duration.
durationchange	The duration has just been changed upon media element load, or after an explicit change of @src and media resource fetching, or when the web browser has a better estimate (e.g., during streaming).	@readyState is HAVE_METADATA or greater for the first time.
timeupdate	The current playback position changed as part of normal playback every 15 to 250 ms. It is also fired when seeking, or when fetching a new media resource. It is also fired when playback has ended, when it is paused, when it is stopped due to an error, orbecause the media resource needs to buffer from the network. Basically, timeupdate is raised whenever something happens where you would want to update your own buffered or played video controls user interface.	@seeking is newly "true" OR @startTime is newly set OR @ended is newly "true" OR @paused is newly "true" OR @readyState newly changed to a value lower than HAVE_FUTURE_DATA without @ended is "true" OR @error is newly non-null with @readyState being HAVE_METADATA or more OR @seeking is "false," @paused is "false," @ended is "false," @readyState is at least HAVE_FUTURE_DATA and the last timeupdate was fired more than 15–250 ms ago.

(*continued*)

Table 3-1. (*continued*)

Event	Is dispatched when...	Preconditions
play	Playback has begun upon media element load with an @autoplay attribute, through user interaction, or after the play() method has returned.	@paused is newly "false."
pause	Playback has been paused either through user interaction, or after the pause() method has returned.	@paused is newly "true."
ratechange	Either the default playback rate or the playback rate has just been updated.	@defaultPlaybackRate or @playbackRate is newly changed.
resize	Either @videoWidth or @videoHeight or both have been changed.	Only works on video elements and when @readyState is not HAVE_NOTHING.
volumechange	Either the volume or the muted state of the media element changed.	@volume or @muted changed.

Third-Party Players

Now that you have had the opportunity to walk through the various bits and pieces of the JavaScript API as it relates to media, let's turn our attention to media players that use the API.

Throughout this book you may have noticed the various browsers use different controller designs to play the video. This is fine for general playback but there will be times where consistency of look across all browsers is important. You have two choices when confronting this requirement: Use a third-party player or "roll your own" custom video player.

There are a number of third-party players out there and choosing which one to use is up to you. There is a comparison chart at http://praegnanz.de/html5video/, which is a fairly comprehensive overview of the major players and their strengths and weaknesses. In this section we will be focusing on two players that made the "Sucks Less Than Others" hit parade: JW Player and Video.js. Both are open source and supported by a commercial entity that can provide hosting and other services to you. We start with the JW Player.

■ **Note** If neither of these appeal to you, take a look at another very popular player, Sublime, which is at www.sublimevideo.net/, or at mediaelement.js at http://mediaelementjs.com/. Sublime is likely the prettiest player out there, but it's not open source. Mediaelement.js is open source and provided by a community developer.

The big advantage with using a third-party media player is not just the consistent controls but that the authors have taken care to make these players work in all environments—including pre-HTML5 browsers and mobile—and for all users—including captions and keyboard control. They thus resolve some of the biggest headaches associated with media controls.

Using the JW Player

JW Player is a veteran in the space of video players. It was already dominant during the time that Flash was the main means of publishing video online and has managed to transition this into the HTML5 space. The basic player is available for free and open source at `https://github.com/jwplayer` and the JWPlayer company is offering hosted video services with an extensive toolset. You can dig into the player API at `http://support.jwplayer.com/customer/portal/articles/1413074-javascript-api-quick-start`.

You will need to sign up for a free account before being able to follow the next steps. Then you follow a three-step process: you simply tell the player where the video is located and what skin to use, and then you copy and paste the scripts into your HTML5 page. Here's how this currently works—the UI may have changed in the meantime.

1. The first step in the process is to click the `Publish A Video Now` button to open the Publish Wizard.

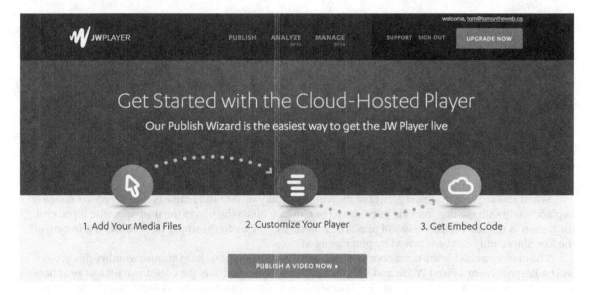

Figure 3-19. *Getting ready to publish a video*

The Publish Wizard offers three choices as to how you want to handle the video to be used.

- Use content from your web site.
- Use content that is currently sitting on your computer.
- Use a YouTube video.

The choice is yours to make, but our video and poster frame are already sitting on a web server so we are going to choose the web site option.

2. Click the `Your Website` button and enter the following:

- Media File: `http://html5videoguide.net/BeginningHTML5Video/CH3/video/Vultures.mp4`

- Poster Image: `http://html5videoguide.net/BeginningHTML5Video/CH3/img/BabyVulture.jpg`

- Media Title: Baby Turkey Vultures

When entering the links (see Figure 3-20), be sure to enter the full path to the content. If everything is correct click the `Publish Video` button to be taken to the Player Configuration page.

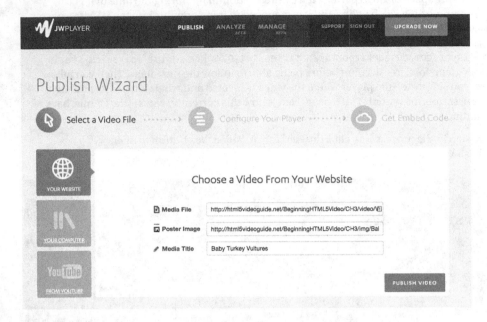

Figure 3-20. *Pointing the JW Player to the content*

When you arrive at the `Configuration` page the first thing you should notice is that the poster image is in place along with the title from the previous screen. In fact, this is the player the user sees and, if you click the button in the screen, the video will play. The watermark you see in the upper right corner is a feature of the free player and can't be removed by purchasing a license.

The choices available are more common sense than confusing. You get to choose whether this project will be Responsive or a Fixed Width and Height. If you choose Responsive, the pop-down list lets you choose a target screen and aspect ratio. Select Fixed Dimensions and you can enter the values into the dialog box.

The Skin area only presents you with a single choice because this is a free account. If you switch over to a paid account you naturally receive a ton of extras including more skins.

The `Playback` options are self-explanatory.

1. Select `Responsive` and `16:9- Wide screen` TV to maintain the video's aspect ratio.

2. In the `Playback` options (see Figure 3-21), select `HTML5` and `Show Controller`. Click the `Get Embed Code` button to open the Embed Code area.

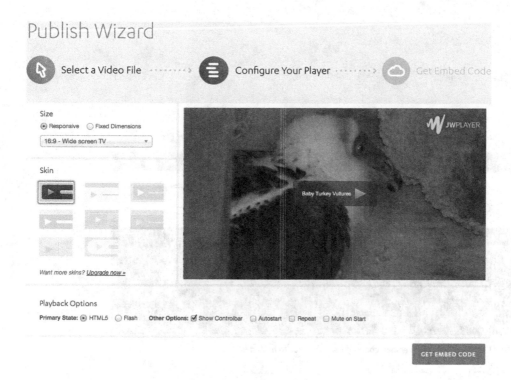

Figure 3-21. *The JW Player is configured*

Figure 3-22 presents two code snippets, and both get copied and pasted into your HTML document. The first snippet gets pasted into the <head></head> element of the HTML page. This little bit of code points to the JW Player's .js library containing the code that creates and controls the Player.

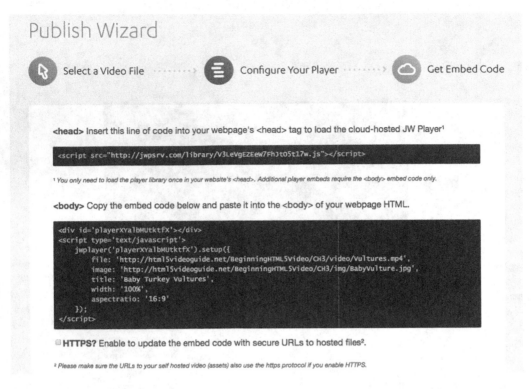

Figure 3-22. *The JW Player embed code*

The second snippet gets pasted into the body of the HTML document. The first line creates the div that will hold the player and the <script> element sets out the parameters for the content entered in the previous two screens.

In our page the final destination for the first snippet was as shown in Listing 3-19a.

Listing 3-19a. Using the JWPlayer

```
<!DOCTYPE html>
<html>
<head>
<meta charset="UTF-8">
<title>JW Player</title>
<script src="http://jwpsrv.com/library/V3LeVgEZEeW7FhJtO5t17w.js"></script>
</head>
```

You may have noticed, when you pointed the player to the video, it only points to the .mp4 version of the file. Obviously, there is a problem. If you want the video to play in Opera you will have to provide a .webm version of the file. Once you have pasted the code into the body here's how you fix that.

1. In the code. Copy this line: file: 'http://html5videoguide.net/ BeginningHTML5Video/CH3/video/Vultures.mp4' to your clipboard.

2. Paste the contents of the clipboard into the Player code after the .mp4 line and change the file extension to .webm as shown in Listing 3-19b.

Listing 3-19h. Using the JWPlayer

```
<div id=' playerXYalbMUtktfx '></div>
<script type='text/javascript'>
    jwplayer(playerXYalbMUtktfx).setup({
        file: 'video/Vultures.mp4',
        file: 'video/Vultures.webm',
        image: 'img/BabyVulture.jpg',
        title: 'JW Player Exercise',
        width: '100%',
        aspectratio: '16:9'
    });
</script>
```

When we browser tested in Opera, the result is what you see in Figure 3-23.

Figure 3-23. *The .webm version plays in Opera*

Using Video.JS

If an open source, easy-to-use and fully customizable player is what you are looking for, then you might want to try out Video JS. This player is made by the folks over at Zencoder and is designed to appeal to all web skill levels from beginner to code warrior.

Though there is a lot under the hood with this player, we will only be showing a very simple example of using this player. Due to its open source nature, Video.JS can be easily customized by either downloading the source files at www.videojs.com and adding them to your web directory or creating your own skin by modifying the LESS or CSS files at http://designer.videojs.com. If you really want to dig into the Video.JS API, you can find the documentation at https://github.com/videojs/video.js/blob/stable/docs/api/vjs.Player.md.

Here's how to play a video using Video JS:

1. Open a browser and navigate to `www.videojs.com`. The home page, shown in Figure 3-24, is where the "magic" happens.

Figure 3-24. *The Video.JS homepage is your only stop*

The player you will be creating is in the middle of the page. The play button, located in the upper left corner, is there for a reason: to keep it out of the way. The slider beside the Embed This Player button lets you control the size of this button and the video controls.

The three colored chips at the bottom allow you to customize the colors of the video controls. From left to right, the following is what these colors affect:

- Gray Chip: changes the color of the icons used in the controls, including the big overlay button.

- Blue Chip: changes the background color for progress and volume bars.

- Black Chip: changes the background color of the player controls.

Be careful here because the colors are contained in a color picker, which is accessed by clicking on a color chip. There is no way, here, to actually enter a hexadecimal or RGBA color value.

■ **Note** If you make bad color choices, you can always reset to the default colors by clicking the Reload button in your browser.

118

2. Click the Embed This Player button to open a window (see Figure 3-25) that presents you with a template for the embed code.

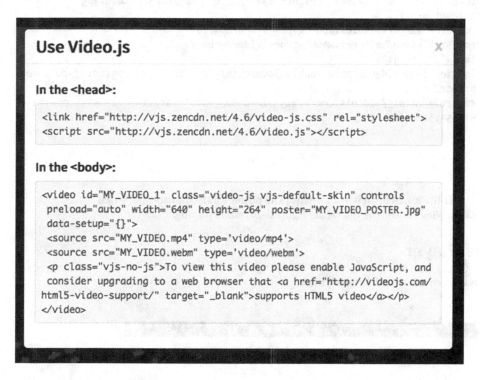

Figure 3-25. *The Video.js embed code*

3. Copy the code in the <head> area and paste it into your HTML page's head. Notice that any changes to the player design resulted in extra CSS to be added to the <head> element.

4. Return to the browser and select the code found in the <body> area. Paste it into the div on the HTML page where the video is to be located.

With the code in place you are going to have to make a few changes to the contents of the <video> element. In our case we:

- Changed the width and height property values to those of the videos.

- Changed the poster value to link to the location of the poster image.

- Changed the source element to link to the .mp4 and .webm versions of the video.

The resulting code is shown in Listing 3-20.

Listing 3-20. Embedding a video.js Player

```
<head>
    <link href="http://vjs.zencdn.net/4.6/video-js.css" rel="stylesheet">
    <script src="http://vjs.zencdn.net/4.6/video.js"></script>
</head>
```

```
<body>
        <video id="MY_VIDEO_1" class="video-js vjs-default-skin" controls
                preload="auto" width="683" height="432" poster="img/BabyVulture.jpg"
                data-setup="{}">
            <source src="video/Vultures.mp4" type='video/mp4'/>
            <source src="video/Vultures.webm" type='video/webm'/>
            <p class="vjs-no-js">
                To view this video please enable JavaScript, and consider upgrading to a web
                browser that
                <a href="http://videojs.com/html5-video-support/" target="_blank">supports
                HTML5 video</a>
            </p>
        </video>
</body>
```

5. Save the HTML file and open it in a browser. The poster frame appears and, when
    you click the Play button, the video (see Figure 3-26) starts playing.

The video.js Player

Use the video.js player to stream video into a web page

Here is the result :

Figure 3-26. *The video playing in the Video JS player*

■ **Tip** If you want to move the Play button to the middle of the video add the following class—`vjs-big-play-centered`—to the video element.

You may have noticed a curious difference between the JWPlayer and Video.js: Video.js is using a native HTML5 <video> element to embed all the control functionality, including Flash fallback, while JWPlayer is using a <div> element. The <video> element approach makes it easier for developers to directly manipulate a video element in JavaScript using the API that we already covered in this book. However, that approach has a downfall in that it avoids the video.js adaptation layer for older browsers that don't support the <video> element. Thus any control calls may not have an effect on the Flash fallback player. JWPlayer avoids this by not even exposing the HTML5 API in the first place. If you don't care about old browsers, the direct use of the browser JavaScript API as in video.js is tempting.

A Custom Player

There will be times when the players used by the various browsers or third-party players just don't fit the design objectives of the project. This could be due to branding, feature set, or even just personal preference. In this case building a custom video player is the only logical choice.

This is where the use of the JavaScript API really shines. Its foremost use case is to "roll your own" controls with a style that looks identical across all browsers. Since this is such a common use case, we provide you with an example on how to do so. It includes a skeleton of the HTML code, some CSS, and the required JavaScript calls to control it.

Our plan is to build the player displayed in Figure 3-27. You might find the controls that we've chosen and their layout a bit unusual. That's because we decided to build a player that targets blind or vision-impaired users with the main buttons they might need. The buttons are deliberately kept large, color-coded, and off the video to be better usable. You can easily tab onto them and activate them using the space bar.

Design inspiration and buttons from http://icant.co.uk/easy-youtube/
Thanks go to Chris Heilmann

Figure 3-27. *A custom accessible video player using the JavaScript API*

Note that in Safari, by default, "tab" is disabled as a navigation means across elements on the page and you have to use option-tab to navigate. To turn on "tab" navigation, open your Preferences and check "Preferences ➤ Advanced ➤ Press tab to highlight each item on a page."

The player consists of several interface elements. It has a progress display (the bar underneath the video), behind which it shows the seconds played and the video duration. Below that is a collection of buttons. The buttons allow the video to start playing (a play/pause toggle), rewind by 5 seconds, stop playback (and reset to file start), increase volume by 10 percentage points, reduce volume by 10 percentage points, and a mute/unmute toggle. To the right of the video is the volume display—it is grayed out when muted and the volume level is shown as a percentage in the bar's height.

■ **Note** If you do decide to construct your own video player, do your research and investigate sites that have done just that. Pay particular attention to the control elements used, their placement in the interface, and their sizes. If you have a User Experience specialist on your team, his or her input will be invaluable when it comes to the design and placement of the various control elements in the Player.

We start implementing this player by providing a skeleton of the HTML code, shown in Listing 3-21a, that creates this player.

Listing 3-21a. HTML Code for the Custom Player

```html
<div id="player">
  <div id="video">
    <video width="400" height="225" poster="img/BabyVulture.jpg">
      <source src="video/Vultures.mp4"  type="video/mp4"/>
      <source src="video/Vultures.webm" type="video/webm"/>
    </video>
    <div id="positionview">
      <div id="transportbar"><div id="position"></div></div>
      <div id="time">
        <span id="curTime">00:00</span>/<span id="duration">00:00</span>
      </div>
    </div>
  </div>

  <div id="volumecontrol">
    <div id="volumebar"><div id="volume"></div></div>
    <div id="vol"></div>
  </div>
  <div style="clear: both;"></div>

  <div id="controls">
    <div><input id="play"    type="image" src="img/0.gif" alt="Play"></div>
    <div><input id="repeat"  type="image" src="img/0.gif" alt="Repeat"></div>
    <div><input id="stop"    type="image" src="img/0.gif" alt="Stop"></div>
    <div><input id="louder"  type="image" src="img/0.gif" alt="Louder"></div>
    <div><input id="quieter" type="image" src="img/0.gif" alt="Quieter"></div>
    <div><input id="mute"    type="image" src="img/0.gif" alt="Mute"></div>
  </div>
</div>
```

A <div> with the id of player encapsulates the code in order that we can later give it a style to show it as an entity. Inside the #*player* div are three main divs: #video, #volumecontrol, and #controls. The #video part contains the video element as well as the transport bar and time displays. The #volumecontrol contains the volume bar and volume number display. The #controls contains all the buttons.

Note that the video element does not have an @controls attribute for the obvious reason that we have our own controls. Also, notice how the <input> elements, representing the buttons, have been made accessible by making them of type "image" and giving them an @alt attribute value. It is a best practice to provide alternative text for image input elements so they are accessible to vision-impaired users. Since we are going to provide the actual buttons in CSS, we have to put a 1 x 1 px gif placeholder into the @src attribute of the <input> elements to ensure they do not appear as broken images.

Next up is styling. In Listing 3-21b we're showing an extract of the CSS.

Listing 3-21b. CSS Styling for the Custom Player

```css
<style type="text/css">
    #player {
      padding: 10px;
      border:    5px solid black;
      border-radius: 15px;
      box-shadow: 10px 10px 5px gray;
      box-sizing: content-box;
      max-width: 455px;
    }
```

```css
#positionview {
  width: 400px; height: 40px;
}
#transportbar {
  height: 20px;
  width: 300px;
  position: relative;
  float: left;
  border: 2px solid black;
}
#position {
  background: #D7BC28;
  height: 20px;
  width: 0px;
}
#time {
  position: relative;
  float: right;
}
#video {
  position: relative;
  float: left;
  padding: 0;
  margin: 0;
}
/* include your own CSS for the volume control here and
   style every button with an offset on buttons.png (we only show one) */
#controls div input {
  background:url('img/buttons.png') no-repeat top left;
  border:none;
  height: 30px;
  width: 30px;
  padding: 5px;
  display: inline-block;
}
#controls div #repeat {
  background-position:0 -901px;
}
</style>
```

The player div gets a nice border, rounded corners and a shadow to make it stand out. This is a classic example of the maxim "Let the software do the work." Were this to be added as a .jpg or .png image, it would require extra resources to be downloaded, which typically reduces the speed of the web page. Also, CSS design is adaptive (i.e., it adapts to different layout sizes without losing quality). That would not be the case when using images, which need to be scaled to different layout sizes.

For the position display we have an outer <div> and an inner <div>, where the outer one provides the box for the duration of the video and the inner one displays the current playback position.

The buttons all use the same .png which includes all the buttons in use (that's called an "image sprite"). To display a particular button, you use an offset and a 30 x 30 px cropping area in CSS. Using image sprites reduces the number of resources that have to be downloaded and thus speeds up web page display again.

Finally we add the JavaScript, as in Listing 3-21c, that adds the functionality. We start by creating the variable names for the elements in the player.

Listing 3-21c. JavaScript Setup of DOM Element Variables

```
<script type="text/javascript">
      var video     = document.getElementsByTagName("video")[0];
      var position  = document.getElementById("position");
      var curTime   = document.getElementById("curTime");
      var duration  = document.getElementById("duration");
      var volume    = document.getElementById("volume");
      var vol       = document.getElementById("vol");
      var play      = document.getElementById("play");
      var repeat    = document.getElementById("repeat");
      var stop      = document.getElementById("stop");
      var louder    = document.getElementById("louder");
      var quieter   = document.getElementById("quieter");
      var mute      = document.getElementById("mute");
```

With that out of the way, we start using the IDL attribute values (see Listing 3-21d) to provide information for the duration and volume value displays:

Listing 3-21d. Loadedmetadata, timeupdate, and volumechange Event Callbacks to Update Duration and Volume Display

```
video.addEventListener("loadedmetadata", init, false);
function init(evt) {
  duration.innerHTML = video.duration.toFixed(2);
  vol.innerHTML      = video.volume.toFixed(2);
}

video.addEventListener("timeupdate", curTimeUpdate, false);
function curTimeUpdate(evt) {
  curTime.innerHTML = video.currentTime.toFixed(2);
  position.style.width = 300*video.currentTime/video.duration + "px";
}

video.addEventListener("volumechange", dispVol, false);
function dispVol(evt) {
  vol.innerHTML = video.volume.toFixed(2);
}
```

Finally, we're ready to actually make the various buttons work using the methods, events, and IDL attributes (see Listing 3-21e) available in the JavaScript API. Note how every button has an onclick event handler that is hooked up to changing video states.

Listing 3-21e. Loadedmetadata, timeupdate, and volumechange Event Callbacks to Update Duration and Volume Display

```
play.addEventListener("click", togglePlay, false);
function togglePlay(evt) {
  if (video.paused == false) {
    video.pause();
    play.style.backgroundPosition = "0 0";
  } else {
    video.play();
```

```
      play.style.backgroundPosition = "0 -151px";
    }
}

repeat.addEventListener("click", rewind, false);
function rewind(evt) {
  video.currentTime = video.currentTime - 2.0;
}

stop.addEventListener("click", restart, false);
function restart(evt) {
  video.pause();
  play.style.backgroundPosition = "0 0";
  video.currentTime = 0;
}

louder.addEventListener("click", volInc, false);
function volInc(evt) {
  changeVolume(video.volume + 0.1);
}

quieter.addEventListener("click", volDec, false);
function volDec(evt) {
  changeVolume(video.volume - 0.1);
}

mute.addEventListener("click", toggleMute, false);
function toggleMute(evt) {
  video.muted = !video.muted;
  if (video.muted) {
    volume.className = 'disabled';
  } else {
    volume.className = '';
  }
}

function changeVolume(changeTo) {
  if (video.muted){
    toggleMute();
  }
  if (changeTo > 1.0) {
    changeTo = 1.0;
  } else if (changeTo < 0.0) {
    changeTo = 0.0;
  }
  volume.style.height = 225*changeTo +'px';
  volume.style.marginTop = 225-(225*changeTo) + 'px';
  video.volume = changeTo;
  }
</script>
```

Take a minute to go through the code. You will notice many familiar IDL attributes—`video.duration`, `video.volume`, `video.currentTime`, `video.paused`, and `video.muted` are all used here to provide the functions behind the buttons. Finally you will also notice the `play()` and `pause()` control methods.

What you have just gone through is the JavaScript that makes this player fully functional. The purpose of the CSS is to manage the presentation. Put those two together and you have a powerful set of tools for creating practically anything.

Summary

This has been a rather longer yet very important chapter. It is critical that you both understand where JavaScript fits into the process and that its purpose is to provide functionality.

In this chapter we covered the following:

- JavaScript API of the <video> and <audio> elements. We have approached this in a structured way, starting with the IDL attributes that represent the content attributes from the HTML markup such as @src, @width, and @height. Then we discussed the IDL attributes that represent resource features such as @currentSrc, @duration, and @volume. Then we looked at the playback-related IDL attributes such as @currentTime, @paused, and @ended.

- The states of a media resource, including the networkState, the readyState, and played, buffered, or seekable time ranges.

- The control methods load(), play(), pause(), and canPlayType().

- A listing of the events the media elements fire. There are a fair number, including loadedmetadata, canplay, playing, pause, seeking, volumechange, durationchange, and ended.

- Third-party solutions for custom players, which all make extensive use of the JavaScript API.

- A practical use case of the JavaScript API: running your own custom controls.

We now have all the tools at hand to successfully use <audio> and <video> in HTML5 applications. We've already started looking at some accessibility issues through the player controls interface at the end of this chapter. The next chapter will dig more into this topic of accessibility, as well as look at internationalization and usability issues. We'll see you there.

CHAPTER 4

■ ■ ■

Accessibility, Internationalization, and Navigation

Accessibility and internationalization are two aspects of usability. The first —accessibility—is for those who have some form of sensory or physical impairment such as blindness. The second—internationalization—appeals to those who don't speak the language used by the audio or the video file.

Since the mid-1990s, the Web has developed a vast set of functionalities to cope with the extra requirements of these users and their needs. Web sites present themselves in multiple languages, and screen readers or Braille devices provide vision-impaired users with the ability to consume web page content. Captioning of video, especially foreign language videos, or use of the @alt attribute for images, has become virtually ubiquitous and the use of @alt for images has been a best practice for a long time.

The introduction of audio and video into the HTML5 specification poses new accessibility challenges and needs to extend this best practice. For the first time, we are publishing audio content that needs to be made accessible to hearing-impaired users and/or users who do not speak the language used in the audio data. We are also publishing, for the first time, HTML imaging content that changes over time which needs to be made accessible to vision-impaired users.

■ **Note** That last sentence may seem to be a bit out of place but video really is nothing more than a series of still images—keyframes separated by delta frames—that change over time.

What we must never forget is the word "World" in the term "World Wide Web." Unlike media broadcasters who can pick and choose their audiences, our audience is composed of a polyglot of able and disabled people as well as varying cultures and languages. Everyone who accesses your video or audio content has just as much a right to have access to it as anyone else and you don't get to pick and choose who views your content.

The primary means of addressing such needs has been the development of so-called alternative content technologies—or alt content—in which users are offered content that gives an alternative representation of the original content in a format they are able to consume. The practice of providing alt content was formalized in 1995 with the introduction of the @alt attribute in HTML 2 and has been a fixture of the specification since then.

When the W3C decided to introduce the `<audio>` and `<video>` tags into HTML5, the question of alt content became a major concern. For example, there are a number of choices for a simple video with a voiceover. They include the following:

- Captions, which are alt content for the audio track for hearing-impaired users.

- Subtitles, which are alt content for the audio track for foreign language users.

- Video descriptions, which are alt content of the video track for vision-impaired users.

When publishing media content, all these alt choices should be published, too, so you don't leave any audience members behind. Don't regard it as a chore: alt content is generally useful as additional content, for example, in the case of subtitles or chapter markers for video, which help any user keep track of what is being spoken and navigate to useful locations within the video file.

In this chapter, we discuss the features offered by HTML5 to satisfy the accessibility and internationalization needs of media users. We start this chapter with a requirements analysis by providing an overview of alternative content technologies for media content. Then we introduce the features that HTML5 offers to satisfy the requirements.

■ **Note** The creation of alt content for videos has important implications for all users on the Web—not just those with special needs or non-native users. The biggest advantage is that text, representing exactly what is happening in the video, is made available and this text is the best means for searches to take place. Just keep in mind, search technology is very advanced when it comes to text, but still quite restricted when it comes to the content of audio or video. It is for this reason that alt content provides the only reliable means of indexing audiovisual content for high-quality search.

Alternative Content Technologies

Throughout this book we have presented the various techniques that can be used to add audio and video assets to HTML5 documents in the form of "Feature-Example-Demonstration." Before we get to this, we will present the many issues that web designers and developers confront in their efforts to cope with the growing demands of accessibility and internationalization.

The first issue to be confronted is legislative in nature.

More and more countries are passing accessibility laws regarding the Web. For example, in the United States, Section 504 of the 1973 Rehabilitation Act was the first civil rights legislation designed to protect the disabled from discrimination based on their disability status. Though the Internet, let alone personal computing, didn't exist, the law applied to any employer or organization that received federal funds and this included government agencies, educational institutions ranging from K-12 to post-secondary, and any other federally funded project. In 1998, when the Internet boom was underway, Section 508 of the Reauthorized Rehabilitation Act created binding and enforceable standards clearly outlining and specifying what is meant by "accessible" electronic and information technology products. The upshot is that any web project developed for a company or organization receiving federal funds in the United States has to comply with Section 508. If you are unfamiliar with Section 508, a good overview is available at `http://webaim.org/articles/laws/usa/`.

Though accessibility policies vary from country to country, most countries —including those in the European Union—have adopted standards based on the W3C's Web Content Accessibility Guidelines (`www.w3.org/TR/WCAG/`)—a set of standardized rules developed by the W3C to explain how to make web content accessible. WCAG was developed because, increasingly, it wasn't only governments that were wrestling with the issue of accessibility but all major web content publishing sites. If you are unfamiliar with the W3C's Web Accessibility Initiative, more information is available at www.w3.org/WAI/. What you do need to know is that many legislative measures are based on this group's work.

The next issue that challenges web developers is the diversity of user requirements for alt content around audio and video, which is quite complex. If you want to learn more about media accessibility requirements, there is also a W3C document published by WAI and coauthored by one of the authors of this book: www.w3.org/WAI/PF/media-a11y-reqs/.

Vision-Impaired Users

For users with poor or no vision, there are two major challenges: how to perceive the visual content of the video, and how to interact with and control media elements.

Perceiving Video Content

The method developed to aid vision-impaired users to consume the imagery content of video is *Described Video*. In this approach, a description of what is happening in the video is made available as the video's time passes and the audio continues to play back. The following approaches are possible:

- **Audio descriptions**: a speaker explains what is visible in the video as the video progresses.

- **Text descriptions**: time-synchronized blocks of text are provided in time with what is happening on screen and a screen reader synthesizes this to speech for the vision-impaired user.

■ **Note**   It may be necessary to introduce pauses into the video to allow the insertion of extra explanations for which there is no time within the main audio track. This will extend the time it takes to consume the video. Therefore, such descriptions are called **extended descriptions**.

Audio descriptions can either be created as a separate audio recording added to the main audio track or mixed into the main audio recording and cannot be extracted again.

Such **mixed-in audio description** tracks can be provided as part of a multitrack video resource as long as they don't extend the video's timeline. One would create one audio track without the audio descriptions and a separate mixed-in track with the audio descriptions, so they can be activated as alternatives to each other.

When extended descriptions are necessary, mixed-in audio descriptions require using a completely separate video element, because they work on a different timeline. The production effort involved in creating such a new video file with mixed-in audio descriptions is, however, enormous. Therefore, mixing-in should only be used if there is no alternative means of providing described video.

Text descriptions are always provided as additional content to be activated on demand.

From a technical viewpoint, there are two ways of publishing described video.

- **In-band**: Audio or text descriptions are provided as a separate track in the media resource to be activated either as an addition to the main audio track or as an alternative to it. Text descriptions are always activated additionally to the main audio track. Audio descriptions that are a separate recording are also activated additionally, while mixed-in descriptions are an alternative to the main audio track. This is actually quite similar to how descriptive audio is traditionally provided through secondary audio programming (see http://en.wikipedia.org/wiki/Second_audio_program).

- **External**: Audio or text descriptions are provided as a separate resource. When the timelines match, HTML5 provides markup mechanisms to link the media resources together. The tracks in the external resource are then handled as "out-of-band" versions of the "in-band" tracks and HTML5 provides the same activation mechanisms as for in-band tracks. Browsers handle the download, interpretation, and synchronization of the separate resources during playback.

The multitrack media API (application programming interface) of HTML5 deals both with in-band and out-of-band audio and text description tracks. In-band captions are supported by Apple in Safari and Quicktime.

Interacting with Content

Vision-impaired users need to interact with described video in several ways.

- **Activate/Deactivate Descriptions.** Where described video is provided through in-band tracks or external resources, the browsers can automatically activate or deactivate description tracks based on user needs specified in user preference settings in browsers. Explicit user control should also be available through interactive controls such as a menu of all available tracks and their activation status. Currently, browsers don't provide such preference settings or menus for video descriptions. They can, however, be developed in JavaScript.

- **Navigate Within and into Media.** Since audiovisual content is a major source of information for vision-impaired users, navigation within and into that content is very important. Sighted users often navigate through video by clicking on time offsets on a playback progress bar. This direct access functionality also needs to be available to vision-impaired users. Jumping straight into temporal offsets or into semantically meaningful sections of content helps the consumption of the content enormously. In addition, a more semantic means of navigating the content along structures such as chapters, scenes, or acts must also be available. Media fragment URIs (uniform resource identifiers) and WebVTT (Web Video Text Tracks) chapters provide for the direct access functionality.

Hard-of-Hearing Users

For users who have trouble hearing, the content of the audio track needs to be made available in an alternative form from audio. Captions, transcripts, and sign language translations have traditionally been used as alternatives. In addition, improvements to the played audio can also help hard-of-hearing people who are not completely deaf to grasp the content of the audio.

For captions, we distinguish between the following:

- **Traditional captions**: blocks of text are synchronized with what is happening on screen and displayed time-synchronously with the video. Often they are overlaid at the bottom of the video viewport, sometimes placed elsewhere in the viewport to avoid overlapping other on-screen text, and sometimes placed underneath the viewport to avoid any overlap at all. Very little, if any, styling is applied to captions to make sure the text is readable with appropriate fonts, colors, and a means to separate it from the video colors through, for example, text outlines or a text background. Some captioned videos introduce color coding for speakers, speaker labeling, and/ or positioning of the text close to the speakers on screen to further improve cognition and reading speed. HTML5 has introduced text tracks of kind "captions" and WebVTT to render captions in browsers.

- **Enhanced captions**: in the modern web environment, captions can be so much more than just text. Animated and formatted text can be displayed in captions. Icons can be used to convey meaning—for example, separate icons for different speakers or sound effects. Hyperlinks can be used to link on-screen URLs to actual web sites or to provide links to further information making it easier to use the audiovisual content as a starting point for navigation. Image overlays can be used in captions to allow displaying timed images with the audiovisual content. To enable this use, general HTML markup is desirable in captions. It is possible to do so using WebVTT with text tracks of the kind "metadata."

For now, we'll concentrate on traditional captions.

Such captions are always authored as text but are sometimes added directly to the video imagery. This technique is called burnt-in captions, or "open captions" because they are always active and open for everyone to see. Traditionally, this approach has been used to deliver captions on TV and in cinemas because it doesn't require any additional technology to be reproduced. This approach is, however, very inflexible. On the Web, this approach is discouraged, since it is easy to provide captions as text. Only legacy content where video without the burnt-in captions is not available should be published in this way. At best, video with burnt-in captions should be made available as a separate track in a multitrack media file or as a separate stream in a MediaSource, such that it is possible for user to choose between the video track with and the one without captions.

From a technical viewpoint, there are two ways of publishing captions.

- **In-band**: burnt-in caption tracks or text captions are provided as a separate track in the media resource. This allows independent activation and deactivation of the captions. It requires web browsers to support handling of multitrack video.

- **External**: text captions are provided as a separate resource and linked to the media resource through HTML markup. Similar to separate tracks, this allows independent activation and deactivation of the captions. It requires browsers to download, interpret, and synchronize the extra resource to the main resource during playback. This is supported in HTML5 through text tracks and WebVTT files.

If you have the choice, publish captions as separate external files because it is much simpler to edit them again later and do other text analysis on them than when they are mashed up with media data.

While we have specified the most common use cases, we must not forget that there are also cases for people with cognitive disabilities (dyslexia) or for learners requiring any of these alternative content technologies.

Transcript

Full-text transcripts of the audio track of audiovisual resources are another means of making this content accessible to hard-of-hearing users and, in fact, to anyone. It can be more efficient to read—or cross-read—a transcript of an audio or video resource rather than having to sit through its full extent. One particularly good example is a site called Metavid, which has full transcripts of US senate proceedings and is fully searchable.

Two types of transcripts are typically used.

- **Plain transcripts**: these are the equivalent of captions but brought together in a single block of text. This block of text can be presented simply as text on the web page somewhere around the video or as a separate resource provided through a link near the video.

- **Interactive transcripts**: these are also equivalent to captions but brought together in a single block of text with a tighter relationship between the text and video. The transcript continues to have time-synchronized blocks such that a click on a specific text cue will navigate the audiovisual resource to that time offset. Also, as the video reaches the next text cue, the transcript will automatically move the new text cue center stage, for example, by making sure it scrolls to a certain on-screen location and/or is highlighted.

Incidentally, the latter type of interactive transcript is also useful for vision-impaired users as a navigation aid when used in conjunction with a screen reader. It is, however, necessary then to mute the audiovisual content while foraging through the interactive transcript, because otherwise it will compete with the sound from the screen reader and make both unintelligible.

Sign Translation

To hard-of-hearing users—in particular to deaf users—sign language is often the most proficient language they speak, followed by the written language of the country in which they live. They often communicate much quicker and more comprehensively in sign language, which—much like Mandarin and similar Asian languages—communicates typically through having a single symbol for semantic entities. Signs exist for letters, too, but sign speaking in letters is very slow and only used in exceptional circumstances. The use of sign language is the fastest and also most expressive means of communicating between hard-of-hearing users.

From a technical viewpoint, there are three ways of realizing sign translation.

- **Mixed-in**: sign translation that is mixed into the main video track of the video can also be called burnt-in sign translation, or "open sign translation," because it is always active and open for everyone to see. Typically, open sign translation is provided as a picture-in-picture (PIP) display, where a small part of the video viewport is used to burn in the sign translation. Traditionally, this approach has been used to deliver sign translation on TV and in cinemas because it doesn't require any additional technology to be reproduced. This approach is, however, very inflexible since it forces all users to consume the sign translation without possibilities for personal choice, in particular without allowing the choice of using a different sign language (from a different country) for the sign translation.

  On the Web, this approach is discouraged. Sign translation that is provided as a small PIP video is particularly hard to see in the small, embedded videos that are typical for Web video. Therefore only legacy content where video without the burnt-in sign translation is not available should be published in this way. Where possible, the sign translation should exist as separate content.

- **In-band**: sign translation is provided as a separate track in the media resource. This allows independent activation and deactivation of the extra information. It requires web browsers to support handling of multitrack video.

- **External**: sign translation is provided as a separate resource and linked to the media resource through HTML markup. Similar to separate tracks, this allows independent activation and deactivation of the extra information. It requires browsers to synchronize the playback of two video resources.

Clear Audio

This is a feature that is not alternative content for the hearing-impaired, but a more generally applicable feature that improves the usability of audio content. It is commonly accepted that speech is the most important part of an audio track, since it conveys the most information. In modern multitrack content, speech is sometimes provided as a separate track apart from the sound environment. A good example would be karaoke music content, but clear audio content can also easily be provided for professionally developed video content, such as movies, animations, or TV series.

Many users have problems understanding the speech in a mixed audio track. But, when the speech is provided in a separate track, it is possible to allow increasing the volume of the speech track independently of the rest of the audio tracks, thus rendering "clearer audio"—that is, more comprehensible speech.

Technically, this can only be realized if there is a separate speech track available, either as a separate in-band track or as a separate external resource.

Deaf-Blind Users

It is very hard to provide alternative content for users who can neither see nor hear. The only means of consumption for them is basically Braille, which requires text-based alternative content.

Individual Consumption

If deaf-blind users consume the audiovisual content by themselves, it makes sense to provide a transcript that contains a description of what is happening both on screen and in the audio. It's basically a combination of a text video description and an audio transcript. The technical realization of this is thus best as a combined transcript. Interestingly, Braille devices are very good at navigating hypertext, so some form of transcript enhanced with navigation markers is also useful.

Shared Viewing Environment

In a shared viewing environment where the deaf-blind user consumes the content together with a seeing and/or hearing person, the combination of text and audio descriptions needs to be provided synchronously with the video playback. A typical Braille reading speed is 60 words per minute. Compare that to the average adult reading speed of around 250 to 300 words per minute or even a usual speaking speed of 130–200 words per minute and you realize that it will be hard for a deaf-blind person to follow along with any normal audiovisual presentation. A summarized version may be necessary, which can still be provided in sync just as text descriptions are provided in sync and can be handed through to a Braille device. The technical realization of this is thus either as an interactive transcript or through a summarized text description.

Learning Support

Some users prefer to slow down the playback speed to assist them in perceiving and understanding audiovisual content; for others, the normal playback speed is too slow. In particular vision-impaired users have learned to digest audio at phenomenal rates. For such users, it is very helpful to be able to slow down or speed up a video or audio resource's playback rate. Such speed changes require keeping the pitch of the audio to maintain its usability.

A feature that can be very helpful to those with learning disabilities is the ability to provide explanations. For example, whenever an uncommon word is used, it can be very helpful to pop up an explanation of the term (e.g., through a link to Wikipedia or to a dictionary). This is somewhat analogous to the aims of enhanced captions and can be provided in the same manner through allowing hyperlinks and/or overlays.

With learning material, we can also provide grammatical markup of the content in time-synchronicity. This is often used for linguistic research but can also help people with learning disabilities to understand the content better. Grammatical markup can be augmented onto captions or subtitles to provide a transcription of the grammatical role of the words in the given context. Alternatively, the grammatical roles can be provided just as markers for time segments, relying on the audio to provide the actual words.

Under the learning category we can also subsume the use case of music lyrics or karaoke. These provide, like captions, a time-synchronized display of the spoken (or sung) text for users to follow along. Here, they help users learn and understand the lyrics. Similar to captions, they can be technically realized through burning-in, in-band multitrack, or external tracks.

Foreign Users

Users who do not speak the language that is used in the audio track of audiovisual content are regarded as *foreign users*. Such users also require alternative content to allow them to comprehend the media content.

Scene Text Translations

The video track typically poses only a small challenge to foreign users. Most scene text is not important enough to be translated or can be comprehended from context. However, sometimes there is on-screen text such as titles that explain the location, for which a translation would be useful. It is recommended to include such text in the subtitles.

Audio Translations

There are two ways in which an audio track can be made accessible to a foreign user.

- **Dubbing**: provide a supplementary audio track that can be used as a replacement for the original audio track. This supplementary audio track can be provided **in-band** with a multitrack audiovisual resource, or **external** as a linked resource, where playback needs to be synchronized.

- **(Enhanced) Subtitles**: provide a text translation of what is being said in the audio track. This supplementary text track can be provided **burnt-in**, **in-band**, or as an **external resource**, just like captions. And just like captions, burnt-in subtitles are discouraged because of their inflexibility.

Technology Summary

When analyzing the different types of technologies that are necessary to provide alternatives to the original content and satisfy special user requirements, we can see that they broadly fall into the following different classes:

- **Burnt-in**: this type of alternative content is actually not provided as an alternative but as part of the main resource. Since there is no means to turn this off (other than through signal processing), no HTML5 specifications need to be developed to support them.

- **Page text**: this type covers the transcriptions that can be consumed either in relation to the video or completely independent of it.

- **Synchronized text**: this type covers text, in-band or external, that is displayed in sync with the content and includes text descriptions, captions, and subtitles.

- **Synchronized media**: this type covers audio or video, in-band or external, that is displayed in sync with the content and includes audio descriptions, sign translation, and dubbing.

- **Navigation**: this is mostly a requirement for vision-impaired users or mobility-impaired users but is generally useful to all users.

With a basic understanding of what we are dealing with and the needs to be satisfied, let's take a look at some methods for making media accessible. We'll start with the obvious: transcripts.

Transcripts

Transcripts are a method designed to provide full-text transcripts—either interactive or plain text—of the audio track found in audiovisual resources. This is a great means of making audiovisual content accessible to hard-of-hearing users and in fact to anyone. It can be more efficient to read—or cross-read—a transcript of an audio or video resource rather than having to sit through its full extent. One site that provides transcripts (see Figure 4-1) with the video content is ted.com.

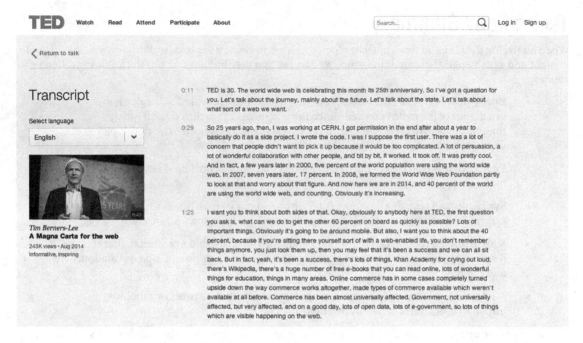

Figure 4-1. *One site that provides transcripts is ted.com*

In the following code listings, we've kept the numbering scheme such that you can easily find the code example on `http://html5videoguide.net/` from the listing number. For example, Listings 4-1a and 4-1b are from example 1 in Chapter 4.

The code block in Listing 4-1a shows an example of how to link a plain transcript to a media element.

Listing 4-1a. Providing a Plain Transcript for a Video Element

```
<video poster="img/ElephantDreams.png" controls>
  <source src="video/ElephantDreams.mp4"  type="video/mp4">
  <source src="video/ElephantDreams.webm" type="video/webm">
</video>
<p>
    <a id="videoTranscript" href="ElephantDreams.html">
    Read the transcript for this video.</a>
</p>
```

In this example the transcript is a linked html document named `ElephantDreams.html`. When the video opens the link appears under the video. This allows a (hearing-impaired) user to read about the content of the video. The transcript, Listing 4-1b, is a very basic HTML document.

Listing 4-1b. The Transcript Is a Very Basic HTML Document

```
<!DOCTYPE html>
<html lang="en">
  <head>
    <title>Media Accessibility Demo</title>
  </head>
```

```
<body>
  <h1>
  Transcript: <a href="../media/video_elephant.ogv">Elephant's Dream</a>
  </h1>
  <p>
    Screen text: "The orange open movie project presents"
  </p>
  <p>
    [Introductory titles are showing on the background of a water pool with
     fishes swimming and mechanical objects lying on a stone floor.]
  </p>
  <p>
    "Elephant's Dream"
  </p>
  <p>
    Proog: At the left we can see... At the right we can see the...the
    head-snarlers. Everything is safe.
    Perfectly safe.
  </p>
  <p>
    [Two people stand on a small bridge.]
  </p>
  <p>
    Proog: Emo? Emo! Watch out!
  </p>
</body>
</html>
```

When you open the file in a browser (see Figure 4-2), you will see the HTML page of the video with the hyperlink underneath it. Click the link and the transcript HTML page opens.

Figure 4-2. *Plain external transcript linked to a video element*

The transcript shown in Figure 4-2 has a transcription of both the spoken text and of what is happening in the video. This makes sense, since the transcript is independent of the video and as such it must contain everything that happens in the video. It also represents both a text description and a transcript, making it suitable for deaf-blind users once rendered into Braille.

Interactive Transcripts

In the previous example the transcript was presented in the form of a separate HTML document that opened in its own window. In many respects this is a static method of providing a transcript. Interactive transcripts provide the experience in a whole different manner. They not only provide a transcription of the spoken text and what is happening in the video but they also move in time with the video and don't require a separate window.

Currently there is no HTML5 specification that provides such an interactive transcript via markup. Therefore, interactivity has to be accomplished through the use of JavaScript and a series of HTML <div> elements to hold the text cues for the screen reader.

The HTML markup of an example can be seen in the following code in Listing 4-2a:

Listing 4-2a. The HTML Provides the Timing and the Transcript

```
<div id="videoBox">
    <video poster="img/ElephantDreams.png" controls>
      <source src="video/ElephantDreams.mp4"  type="video/mp4">
      <source src="video/ElephantDreams.webm" type="video/webm">
    </video>
</div>
<div id="speaking" aria-live="rude">
</div>
<div id="transcriptBox">
  <h4>Interactive Transcript</h4>
  <p style="font:small;">Click on text to play video from there.</p>
  <div id="transcriptText">
    <p id="c1" class="cue" data-time="0.0" aria-live="rude" tabindex="1">
    [Screen text: "The orange open movie project presents"]
    </p>
    <p id="c2" class="cue" data-time="5.0" aria-live="rude" tabindex="1">
    [Introductory titles are showing on the background of a water pool
     with fishes swimming and mechanical objects lying on a stone floor.]
    </p>
    <p id="c3" class="cue" data-time="12.0" aria-live="rude" tabindex="1">
    [Screen text: "Elephant's Dream"]
    </p>
    <p id="c4" class="cue" data-time="15.0" tabindex="1">
    Proog: At the left we can see...  At the right we can see the... the
    head-snarlers.
    Everything is safe. Perfectly safe. Emo? Emo!
    </p>
...
</div>
</div>
```

Next to the <video> element, we provide a <div> element with the id of speaking. This element is given the text cues that a screenreader should read out. It has an @aria-live attribute for this, which tells the screenreader to read out whatever text has changed inside the element as soon as the change happens. This provides a simple means of rendering text descriptions for vision-impaired users.

Next, we provide a scrollable <div> named transcriptBox to display the transcript in. Each cue within transcriptBox is provided with a @data-time attribute, which contains its start time and a @tabindex to allow vision-impaired users to navigate through it by pressing the Tab key. A cue implicitly ends with the next cue.

Figure 4-3 shows the result that we want to achieve.

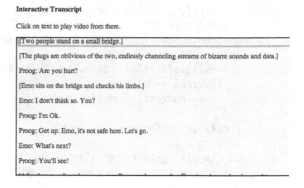

Figure 4-3. *Interactive transcript for a video element*

The JavaScript that creates the interactivity and the renders the text descriptions is shown in Listing 4-2b.

Listing 4-2b. JavaScript Provides the Interactivity for a Transcript

```
window.onload = function() {
  // get video element
  var video = document.getElementsByTagName("video")[0];
  var transcript = document.getElementById("transcriptBox");
  var trans_text = document.getElementById("transcriptText");
  var speaking = document.getElementById("speaking");
  var current = -1;

  // register events for the clicks on the text
  var cues = document.getElementsByClassName("cue");
  for (var i=0; i<cues.length; i++) {
    cues[i].addEventListener("click", function(evt) {
      var start = parseFloat(this.getAttribute("data-time"));
      video.currentTime = start;
      video.play();
    }, false);
  }

  // pause video as you mouse over transcript
  transcript.addEventListener("mouseover", function(evt) {
    video.pause();
  }, false);

  // scroll to text as video time changes
  video.addEventListener("timeupdate", function(evt) {
    if (video.paused || video.ended) {
      return;
    }
```

```
    // scroll to currently playing time offset
    for (var i=0; i<cues.length; i++) {
      var cueTime = cues[i].getAttribute("data-time");
      if (cues[i].className.indexOf("current") == -1 &&
          video.currentTime >= parseFloat(cueTime) &&
          video.currentTime < parseFloat(cueTime)) {
        trans_text.scrollTop =
          cues[i].offsetTop - trans_text.offsetTop;
        if (current >= 0) {
            cues[current].classList.remove("current");
        }
        cues[i].className += " current";
        current = i;
        if (cues[i].getAttribute("aria-live") == "rude") {
          speaking.innerHTML = cues[i].innerHTML;
        }
      }
    }
  }
  }, false);
};
```

As you can see, the JavaScript handles the following functions:

- Register an onclick event handler on the cues, such that it is possible to use them to navigate around the video.

- Register an onmouseover event handler on the transcription box, such that the video is paused as soon as you move the mouse into the transcription box for navigation.

- Register an ontimeupdate event handler on the video, which checks the scrolling position of the text and scrolls it up as necessary, sets a background color on the currently active cue, and also checks the value of the @aria-live attribute of the cue, such that if it's not spoken in the video, the respective content is read out by a screenreader.

The elements, as designed here, work both for vision- and hearing-impaired users. As you click the Play button on the video, the video plays back normally and the caption text that is part of the interactive transcript is displayed in a scrolling display on the right, highlighting the current cue. If you have a screenreader enabled, the markup in the transcript that has been marked with an @aria-live attribute is copied to the screenreader to be read out at the appropriate time. Click on a piece of text and the video moves to that position in the playback.

The <track> Element: Subtitles, Captions, and Text Descriptions

Now that you know how transcripts can be included with your video projects, let's turn our attention to captions, subtitles, and descriptions, which are typically authored separately from your web page. As such, HTML5 has introduced special markup and APIs (application programming interfaces) to automatically synchronize these external files with the video's timeline.

In this section we focus on the <track> element and its API. They have been introduced into HTML and let you associate a time-based text file with a media resource. This text file—usually a *WebVTT or* .vtt file—can be used in a number of ways including adding subtitles, captions, and text descriptions of the media content.

■ **Note**   It is worth mentioning that browsers may also support other file formats in the <track> element. For example, IE10 supports both WebVTT and TTML (Timed Text Markup Language). TTML is often used by the captioning industry to interchange captions between authoring systems, see www.w3.org/TR/ttml1/. We won't discuss TTML in more detail here, because it is only supported in IE and other browsers have explicitly stated that they are not interested in implementing support for it.

WebVTT is a new standard and is supported by all browsers implementing the <track> element. WebVTT provides a simple, extensible, and human-readable format on which to build text tracks.

We are going to get deeper into the details of the WebVTT format's features in the next section. However, to make use of the <track> element, you will need to use a basic .vtt file. If you are unfamiliar with this format, a basic understanding is helpful. WebVTT files are UTF-8 text files that consist simply of a "WEBVTT" file identifier followed by a series of so-called *cues* containing a start and end time and some cue text. Cues need to be separated from each other by empty lines. For example, a simple WebVTT file would be

```
WEBVTT

00:00:15.000 --> 00:00:17.951
At the left we can see...

00:00:18.166 --> 00:00:20.083
At the right we can see the...
```

The first line—WEBVTT—must be in all capital letters and is used by the browser to check if it really is a .vtt file. IE10 actually requires this header to be "WEBVTT FILE" and since other browsers ignore the extra text, you might as well always author files with that identifier.

The time markers in the cues provide the duration of the cues expressed as *hr:min:sec.mms* and the cue text is the text appears on the screen. In this case, the words *"At the left we can see..."* will be visible from 15 seconds to 17.951 seconds of the video's playback timeline. Any word processor or editor that creates a plain text file can be used to create a .vtt file.

■ **Note**   WebVTT is the modern version of what was formerly called WebSRT. For those of you who already have projects containing subtitles in SRT, you will find VTT follows a very similar approach. There is a no-frills converter available at https://atelier.u-sub.net/srt2vtt/.

With the .vtt file created, it needs to be tied to the <track> element. This element is placed inside either the <audio> or <video> elements and references external time-synchronized text resources—a .vtt file—that align with the <audio> or <video> element's timeline. In <video> elements, captions and subtitles are rendered on top of the video viewport. Since <audio> elements have no viewport, <track> elements that are children of <audio> elements are not rendered and just made available to script.

■ **Note**   IE10 requires that .vtt files are served with a mime type of "text/vtt"; otherwise it will ignore them. So, make sure your Web server has this configuration (e.g., for Apache you need to add this to the mime.types file). In your browser page inspector, you can check the "content-type" HTTP header that the Web browser downloads for a .vtt file to confirm that your server is providing the correct mime type.

Let's look at the <track> element's content attributes.

@src

Naturally, this attribute references an external text track file. Listing 4-3 is a simple code example of a track element with a reference to a WebVTT file.

Listing 4-3. Example of <track> Markup with a .vtt File

```
<video controls poster="img/ElephantDreams.png">
  <source src="video/ElephantDreams.mp4"  type="video/mp4">
  <source src="video/ElephantDreams.webm" type="video/webm">
  <track src="tracks/ElephantDreams_en.vtt">
</video>
```

The @src attribute only creates the reference to an external text track file. It does not activate it, but it allows browsers to make a listing of the referenced tracks available to the user. This is normally displayed via a menu in the video's controls.

■ **Note**   If you are working along with us, it is important to run the <track> examples on a Web server and not locally. Documents loaded from file URLs have special security restrictions in blink-based browsers to stop malicious scripts you may have saved to your desktop from doing bad things. For Chrome, you can also run it with a command-line flag like this to avoid the issue: `chrome --disable-web-security`.

Figure 4-4 shows the resulting display of Listing 4-3 in Safari (left) and Google Chrome (right).

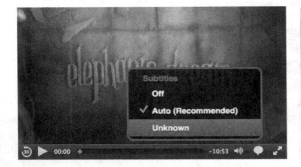 

Figure 4-4. *Video element with a track child element in Safari and Google Chrome*

Safari, as shown on the left in Figure 4-4, has a menu behind a speech bubble on the video controls. You activate the menu by clicking on the speech bubble. The track we defined is listed as "Unknown" in the menu. Activate that track by clicking on it and you can watch the rendered subtitles.

Google Chrome, on the right, shows a "CC" button through which you can activate captions and subtitles. If you click that button and watch the video, you will be able to see the subtitles that loaded from the .vtt file rendered on top of the video.

Opera looks identical to Google Chrome. In Firefox, no subtitle activation button is available as yet. We will explain how you can still activate a subtitle track via markup next. Alternatively, you can also do so from JavaScript, which we will also look at later in this chapter.

Internet Explorer (see Figure 4-5) is a combination of Safari and Chrome. It includes the CC button which, when clicked, shows you the name of the track. Click the name and the subtitles are rendered.

Figure 4-5. *Video element with a track child element in Internet Explorer*

■ **Note**   You may have noticed Safari and Internet Explorer provide the most useful visual activation and selection mechanisms for text tracks: a menu activated from the video controls. All browsers intend to implement this feature, but not all of them have reached that state. Google Chrome and Opera show a single "CC" button for now, which activates the most appropriate subtitle track (e.g., English if your browser language is set to English).

@default

The next attribute—@default—allows a Web page author to pick a text track and mark it as activated by default. It's a Boolean attribute meaning the default has the same value as the Boolean true value. Here, Listing 4-4 provides an example:

Listing 4-4. Example of <track> Markup with a .vtt File, Activated with @default

```
<video controls poster="img/ElephantDreams.png">
  <source src="video/ElephantDreams.mp4"  type="video/mp4">
  <source src="video/ElephantDreams.webm" type="video/webm">
  <track src="tracks/ElephantDreams_en.vtt" default>
</video>
```

You can see in Figure 4-6 how the "CC" button in Opera on the left and the menu selection in Safari on the right are automatically turned on. Google Chrome, like Opera, automatically turns on the "CC" button.

Figure 4-6. *Video element with @default activated track child element in Opera (left) and Safari (right)*

Now you can also play back the video in Firefox and see the subtitles display unlike the results in the previous example. By using the `@default` attribute, the subtitles, as shown in Figure 4-7, contained in the `.vtt` file are now activated. Just be aware that the subtitles will be hidden by the video controls if the user places the cursor at the bottom of the video.

Internet Explorer, as shown in Figure 4-7, not only activates captions but shows you the default track that is playing. It's currently called "untitled," so we need to give it a proper name.

Figure 4-7. *Video element with @default activated track child element in Firefox and Internet Explorer*

@label

We just learned that tracks not given a name are given a random label of "Unknown" or "untitled" in their track selection menu. We can fix this by providing an explicit `@label` attribute.

Listing 4-5 provides an example.

Listing 4-5. Example of <track> Markup with a .vtt File and a @label

```
<video controls poster="img/ElephantDreams.png">
  <source src="video/ElephantDreams.mp4"  type="video/mp4">
  <source src="video/ElephantDreams.webm" type="video/webm">
  <track src="tracks/ElephantDreams_en.vtt" default label="English">
</video>
```

Figure 4-8 shows how the label renders in Safari. "English" is much more obvious and understandable than "Unknown."

Figure 4-8. *Video element with a named track child element using @label in Safari left) and Internet Explorer (right)*

@srclang

Now that the track has a label, the user can tell that it's an English track. This is important information that should not be hidden from the browser. If we let the browser know that we're dealing with an English track, then the browser can decide to autoactivate this track when a user starts watching videos with subtitles in their preferred language: "English." The browser retrieves such user preferences from the browser's or the operating system's settings. To enable browsers to pick the right tracks for the user's preferences, we have the @srclang attribute, which is given an IETF (Internet Engineering Task Force) language code according to BCP47 to distinguish different tracks from each other.

■ **Note**   Browsers haven't yet extended their browser preferences to include preference settings about the activation of text tracks. However, some browsers use platform settings to deal with this, in particular Safari.

Also note that there are other valid uses for providing information about the track resource's language in @srclang (e.g., Google indexing or automatic translation).

Listing 4-6 shows an example of how to use @srclang.

Listing 4-6. Example of <track> Markup with a .vtt File and a @label

```
<video controls poster="img/ElephantDreams.png">
  <source src="video/ElephantDreams.mp4"  type="video/mp4">
  <source src="video/ElephantDreams.webm" type="video/webm">
  <track src="tracks/ElephantDreams_en.vtt" srclang="en">
</video>
```

A key aspect of Listing 4-6 is that it doesn't include the @label or @default attributes. The only attribute is @srclang. When rendered in Safari, the track, as shown in Figure 4-9, is still labeled "English" in the menu. This figure also shows the native OSX Accessibility Preference settings for captions. In this case captions appear as large text in Safari, and this choice also turns the "Auto (Recommended)" track selection on which, in turn, activates the English track.

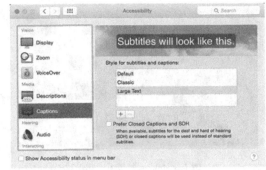

Figure 4-9. *Video element with a @srclang attribute and default activation on the platform*

@kind

The @kind attribute specifies the type of text track you are dealing with and the available @kind attribute values. These values are:

- **subtitles:** transcription or translation of the dialogue, suitable for when the sound is available but not understood (e.g., The user does not understand the language of the media resource's soundtrack). Such tracks are suitable for internationalization purposes.

- **captions:** transcription or translation of the dialog, sound effects, relevant musical cues, and other relevant audio information, suitable for when the soundtrack is unavailable (e.g., the dialog is muted, drowned-out by ambient noise, or because the user is deaf). Such tracks are suitable for hard-of-hearing users.

- **descriptions:** textual descriptions of the video component of the media resource, useful for audio synthesis when the visual component is obscured, unavailable, or not usable (e.g., the user is interacting with the application because the user is blind). To be synthesized as audio. Such tracks are suitable for vision-impaired users.

- **chapters:** chapter titles are to be used for navigating the media resource. Such tracks are displayed as an interactive (potentially nested) list in the browser's interface.

- **metadata:** tracks intended for use from JavaScript. The browser does not render these tracks.

If no @kind attribute is specified, the value defaults to "subtitles," which is what we experienced in the previous examples.

Tracks that are marked as *subtitles* or *captions* will be rendered, if activated, in the video viewport. Only one caption or subtitle track can be activated at any one point in time. This also means that only one of these tracks should be authored with a @default attribute—otherwise the browser does not have a clue which one gets activated by default.

Tracks marked as *descriptions*, if activated, will synthesize their cues into audio—possibly via the screen reader API. Since screen readers are also the intermediaries to Braille devices, this is sufficient to make the descriptions accessible to vision-impaired users. Only one *descriptions* track can be active at any one time.

> ■ **Note** At the time of this writing, no browser supports such "rendering" of descriptions. There are, however, two Chrome extensions that render descriptions: one that uses Chrome's text-to-speech API (`https://chrome.google.com/webstore/detail/html5-audio-description-v/jafenodgdcelmajjnbcchlfjomlkaifp`) and one that uses a screenreader (if installed): (`https://chrome.google.com/webstore/detail/html5-audio-description-v/mipjggdmdaagfmpnomakdcgchdcgfbdg`).

Tracks marked as *chapters* are provided for navigation purposes. It is expected this feature will be realized in browsers through a menu or other form of navigation markers on the media controls' timeline. No browser, as of yet, natively supports chapter rendering.

Finally, tracks marked as *metadata* will not be rendered visually, but only exposed to JavaScript. A web developer can do anything with this metadata, which can consist of any text web page scripts can decode. This includes JSON, XML, or any other special-purpose markup as well as image URLs to provide thumbnails of the video for navigation or subtitles with hyperlinks such as those used in advertising.

Listing 4-7 is a code example containing each of these track types.

Listing 4-7. Example of <track> Markup with a Track of Each @kind

```
<video controls poster="img/ElephantDreams.png">
  <source src="video/ElephantDreams.mp4"  type="video/mp4">
      <source src="video/ElephantDreams.webm" type="video/webm">
      <track src="tracks/ElephantDreams_zh.vtt" srclang="zh" kind="subtitles">
      <track src="tracks/ElephantDreams_jp.vtt" srclang="ja" kind="captions">
      <track src="tracks/ElephantDreams_en.vtt"
              srclang="en" kind="metadata" label="Metadata">
      <track src="tracks/ElephantDreams_chapters_en.vtt"
              srclang="en" kind="chapters"  label="Chapters">
      <track src="tracks/ElephantDreams_audesc_en.vtt"
              srclang="en" kind="descriptions" label="Descriptions">
  </video>
```

This example contains the following:

- Chinese subtitles: `srclang="zh" kind="subtitles"`
- Japanese captions: `srclang="ja" kind="captions"`
- English metadata: `srclang="en" kind="metadata" label="Metadata"`
- English Chapters: `srclang="en" kind="chapters" label="Chapters"`
- English Descriptions: `srclang="en" kind="descriptions" label="Descriptions"`

When viewed in Safari (see Figure 4-10), all of the tracks are exposed. Selecting any of the chapters, descriptions, or metadata tracks don't result in any rendering. It is surprising Safari even lists them in the menu.

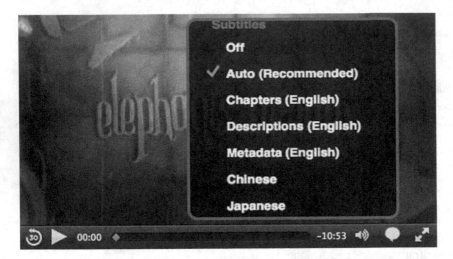

Figure 4-10. *Video element in Safari with multiple tracks of different @kind*

After selecting the Japanese caption track, we can see (Figure 4-11) the UTF-8 encoded characters rendered correctly on top of the video viewport.

Figure 4-11. *Video element with Japanese caption track activated*

Despite browsers being a bit behind in implementing the buttons and menus for controlling text tracks, third-party players have started taking advantage of the <track> element and its rendering of captions and subtitles.

For example, JWPlayer, which we explored in Chapter 3, supports captions, chapters, and thumbnails in a "metadata" track contained in a WebVTT file. As shown in Figure 4-12, it renders them with no frills. You can see that chapters are rendered with little markers on the timeline and when you hover over them you get the title of that chapter. You can also see, when you hover over the JWPlayer timeline, when thumbnails are provided, they pop up.

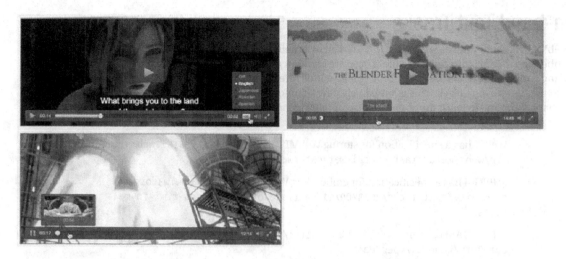

Figure 4-12. *JWPlayer rendering captions, chapters tracks, and preview thumbnails via WebVTT*

■ **Note**   Examples of WebVTT for JWPlayer are at `http://support.jwplayer.com/customer/portal/`
`articles/1407438-adding-closed-captions`, `http://support.jwplayer.com/customer/portal/`
`articles/1407454-adding-chapter-markers`, and `http://support.jwplayer.com/customer/portal/`
`articles/1407439-adding-preview-thumbnails`.

The WebVTT markup used for the thumbnail timeline is as follows in Listing 4-8:

Listing 4-8. Example WebVTT File for a Track of Kind "Metadata" with Thumbnails

```
WEBVTT

00:00:00.000 --> 00:00:30.000
/path/thumb1.png

00:01:00.000 --> 00:01:30.000
/path/thumb2.png
```

The thumbnails were created with the following command-line ffmpeg command, one every 30 seconds:

```
$ ffmpeg -i video.mp4 -f image2 -vf fps=fps=1/30 thumb%d.png
```

In-band Text Tracks

WebVTT files don't necessarily have to be linked externally through the <track> element. They can also be embedded directly into the video file. These are known as ***in-band tracks***. Due to the mp4 and webm formats being container formats, a WebVTT file can be added directly to the container, typically by being multiplexed into the file as a data track. This is a relatively new technique and the browsers are just now starting to add in-band support. To learn more about this emerging technique for the various formats we suggest you start with the following sites:

- WebM has a specification for storing WebVTT in-band: `http://wiki.webmproject.org/webm-metadata/temporal-metadata/webvtt-in-webm`

- MPEG-4 has a specification for embedding WebVTT in-band: `www.w3.org/community/texttracks/2013/09/11/carriage-of-webvtt-and-ttml-in-mp4-files/`

- MPEG DASH can deal with WebVTT: `http://concolato.wp.mines-telecom.fr/category/general/mpeg/dash/`

- and so can Apple's HLS: `http://tools.ietf.org/html/draft-pantos-http-live-streaming-09`

At the moment there are no visual editors that will embed a WebVTT track into a media file. There are, however, a couple of command line approaches to adding these tracks to an mp4 or webm file.

You can use MP4Box (`http://concolato.wp.mines-telecom.fr/2013/07/28/webvtt-mp4-files-dash-and-gpac/`) to author WebVTT in MPEG-4 and ffmpeg to author WebVTT in WebM.

Here is an example for how to create a mp4 file with a WebVTT track using mp4box:

```
$ mp4box -add Monty_subs_en.vtt:FMT=VTT:lang=en Monty_subtitles.mp4
```

This command adds the `monty_subs_en.vtt` subtitle track to `Monty_subtitles.mp4`.

Following is an example for how to create a webm file with a WebVTT track using ffmpeg:

```
$ ffmpeg -i Monty.mp4 -i Monty_subs_en.vtt -metadata:s:s:0 kind="captions" \
         -scodec copy Monty_subtitles.webm
```

It tells ffmpeg to use `Monty.mp4` as the input media file, tells it to use `Monty_subs_en.vtt` as the input file for WebVTT captions to be copied into the WebM file, and gives the subtitle track a kind of "captions."

Though this is a relatively new technique, HTML5 has made it such that in-band text tracks are exposed in Web browsers identically to external tracks that are defined in <track>. This means that the same JavaScript API is available regardless of the text-track's origin.

■ **Note**   As a Web developer you can choose to publish your WebVTT files as independent files or make use of video files that have WebVTT in-band. Browser support, at the time of this writing, is not consistent. With this in mind we recommend using external text track files—.vtt files—not in-band tracks, until such time the browsers have a consistent implementation of in-band text tracks.

JavaScript API: Flexibility for Web Developers

As we pointed out in Chapter 3, JavaScript can be used to extend the functionality of the various elements of a web page. In this case JavaScript can be used to manipulate the text tracks used in a media source whether that text track is in-band or external to the media. This opens up a number of creative possibilities to web developers and designers looking to produce accessible video or audio content. In this section we review the JavaScript API as it pertains to external text tracks.

We start with the <track> element.

Track Element

The IDL (Interface Definition Language) interface of the track element looks as follows:

```
interface HTMLTrackElement : HTMLElement {
         attribute DOMString kind;
         attribute DOMString src;
         attribute DOMString srclang;
         attribute DOMString label;
         attribute boolean default;
  const unsigned short NONE = 0;
  const unsigned short LOADING = 1;
  const unsigned short LOADED = 2;
  const unsigned short ERROR = 3;
  readonly attribute unsigned short readyState;
  readonly attribute TextTrack track;
};
```

This IDL is the object that represents a <track> element. It is available when external text tracks are listed. The IDL attributes kind, src, srclang, label, and default contain the value of the content attributes of the same names as introduced earlier. As with the audio and video element, the remaining DOM attributes reflect the current state of the track element.

@readyState

The @readyState IDL is a read-only attribute that represents the current readiness state of the track element. The available states are as follows:

- NONE(0): indicates that the text track's cues have not been obtained.

- LOADING(1): indicates that the text track is loading and there have been no fatal errors encountered so far. Further cues might still be added to the track by the parser.

- LOADED(2): indicates that the text track has been loaded with no fatal errors.

- ERROR(3): indicates that the text track was enabled, but when the user agent attempted to obtain it, this failed in some way (e.g., URL could not be resolved, network error, and unknown text track format). Some or all of the cues are likely missing and will not be obtained.

The readiness state of a text track changes dynamically as the track is obtained.

It is useful, as a JavaScript developer, for you to make sure all of the text tracks that are expected to be loaded actually did load and didn't result in an ERROR. If you are displaying your own menu of available subtitle tracks, this is particularly important since you may only want to display tracks for selection if they can actually be loaded.

@track

As discussed earlier, the objects that are created by In-band text tracks and external <track> referenced text tracks is identical. They are instantiations of the *TextTrack* object. This attribute links to the TextTrack object of the respective <track> element.

■ **Note** In the next examples we are going to be using an extract of a video called "A Digital Media Primer for Geeks" by Monty Montgomery (published under the Creative Commons Attribution NonCommercial ShareAlike License; see http://xiph.org/video/vid1.shtml). We thank the Xiph.org Foundation for making this video available—the full video and others in the series are well worth checking out.

To get a better feeling for how the attributes in the Track Element's IDL work together, Listing 4-9 displays the value of all the IDL attributes of a track element on load and then the readyState just after playback starts.

Listing 4-9. IDL Attributes of the <track> Element

```
<video poster="img/Monty.jpg" controls width="50%">
  <source src="video/Monty.mp4"  type="video/mp4">
  <source src="video/Monty.webm" type="video/webm">

  <track label="English" src="tracks/Monty_subs_en.vtt" kind="subtitles"
         srclang="en" default>
</video>
<h3>Attribute values:</h3>
<p id="values"></p>
<script>
var video = document.getElementsByTagName('video')[0];
var track = document.getElementsByTagName('track')[0];
var values = document.getElementById('values');
values.innerHTML += "Kind: " + track.kind + "<br/>";
values.innerHTML += "Src: " + track.src + "<br/>";
values.innerHTML += "Srclang: " + track.srclang + "<br/>";
values.innerHTML += "Label: " + track.label + "<br/>";
values.innerHTML += "Default: " + track.default + "<br/>";
values.innerHTML += "ReadyState: " + track.readyState + "<br/>";
values.innerHTML += "Track: " + track.track + "<br/>";

function loaded() {
    values.innerHTML += "ReadyState: " + track.readyState + "<br/>";
}
video.addEventListener("loadedmetadata", loaded, false);
</script>
```

Figure 4-13 shows the result from Firefox.

Attribute values:

Kind: subtitles
Src: http://html5videoguide.net/NEW/CH4/tracks/Monty_subs_en.vtt
Srclang: en
Label: English
Default: true
ReadyState: 1
Track: [object TextTrack]
ReadyState: 1

Figure 4-13. *IDL attributes of a <track> element that is activated by default*

All the information regarding the <track> element's attribute values, including kind, src, srclang, label, and default are represented. You can also see the readyState is, at first, LOADING(1) and when the video starts playing, it changes to LOADED(2).

Before we get to the content of the track attribute, let's briefly list the events that may be fired at the <track> element.

onload

An onload event is fired at the HTMLTrackElement when the resource referenced in the @src attribute is successfully loaded by the browser—the readyState then also changes to LOADED(2).

onerror

An onerror event is fired at the HTMLTrackElement when the resource referenced in the @src attribute fails to load. The readyState then also changes to ERROR(3).

oncuechange

An oncuechange event is fired at the HTMLTrackElement when a cue in that track becomes active or stops being active.

Listing 4-10 is a good example of a code block that captures these events.

Listing 4-10. Catching Events on the <track> Element

```
<video poster="img/Monty.jpg" controls width="50%" autoplay>
  <source src="video/Monty.mp4"  type="video/mp4">
  <source src="video/Monty.webm" type="video/webm">

  <track label="Australian" src="tracks/Monty_subs_au.vtt" kind="subtitles"
        srclang="en-au" default>
  <track label="English" src="tracks/Monty_subs_en.vtt" kind="subtitles"
        srclang="en">
</video>
<h3>Events:</h3>
<p id="values"></p>
<script>
var video = document.getElementsByTagName('video')[0];
var tracks = document.getElementsByTagName('track');
var values = document.getElementById('values');

function trackloaded(evt) {
    values.innerHTML += "Track loaded: " + evt.target.label
                      + " track<br/>";
}
function trackerror(evt) {
    values.innerHTML += "Track error: " + evt.target.label + " track<br/>";
    tracks[1].track.mode = "showing";
}
function cuechange(evt) {
    values.innerHTML += "Cue change: " + evt.target.label + " track<br/>";
    video.pause();
}
for (var i=0; i < tracks.length; i++) {
    tracks[i].onload = trackloaded;
    tracks[i].onerror = trackerror;
    tracks[i].oncuechange = cuechange;
}
</script>
```

We've deliberately defined and activated by @default a first text track whose @src resource—Monty_subs_au.vtt—does not exist. The result is the triggering of that first error event mentioning the Australian track. In the error event callback we're activating the second track—Monty_subs_en.vtt—which, in turn, activates the load callback. Then later, when the video playback reaches the first cue, the cuechange event is activated and pauses the video.

Running this in Google Chrome gives us the result shown in Figure 4-14.

Events:

Track error: Australian track

Track loaded: English track

Cue change: English track

Figure 4-14. *Catching events on the <track> element*

■ **Note** There are bugs in the implementation of these events in browsers. For example, Firefox doesn't seem to raise the load and cuechange events, and Safari doesn't raise the cuechange event.

Now that we understand the events that can be fired at the HTMLTrackElement, we can turn our attention to the content of the @track attribute, which is a TextTrack object.

TextTrack Object

A TextTrack object is created for every text track that is associated with a media element. This object is created regardless of whether

- it comes from an external file through the <track> element,

- it comes through an in-band text track of a media resource; or

- it is created completely in JavaScript via the addTextTrack() method of the HTMLMediaElement which we will get to later in this chapter.

A TextTrack object's attribute values are thus sourced either from the HTMLTrackElement's attribute values, from in-band values (see http://dev.w3.org/html5/html-sourcing-inband-tracks/), or from the parameters of the addTextTrack() method.

■ **Note** A TextTrack object originating from a <track> element is linked both from the HTMLTrackElement object and from the TextTrackList of the media element, which is a child of the <track> element. In-band tracks and script-created tracks only exist in the TextTrackList of the media element.

The IDL of the TextTrack object looks as follows:

```
enum TextTrackMode { "disabled", "hidden", "showing" };
enum TextTrackKind { "subtitles", "captions", "descriptions", "chapters", "metadata" };

interface TextTrack : EventTarget {
    readonly attribute TextTrackKind kind;
    readonly attribute DOMString label;
    readonly attribute DOMString language;
    readonly attribute DOMString id;
    readonly attribute DOMString inBandMetadataTrackDispatchType;
             attribute TextTrackMode mode;
    readonly attribute TextTrackCueList? cues;
    readonly attribute TextTrackCueList? activeCues;
    void addCue(TextTrackCue cue);
    void removeCue(TextTrackCue cue);
             attribute EventHandler oncuechange;
};
```

The first four attributes are as follows:

- The @kind attribute is restricted by the TextTrackKind object to the legal values that we learned earlier in the <track> element.

- The @label attribute contains the label string as provided from either the <track> element's @label attribute, from a field of an in-band track, or from the label parameter of the addTextTrack() method of the HTMLMediaElement.

- The @language attribute contains the language string either provided from the <track> element's @srclang attribute, from a field of an in-band track, or from the language parameter of the addTextTrack() method of the HTMLMediaElement.

- The @id attribute contains the identifier string as provided either from the <track> element's @id attribute (every element has such an attribute), or from an identifier field of an in-band track.

The remaining attributes in the IDL need a bit more explanation.

@inBandMetadataTrackDispatchType

This is a string extracted from the media resource specifically for a text track of @kind "metadata." This string explains the exact format of the data in the cues, so adequate JavaScript functions can be set to parse and display that data.

For example, text tracks with particular content formats could contain metadata for ad targeting, trivia game data during game shows, play states during sports games, or recipe information during cooking shows. As such, dedicated script modules could be bound to parsing such tracks using the value of this attribute.

How the data formats are identified is specified in `http://dev.w3.org/html5/html-sourcing-inband-tracks/`. Since this attribute is very specific to particular kinds of applications and has a rather negligible impact on accessibility, further discussion of this attribute is beyond the scope of this book.

@mode

As defined by the `TextTrackMode` type, a `TextTrack` object can have three different modes.

- *Disabled:* indicates the text track is not active. In this case, the browser has identified the existence of a <track> element, but it hasn't downloaded the external track file or parsed it. No cues are active and no events are fired. <track>-defined text tracks that are not activated by default end up in this state initially.

- *Hidden:* indicates that the text track's cues have been or should be obtained, but they are not being shown. The browser is maintaining a list of which cues are active, and events are being fired accordingly. In-band text tracks and JavaScript-created text tracks end up in this state initially.

- *Showing:* indicates that the text track's cues have been or should be obtained and are being displayed if they are of an `@kind` that renders. The browser is maintaining a list of which cues are active and which events are being fired accordingly. <track>-defined text tracks that are activated with the `@default` attribute end up in this state initially.

@cues

This is the list of loaded `TextTrackCues` once the `TextTrack` has become active (i.e., mode is hidden or showing). For continuously loading media files, this list may update continuously as the media resource continuous to parse the in-band text track.

@activeCues

This is the list of `TextTrackCues` on the `TextTrack` that are currently active. Active cues are those that start before the current playback position and end after the playback position.

Before we move on to the methods and events used by the `TextTrack` object, Listing 4-11 gives us an opportunity to inspect the <track> element's IDL attributes.

Listing 4-11. IDL Attributes of <track> Element's @track Attribute

```
<video poster="img/Monty.jpg" controls width="50%">
  <source src="video/Monty.mp4"  type="video/mp4">
  <source src="video/Monty.webm" type="video/webm">

  <track id="track1" label="English" src="tracks/Monty_subs_en.vtt"
         kind="subtitles" srclang="en" default>
</video>
<h3>TextTrack object:</h3>
<p id="values"><b>Before loading:</b><br/></p>
<script>
var video = document.getElementsByTagName('video')[0];
var track = document.getElementsByTagName('track')[0];
```

```
var values = document.getElementById('values');
values.innerHTML += JSON.stringify(track.track, undefined, 4) + "<br/>";
values.innerHTML += "track.cues length: " + track.track.cues.length
                     + "<br/>";

function loaded() {
    values.innerHTML += "<b>After loading:</b><br/>";
    values.innerHTML += "track.cues[0]: " + track.track.cues[0] + "<br/>";
    values.innerHTML += "track.cues length: " + track.track.cues.length;
}
video.addEventListener("loadeddata", loaded, false);
</script>
```

Figure 4-15 shows the value of the TextTrack object in the @track attribute before the <track> element is loaded and the number of cues after it's loaded in Google Chrome. You'll see that the length of @cues is 0 (because "cues" is null before loading and 51 afterward).

TextTrack object:

Before loading:
{ "oncuechange": null, "activeCues": null, "cues": { "length": 0 }, "mode": "showing", "id": "track1", "language": "en", "label": "English", "kind": "subtitles" }
After loading:
track.cues[0]: [object VTTCue]
track.cues length: 51

Figure 4-15. *IDL attribute values of <track> element's @track attribute shown in Opera*

Firefox doesn't actually create the TextTrack object that early which means the @track attribute is still an empty object prior to loading, but it reports on the number of cues consistently.

addCue()

This method adds a TextTrackCue object to the text track's list of cues. That means that the object is added to @cues, and also to @activeCues if the media element's current time is within that cue's time interval. Note that if the given cue is already in another text track list of cues, then it is removed from that text track list of cues before it is added to this one.

removeCue()

This method removes a TextTrackCue object from the text track's list of cues.

onCueChange Event

The cueChange event is raised when one or more cues in the track have become active or stopped being active.

Listing 4-12 provides a JavaScript example of applying the addCue() and removeCue() methods on a TextTrack of a <track> element and capturing the resulting cuechange event.

Listing 4-12. Methods and Events of a <track> Element's @track Attribute

```
var video = document.getElementsByTagName('video')[0];
var track = document.getElementsByTagName('track')[0];
var values = document.getElementById('values');

function loaded() {
    var cue = new VTTCue(0.00, 5.00, "This is a script created cue.");
    values.innerHTML += "Number of cues: " + track.track.cues.length
                        + "<br/>";
    values.innerHTML += "<b>After adding cue:</b><br/>"
    track.track.addCue(cue);
    values.innerHTML += "Number of cues: " + track.track.cues.length
                        + "<br/>";
}
video.addEventListener("loadedmetadata", loaded, false);

function playing() {
    values.innerHTML += "<b>After play start:</b><br/>"
    values.innerHTML += "Number of cues: " + track.track.cues.length
                        + "<br/>";
    values.innerHTML += "First cue: "
                        + JSON.stringify(track.track.cues[0].text) + "<br/>";
    function cuechanged() {
        track.track.removeCue(track.track.cues[1]);
        values.innerHTML += "<b>After removing cue:</b><br/>"
        values.innerHTML += "Number of cues: " + track.track.cues.length
                        + "<br/>";
        video.pause();
    }
    track.track.addEventListener("cuechange", cuechanged, false);
}
video.addEventListener("play", playing, false);
```

After loading the video, we create a VTTCue—new VTTCue—which is a kind of TextTrackCue. We start with 51 cues and end up with 52. After starting playback, we have all the 52 cues loaded and then register a cuechange event upon which cue 1 is removed to get back to 51 cues. Figure 4-16 shows the result in Google Chrome. Also note that the first cue is the script created cue in the list of 52 cues.

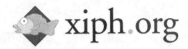

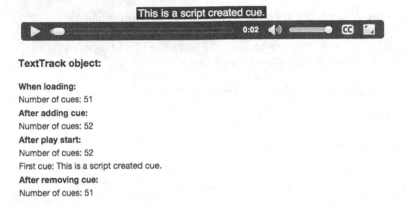

TextTrack object:

When loading:
Number of cues: 51
After adding cue:
Number of cues: 52
After play start:
Number of cues: 52
First cue: This is a script created cue.
After removing cue:
Number of cues: 51

Figure 4-16. *Methods and events of a TextTrack object*

■ **Note**   This example doesn't work correctly in Firefox because Firefox doesn't support the `oncuechange` event on the `TextTrack` object yet.

TextTrackCue

The cues in the @cues and @activeCues attributes of the TextTrack IDL have the following format:

```
interface TextTrackCue : EventTarget {
    readonly attribute TextTrack? track;
            attribute DOMString id;
            attribute double startTime;
            attribute double endTime;
            attribute boolean pauseOnExit;
            attribute EventHandler onenter;
            attribute EventHandler onexit;
};
```

These are the basic attributes of a cue. Specific cue formats such as VTTCue can further extend these attributes. Here's a quick review of the TextTrackCue attributes.

@track

This is the `TextTrack` object to which this cue belongs, if any, or `null` otherwise.

@id

This is an identifying string for the cue.

@startTime, @endTime

These are the start and end times of the cue. They relate to the media element's playback time and define the cue's active time range.

@pauseOnExit

The `@pauseOnExit` flag is a Boolean that indicates whether playback of the media resource is to pause when the end of the cue's active time range is reached. It may, for example, be used to pause a video when reaching the end of a cue in order to introduce advertising.

onenter and onexit Events

The `enter` event is raised when the cue becomes active and the `exit` event is raised when it stops being active.

TextTrackCueList

The `@cues` and `@activeCues` attributes of the `TextTrack` IDL are `TextTrackCueList` objects of the following format:

```
interface TextTrackCueList {
    readonly attribute unsigned long length;
    getter TextTrackCue (unsigned long index);
    TextTrackCue? getCueById(DOMString id);
};
```

`@length` returns the length of the list.
The getter makes it possible to access a cue list element by index (e.g., `cues[i]`).
The `getCueById()` function allows retrieving a `TextTrackCue` by providing its id string.
Listing 4-13 demonstrates how one can go through the list of cues of a track and access the cue attributes.

Listing 4-13. Access the Attributes of All the Cues of a Text Track

```
<video poster="img/Monty.jpg" controls width="50%">
  <source src="video/Monty.mp4"  type="video/mp4">
  <source src="video/Monty.webm" type="video/webm">

  <track id="track1" label="English" src="tracks/Monty_subs_en.vtt"
         kind="subtitles" srclang="en" default>
</video>
```

```
<h3>TextTrack object:</h3>
<table>
    <thead>
        <tr>
            <td>Cue Number</td>
            <td>ID</td>
            <td>StartTime</td>
            <td>EndTime</td>
            <td>Text</td>
        </tr>
    </thead>
    <tbody id="values">
    </tbody>
</table>
<script>
var video = document.getElementsByTagName('video')[0];
var track = document.getElementsByTagName('track')[0];
var values = document.getElementById('values');
var content;

function loaded() {
    for (var i=0; i < track.track.cues.length; i++) {
        content = "<tr>";
        content += "<td>" + i + "</td>";
        content += "<td>" + track.track.cues[i].id + "</td>";
        content += "<td>" + track.track.cues[i].startTime + "</td>";
        content += "<td>" + track.track.cues[i].endTime + "</td>";
        content += "<td>" + track.track.cues[i].text + "</td></tr>";
        values.innerHTML += content;
    }
}
video.addEventListener("loadedmetadata", loaded, false);
</script>
```

When you test this in the browser, as shown in Figure 4-17, you will see that this technique helps to quickly introspect the cues to ensure the order, timing, and text spelling is correct.

TextTrack object:

Cue Number	ID	StartTime	EndTime	Text
0	1	8.124	10.742	Workstations and high end personal computers have been able to
1	2	10.742	14.749	manipulate digital audio pretty easily for about fifteen years now.
2	3	14.749	17.47	It's only been about five years that a decent workstation's been able
3	4	17.47	21.643	to handle raw video without a lot of expensive special purpose hardware.
4	5	21.643	25.4	But today even most cheap home PCs have the processor power and
5	6	25.4	28.092	storage necessary to really toss raw video around,
6	7	28.092	30.479	at least without too much of a struggle.
7	8	30.479	33.579	So now that everyone has all of this cheap capable hardware,

Figure 4-17. *Listing all cues of a text track*

Media Element

We've seen how we can access <track> elements, their list of cues, and the content of each of the cues. Now we will take a step away from <track> elements alone and return to the media element's list of text tracks. This will include in-band text tracks and script-created tracks, too.

TextTrackList

First we need to understand the TextTrackList object:

```
interface TextTrackList : EventTarget {
    readonly attribute unsigned long length;
    getter TextTrack (unsigned long index);
    TextTrack? getTrackById(DOMString id);
            attribute EventHandler onchange;
            attribute EventHandler onaddtrack;
            attribute EventHandler onremovetrack;
};
```

Similar to the TextTrackCueList object, a TextTrackList is a list of TextTrack objects. The list's length is given in the @length attribute.

Individual tracks can be accessed by index (e.g., track[i]).

The getTrackById() method allows retrieving a TextTrack by providing its id string.

In addition, a "change" event is raised whenever one or more tracks in the list have ben enabled or disabled, an addtrack event is raised whenever a track has been added to the track list, and a removetrack event whenever a track has been removed.

To get access to all the text tracks that are associated with an audio or video element, the IDL of the MediaElement is extended with the following attribute and method:

```
interface HTMLMediaElement : HTMLElement {

...
  readonly attribute TextTrackList textTracks;
  TextTrack addTextTrack(TextTrackKind kind, optional DOMString label = "",
                         optional DOMString language = "");
};
```

@textTracks

The @textTracks attribute of media elements is a TextTrackList object that contains the list of text tracks that are available for the media element.

addTextTrack()

This new method for media elements **addTextTrack (*kind*, *label*, *language*)** is used to create a new text track for a media element purely from JavaScript with the given kind, label, and language attribute settings. The new track, if valid, is immediately in the LOADED(2) @readyState and in "hidden" @mode with an empty @cues TextTrackCueList.

We mentioned earlier that @textTracks contains all tracks that are associated with a media element, regardless of whether they were created by a <track> element, exposed from an in-band text track, or created by JavaScript through the addTextTrack() method. The tracks are actually always accessed in the following order:

1. <track> created TextTrack objects, in the order that they are in the DOM.

2. addTextTrack() created TextTrack objects, in the order they were added, oldest first.

3. In-band text tracks, in the order given in the media resource.

In Listing 4-14 we have a subtitle track created via a <track> element and a script-created chapters track.

Listing 4-14. List and Access All the Text Tracks of a Video Element

```
<video poster="img/Monty.jpg" controls width="50%">
  <source src="video/Monty.mp4"  type="video/mp4">
  <source src="video/Monty.webm" type="video/webm">
  <track id="track1" label="English" src="tracks/Monty_subs_en.vtt"
        kind="subtitles" srclang="en" default>
</video>
```

```
<h3>TextTrack object:</h3>
<p id="values"></p>
<script>
var video = document.getElementsByTagName('video')[0];
var values = document.getElementById('values');
var new_track = video.addTextTrack("chapters", "English Chapters", "en");

var cue;
cue = new VTTCue(0.00, 7.298, "Opening Credits");
new_track.addCue(cue);
cue = new VTTCue(7.298, 204.142, "Introduction");
new_track.addCue(cue);

function loaded() {
    values.innerHTML += "Number of text tracks: "
                        + video.textTracks.length + "</br>";
    for (var i=0; i < video.textTracks.length; i++) {
        values.innerHTML += "<b>Track[" + i + "]:</b></br>";
        values.innerHTML += "Number of cues: "
                        + video.textTracks[i].cues.length + "<br/>";
        values.innerHTML += "First cue: "
                        + video.textTracks[i].cues[0].text + "<br/>";
    }
}
video.addEventListener("loadedmetadata", loaded, false);
</script>
```

When the video has finished loading, we display the number of text tracks and, for each of them, their number of cues and the text within the first cue. Figure 4-18 shows the result.

TextTrack object:

Number of text tracks: 2
Track[0]:
Number of cues: 51
First cue: Workstations and high end personal computers have been able to
Track[1]:
Number of cues: 2
First cue: Opening Credits

Figure 4-18. Listing all the text tracks of a video element

This concludes the description of the JavaScript objects and their APIs, which allow us to deal with general text tracks and retrieve relevant information or react to specific events.

WebVTT: Authoring Subtitles, Captions, Text Descriptions and Chapters

Though we provided a quick look at WebVTT and how it can be used earlier in this chapter, we are going to devote this section of the chapter to a deep-dive into this subject. This will include formatting the cues and captions and positioning them on the video.

As we pointed out, WebVTT is a file format specifically defined to allow authors to create text track cues independently of web pages and to distribute them in separate files. A web page author does not typically create video content; therefore, it would make no sense to require subtitles to be authored as part of web pages.

We have also seen that a simple WebVTT file is a text file consisting of a WEBVTT string signature followed by a list of cues separated by empty lines. Following is an example file:

```
WEBVTT

1 this is an identifier
00:00:08.124 --> 00:00:10.742
Workstations and high end personal computers have been able to

transcription-line
00:00:10.742 --> 00:00:14.749
manipulate digital audio pretty easily for about fifteen years now.

3
00:00:14.749 --> 00:00:17.470
It's only been about five years that a decent workstation's been able
```

As you can see, each cue starts with string, which is the optional identifier. The next line contains the start and end times for the display of the cue expressed in the form of hh:min:sec.mms and separated by the "-->" string. Just be aware each of hour and minute segments must consist of two digits such as 01 for one hour or one minute. The second segment must consist of two digits and three decimal places for the milliseconds.

The next line or lines of text are the actual cue content, which is the text to be rendered.

This file, which will be referenced by the <track> element, is nothing more than a simple text file with the .vtt extension in the file name. When the cues are displayed and are of kind "subtitles" or "captions," they appear in a black box over the bottom middle of the video viewport. Naturally, this raises an obvious question: can these cues be "jazzed" up? The answer is: "Yes." Let's look at some ways of working with these cues.

Cue Styling

Cues in the WebVTT format can be styled using CSS, once they are available to a web page. Using the preceding example, you could use the ::cue pseudo-selector to:

- style the first cue using

  `video::cue(#\31\ this\ is\ an\ identifier) { color: green; }`

- style the second cue using

  `video::cue(#transcription\-line) { color: red; }`

- style the third cue using

  `video::cue(#\33) { color: blue; }`

- style all cues using

  `video::cue { background-color: lime; }`

■ **Note** CSS allows less freedom in the selector strings than WebVTT, so you need to escape some characters in your identifiers to make this work. See `https://mathiasbynens.be/notes/css-escapes` for more information.

The CSS properties that can be applied to the text in cue and are used with `::cue` include:

- "color"
- "opacity"
- "visibility"
- "text-decoration"
- "text-shadow"
- the properties corresponding to the "background" shorthand
- the properties corresponding to the "outline" shorthand
- the properties corresponding to the "font" shorthand, including
  - "line-height"
  - "whitespace"

With `::cue()` you can additionally style all the properties relating to the transition and animation features.

Cue Markup

Cues are of the kind "metadata" and can contain anything in the cue content. This includes things like JSON (JavaScript Object Notation), XML, or data URLs.

Cues of other kinds contain restricted cue text. Cue text contains plain text in UTF-8 plus a limited set of tags. The ampersand (&) and the less-than sign (<) have to be escaped as characters because they represent the start of an escaped character sequence or a tag. The following escaped entities are used, just like they are in HTML: & (&), < (<), > (>), ‎ (left-right-mark), ‏ (right-left-mark), and   (non-breaking space). The left-right and right-left marks are non-printing characters that allow for changing the directionality of the text as part of internationalization and bidirectional text. This is critically important when marking up script in languages such as Hebrew or Arabic, which render words from right to left, or when marking up mixed-language text.

Next, we'll list the currently defined tags and give simple examples on how to address them with CSS from an HTML page once such a cue is included and displayed on a web page. The tags are:

- **Class span** `<c>`: to mark up a section of text for styling, for example,

  `<c.myClass>Apply styling to this text</c>`

  This will allow using CSS selectors like the following:

  `::cue(.myClass) { font-size: 2em; }`

  You can use a `.myClass` class attribution on all tags.

- **Italics span** `<i>`: to mark up a section of italicized text, for example,

  `<i>Apply italics to this text</i>`

  This also allows using CSS selectors like the following:

  `::cue(i) { color: green; }`

- **Bold span** `<b>`: to mark up a section of bold text, for example,

  ```
  <b>Apply bold to this text</b>
  ```

  This also allows using CSS selectors like the following:

  ```
  ::cue(b) { color: red; }
  ```

- **Underline span** `<u>`: to mark up a section of underlined text, for example,

  ```
  <u>Apply underlines to this text</u>
  ```

  This also allows using CSS selectors like the following:

  ```
  ::cue(u) { color: blue; }
  ```

- **Ruby span** `<ruby>`: to mark up a section of ruby annotations.

  Ruby annotations are short runs of text presented alongside base text, primarily used in East Asian typography as a guide for pronunciation or to include other annotations. Following is a markup example:

  ```
  <ruby>日<rt>に</rt></ruby>
  ```

  This also allows using CSS selectors like the following:

  ```
  ::cue(ruby) { font-weight: bold; }
  ::cue(rt) { font-weight: normal; }
  ```

- **Voice span** `<v>`: to mark up a section of text with a voice and speaker annotation, for example,

  ```
  <v Fred>How are you?</v>
  ```

  This also allows using CSS selectors like the following, once the cue is included in an HTML page:

  ```
  ::cue(v[voice="Fred"]) { font-style: italic; }
  ```

- **Language span** `<lang>`: to mark up a section of text in a specific language, for example,

  ```
  <lang de>Wie geht es Dir?</lang>
  ```

  This also allows using CSS selectors like the following, once the cue is included in an HTML page:

  ```
  ::cue(lang[lang="de"]) { font-style: oblique; }
  ```

  ```
  ::cue(:lang(ru)) { color: lime; }
  ```

- **Timestamps** `<hh:mm:ss.mss>`: to mark up a section of text with timestamps.

  The beauty of timestamps is they give you the opportunity to style cues at precise points in time rather than accepting the white text on a black background we have used to this point in the chapter. An example of the use of a timestamp is shown the following code block:

  ```
  <00:01:00.000><c>Wie </c><00:01:00.200><c>geht </c><00:01:00.400><c>es
  </c><00:01:00.600><c>Dir? </c><00:01:00.800>
  ```

  In this example the words "Wie," "geht," "es," and "Dir" will appear onscreen at the times indicated.

171

This also allows using CSS selectors, as follows, once the cue is included in an HTML page:

```
::cue(:past) { color: lime; }
::cue(:future) { color: gray; }
```

You can use timestamps, for example, to mark up karaoke cues or for paint-on captions. What is a "paint-on" caption? Paint-on captions are individual words that are "painted on" the screen. They appear as the individual words that make up the caption single words, appear from left to right, and are usually are verbatim.

■ **Note**   Until further notice, you need to use <c> tags to enclose the text between timestamps to make CSS selectors take effect (until `www.w3.org/Bugs/Public/show_bug.cgi?id=16875` gets resolved).

The following is a rather interesting demonstration of the use of the tags and CSS, applied to a music video by Tay Zonday. This video, "Chocolate Rain," went viral on YouTube a few years ago and is now licensed under Creative Commons.

We start with the WebVTT markup as shown in Listing 4-15a.

Listing 4-15a. WebVTT File for "Chocolate Rain"

```
WEBVTT

1 first cue
00:00:10.000 --> 00:00:21.710
<v Tay Zonday>Chocolate Rain</v>

2
00:00:12.210 --> 00:00:21.710
<b>Some </b><i>stay </i><u>dry </u>and others feel the pain

3
00:00:15.920 --> 00:00:21.170
<c.brown>Chocolate </c><u>Rain</u>

4
00:00:18.000 --> 00:00:21.170
<00:00:18.250><c>A </c><00:00:18.500><c>baby </c><00:00:19.000><c>born
</c><00:00:19.250><c>will </c><00:00:19.500><c>die </c><00:00:19.750><c>before
</c><00:00:20.500><c>the </c><00:00:20.750><c>sin</c>
```

and apply the appropriate CSS markup to the HTML in Listing 4-15b.

Listing 4-15b. The Cues Are Styled in the HTML page for "Chocolate Rain"

```
<style>
video::cue {color: lime;}
video::cue(#\31\ first\ cue) {background-color: blue;}
video::cue(v[voice="Tay Zonday"]) {color: red !important;}
video::cue(:past) {color: lime;}
video::cue(:future) {color: gray;}
video::cue(c.brown) {color:brown; background-color: white;}
</style>
```

```
<video poster="img/chocolate_rain.png" controls>
  <source src="video/chocolate_rain.mp4"  type="video/mp4">
  <source src="video/chocolate_rain.webm" type="video/webm">
  <track id="track1" label="English" src="tracks/chocolate_rain.vtt"
         kind="subtitles" srclang="en" default>
</video>
```

As you can see, the cues are created in the VTT document and styled in the HTML using inline CSS and a variety of styles from the cue markup. The styling could just as easily be contained in an external CSS style sheet. The result, as shown in Figure 4-19, is not exactly consistent between the browsers and is something you need to be aware of when undertaking a project of this sort.

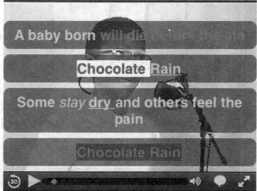

Figure 4-19. Rendering of "Chocolate Rain" example in Google Chrome (left) and Safari (right)

■ **Note**   Google Chrome and Safari currently have the best styling support. Firefox doesn't support the ::cue pseudo-selector and Internet Explorer already fails at parsing marked up cue text.

Cue Settings

Now that you know how to style cue content, let's deal with another question you may have: "Do they always have to be at the bottom of the screen?" The short answer is: "No." You can choose where to place them and that is the subject of this, the final part of the section "WebVTT: Authoring Subtitles, Captions, Text Descriptions, and Chapter."

This is accomplished due to WebVTT introducing "cue settings." These are directives that are added behind the end time specification of the cue on the same line and consist of name-value pairs separated by a colon (:).

We'll start with vertical cues.

Vertical Cues

Some languages render their script vertically rather than horizontally. This is especially true of many Asian languages. Mongolian, for example, is written vertically with lines added to the right. Most other vertical script is written with lines added to the left, such as traditional Chinese, Japanese, and Korean.

The WebVTT cue setting for vertical cues is as follows:

```
vertical:rl
vertical:lr
```

The first cue setting specifies vertical text growing right to left, and the second cue setting has the text growing left to right.

Listing 4-16 shows an example of Japanese text and Figure 4-20 a rendering in Safari. Note how the <ruby> markup is not yet supported.

Listing 4-16. WebVTT File with Vertical Text Cues

```
WEBVTT

00:00:15.042 --> 00:00:20.333 vertical:rl
<ruby>左<rt>ひだり</rt></ruby>に<ruby> 見<rt>み</rt></ruby>えるのは...

00:00:18.750 --> 00:00:20.333 vertical:lr
<ruby>右<rt>みぎ</rt></ruby>に<ruby> 見<rt>み</rt></ruby>えるのは...
```

As you can see, in Figure 4-20, the vertical cues are added. There is one small problem. Chrome and Opera currently have rl and lr mixed up and Firefox and Internet Explorer have yet to support vertical rendering. Only Safari gets this right.

Figure 4-20. *Rendering of vertical text cues in Safari*

Line Positioning

Cue lines are, by default, rendered in the bottom center of the video viewport. However, sometimes WebVTT authors will want to move the text to another position—for example, when burnt-in text is being shown on the video in that location or when most of the action is in that position, as is the case in a soccer match. In those situations you may decide to position the cues at the top of the video viewport or in any other position between the top and bottom of the viewport.

The top of the viewport is the right side for rl and the left side for lr vertical cues with the space between the left and right of the viewport being calculated in much the same manner as horizontal text.

A typical WebVTT cue setting for line positioning looks as follows:

```
line:0
line:-1
```

The first version specifies the first line at the top of the video viewport —any successive numbers continuing down from there (e.g., 4 is the fifth line from the top of the viewport). The second one specifies the first line at the bottom of the viewport with decreasing numbers counting up from there (e.g., -5 is the fifth line from the bottom).

You can also specify percentage positioning from the top of the video viewport.

```
line:10%
```

If we assume the video is 720 pixels high, the caption would appear 72 pixels down from the top of the video viewport.

As you have seen, the line cue setting allows you three different ways of positioning a cue top and bottom: counting lines from the top, counting lines from the bottom, and percentage positioning from the top.

Cue Alignment

The text within a cue can be left, middle, or right aligned, within the cue box, through an align setting.

```
align:left
align:middle
align:right
align:start
align:end
```

The start and end settings are for the case where the alignment should be with the start/end of the text, independent of the text being of directionality left to right or right to left.

Text Positioning

Sometimes WebVTT authors will want to move the cue box away from the center position. For example, the position chosen covers the speaker's face. In this case the cue should be moved either to the left, right or below the speaker.

The WebVTT cue setting for text positioning would be:

```
position:60%
```

This aligns a horizontal cue to a potion that is 60% of the distance from the left edge of the video viewport.

■ **Note**   Be careful with text positioning because the final position of the cue is dependent on the alignment of the text. For example, if a cue is middle aligned, the origin point for the text position will be the center of the text block. For right-aligned text it will be the right edge of the block, and so on. If you get inconsistent results, the first place to look is the cue alignment property.

Cue Size

Being able to change the cue position in the viewport is a good feature, but there is also the risk that the caption may actually be too wide. This is where the size property—always expressed as a percentage—is useful. For example, positioning a cue on the left below a speaker would require you to also limit the cue width as shown here.

```
position:10% align:left size:40%
```

To get a better understanding of the effect of all these cue settings, Listing 4-17 shows an example of cues that use the line, align, position, and size settings to accommodate changing cue positions and widths.

Listing 4-17. WebVTT File with Cues with Cue Settings

```
WEBVTT

1a
00:00:08.124 --> 00:00:10.742 line:0 position:10% align:left
Workstations

1b
00:00:08.124 --> 00:00:10.742 line:50% position:50%
and high end personal computers

1c
00:00:08.124 --> 00:00:10.742 align:right size:10% position:100%
have been able to
```

The first cue—1a—is rendered in the first line of the video viewport and left aligned at a 10% offset. The second cue—1b—is rendered right in the middle. The third cue—1c—is 10% of the viewport width, rendered right aligned at the right edge.

Figure 4-21 shows the result in Chrome (left) and Safari (right).

Figure 4-21. Rendering of cues with cue settings in Chrome and Safari

Chrome, Opera, and Firefox essentially render the cues in the same manner. Safari's positioning has a somewhat different interpretation. IE doesn't support any cue settings.

Other WebVTT Features

To this point we have outlined the most important WebVTT features. We'd also like to mention a few others before we finish.

- **Comments**: you can author comments in a WebVTT file—basically, they are a cue without an identifier or a timing line, and the text block starts with "NOTE."

- **Regions**: this is a feature under discussion to allow more detailed positioning, allow providing a background color on the cue, and allow for scrolling text (roll-up captions). It is not clear yet whether browsers will implement this part of the spec.

- **Nested cues**: a track of @kind='chapters' allows definition of nested cues (i.e., cues that are fully contained in other cues). This is useful for a track, which distinguishes between chapters, sections, subsections, and so on, where each lower hierarchy is fully contained within the higher one. Thus, chapter tracks can be used for navigation at different resolutions, though it is difficult to imagine how that would be rendered in browsers.

To this point we have focused on a single video and shown you how to add transcripts, subtitles, captions, chapters, and text descriptions. As you have discovered, they are all key aspects in making video and audio accessible to various audiences. Still, we have all seen video on TV where, at a news conference, someone is just off to the side using sign language to translate what is being said to deaf users. Thus, there are instances where the video being streamed will also require the use of a separate video of a "signer." This is where you will need to create a video with multiple synchronized audio and video tracks.

Multiple Audio and Video Tracks: Audio Descriptions and Sign Language Video

We have talked a lot about how to publish text alternatives for video, including transcripts, captions, subtitles, and text descriptions. However, vision-impaired video viewers are used to consuming audio descriptions with their videos, and many deaf users find it easier to read/watch sign language rather than text. Similarly, international users have become accustomed to dubbed audio tracks such as the clear audio tracks reviewed earlier. This presents us with a rather interesting challenge where a video doesn't have just one video and one audio track but multiple video and audio tracks.

This challenge can be met in two ways. The first is to prepare separate audio and video files that are synchronized to each other. The second method is to produce a single multiplexed video file from which we retrieve the tracks relevant to the particular user. HTML5 provides both options. The first is supported via the MediaController API, the latter via multitrack media files.

■ **Note**   Media with multiple time-synchronized audio and video tracks is also common in professional video production where scenes are often recorded from multiple angles and with multiple microphones, or the director's comments may be available.

Multitrack Media

When referencing a video containing multiple audio and video tracks in a <video> element, browsers only display one video track and render all enabled audio tracks. To get access to all the audio and video tracks that are associated with an <audio> or <video> element, the IDL of the MediaElement is extended with the following attributes:

```
interface HTMLMediaElement : HTMLElement {
...
  readonly attribute AudioTrackList audioTracks;
  readonly attribute VideoTrackList videoTracks;
};
```

@audioTracks

The @audioTracks attribute of media elements is an AudioTrackList object that contains the list of audio tracks that are available for the media element together with their activation status.

@videoTracks

The @videoTracks attribute of media elements is a VideoTrackList object that contains the list of video tracks that are available for the media element together with their activation status.

Audio and Video Tracks

The AudioTrackList object and the AudioTrack objects contained therein are defined as follows:

```
interface AudioTrackList : EventTarget {
    readonly attribute unsigned long length;
    getter AudioTrack (unsigned long index);
    AudioTrack? getTrackById(DOMString id);
            attribute EventHandler onchange;
            attribute EventHandler onaddtrack;
            attribute EventHandler onremovetrack;
};

interface AudioTrack {
    readonly attribute DOMString id;
    readonly attribute DOMString kind;
    readonly attribute DOMString label;
    readonly attribute DOMString language;
            attribute boolean enabled;
};
```

The VideoTrackList object and its VideoTrack objects are very similar:

```
interface VideoTrackList : EventTarget {
    readonly attribute unsigned long length;
    getter VideoTrack (unsigned long index);
    VideoTrack? getTrackById(DOMString id);
```

```
readonly attribute long selectedIndex;
        attribute EventHandler onchange;
        attribute EventHandler onaddtrack;
        attribute EventHandler onremovetrack;
};

interface VideoTrack {
  readonly attribute DOMString id;
  readonly attribute DOMString kind;
  readonly attribute DOMString label;
  readonly attribute DOMString language;
        attribute boolean selected;
};
```

An AudioTrackList is a list of AudioTrack objects. The list's length is provided by the @length attribute. Individual tracks can be accessed by their index number (e.g., track[i]), and the getTrackById() method allows retrieving an AudioTrack by providing its id string. In addition, a change event is raised whenever one or more tracks in the list have ben enabled or disabled, an addtrack event is raised whenever a track has been added to the track list, and a removetrack event whenever a track has been removed.

The VideoTrackList is identical, only applied to VideoTrack objects. It has one additional attribute: @selectedIndex, which specifies which track in the list is selected and rendered when used in a <video> element.

Both the AudioTrack and VideoTrack objects consist of the following attributes:

- @id: an optional identifier string,

- @kind: an optional category of the track,

- @label: an optional human-readable string with a brief description of the content of the track,

- @language: an optional IETF Language code according to BCP47 specifying the language used in the track, which could be a sign language code.

The AudioTrack object also has an @enabled attribute used to turn the audio track on or off. This, incidentally, fires an onchange event at the list containing the AudioTrack.

The VideoTrack object additionally has an @selected attribute through which a video track can be turned on When the video track is turned on it automatically turns off any other video tracks in the VideoTrackList and fires a onchange event at that list.

The following @kind values are defined for audio tracks:

- "main": the primary audio track,

- "alternative": an alternative version to the main audio track (e.g., a clean audio version),

- "descriptions": audio descriptions for the main video track,

- "main-desc": the primary audio track mixed with audio descriptions,

- "translation": a dubbed version of the main audio track,

- "commentary": a director's commentary on the main video and audio track.

The following @kind values are defined for video tracks:

- "main": the primary video track,

- "alternative": an alternative version to the main video track (e.g., a different angle),

- "captions": the main video track with burnt-in captions,

- "subtitles": the main video track with burnt-in subtitles,

- "sign": a sign language interpretation of the main audio track,

- "commentary": a director's commentary on the main video and audio track.

Creating Multitrack Media Files

You can use MP4Box (http://concolato.wp.mines-telecom.fr/2013/07/28/webvtt-mp4-files-dash-and-gpac/) to author multitrack MPEG-4 files. Following is an example:

```
$ MP4Box -new ElephantDreams.mux.mp4 -add ElephantDreams.mp4 \
        -add ElephantDreams.sasl.mp4 -add ElephantDreams.audesc.mp3
```

This command adds the ElephantDrams.sasl.mp4 and ElephantDreams.audesc.mp3 files to the ElephantDrams.mp4 file thus creating both a SASL (South African Sign Language) and an audio description track.

To check that it all worked you could use

```
$ MP4Box -info ElephantDreams.mux.mp4
```

. . . to confirm the mux file has four tracks.

For WebM files, you would use mkvmerge (see also http://mkvtoolnix.en.softonic.com/ for a GUI application). Following is an example:

```
$ mkvmerge -w -o ElephantDreams.mux.webm ElephantDreams.webm \
  ElephantDreams.sasl.webm ElephantDreams.audesc.ogg
```

This command adds the ElephantDreams.sasl.webm sign language file and the ElephantDreams.audesc.ogg audio description file to ElephantDreams.webm.

To check that it all worked you could use

```
$ mkvinfo ElephantDreams.mux.webm
```

which confirms the mux file has four tracks.

You can play back these files in VLC—it will show both video tracks and synchronize them. Unfortunately, VLC allows only one audio track to be active at one time, so you can only listen to the main audio track or the audio description track.

Now let's put it all together in an example the HTML file, shown in Listing 4-18.

Listing 4-18. Inspection of Multitrack Video Files

```
<video poster="img/ElephantDreams.png" controls width="50%">
  <source src="video/ElephantDreams.mux.webm" type="video/webm">
  <source src="video/ElephantDreams.mux.mp4"  type="video/mp4">
</video>
```

```
<h3>Attribute values:</h3>
<p id="values"></p>
<script>
  var video = document.getElementsByTagName("video")[0];
  var values = document.getElementById('values');

  function start() {
    if (video.videoTracks) {
      values.innerHTML += "videoTracks.length: "
                        + video.videoTracks.length + "<br/>";
      values.innerHTML += "audioTracks.length: "
                        + video.audioTracks.length;
    } else {
      values.innerHTML += "Browser does not support multitrack audio and video.";
    }
    video.pause();
  }
  video.addEventListener("play", start, false);
  video.play();
</script>
```

We are trying to extract the content of the @videoTracks and @audioTracks attributes in Listing 4-19, so we may be able to manipulate which audio or video track is active. However, Figure 4-22 shows that we're not very lucky with that—Safari only ever shows 0 video and audio tracks.

Attribute values:

videoTracks.length: 0
audioTracks.length: 0

Figure 4-22. *Rendering of @videoTracks and @audioTracks in Safari*

Unfortunately, the other browsers are worse and don't even support that attribute. For now it is not suggested that you try to use multitrack media resources in HTML5. Browsers have mostly decided that multitrack resources are not a good way to deal with multiple synchronized audio and video tracks, because it incurs the cost of having to transmit audio and video tracks out of which only a small number is ever rendered to the user.

The preferred approach today is to use the new MediaSource extensions to deliver multitrack media resources. With MediaSource extensions, a manifest file is transmitted at the start of media playback, which describes which tracks are available for a resource. Then, only data from those tracks that are actually activated by the user will be transmitted. MediaSource extensions are outside the scope of this book.

The HTML5 specification provides another approach to the synchronization of separate media files with each other, which we will explore next.

MediaController: Synchronizing Independent Media Elements

MediaController is an object that coordinates the playback of multiple media elements such as synchronizing a sign-language video to the main video. Every media element can be attached—or slaved—to a MediaController. When that happens, the MediaController modifies the playback rate and the volume of each of the media elements slaved to it, and ensures, when any of the media it controls stall, that the others are stopped at the same time. One other point to keep in mind is that when the MediaController is used, looping is disabled.

By default a media element has no MediaController. Thus a MediaController has to be created declaratively using the @mediagroup attribute or by explicitly setting a controller attribute of the IDL of the MediaElement:

```
interface HTMLMediaElement : HTMLElement {
...
        attribute DOMString mediaGroup;
        attribute MediaController? controller;
};
```

@mediaGroup

The mediaGroup IDL attribute reflects the value of the @mediagroup content attribute. The @mediagroup attribute contains a string value. We can pick the name of the string at random—it just has to be the same between the media elements that we are trying to synchronize. All media elements that have a @mediagroup attribute with the same string value are slaved to the same MediaController.

Listing 4-19 shows an example of how all of this works.

Listing 4-19. Slaving a Main Video and a Sign Language Video Together

```
<video poster="img/ElephantDreams.png" controls width="50%" mediagroup="sync">
  <source src="video/ElephantDreams.webm" type="video/webm">
  <source src="video/ElephantDreams.mp4"  type="video/mp4">
</video>
<video poster="img/ElephantDreams.sasl.png" width="35%" mediagroup="sync">
  <source src="video/ElephantDreams.sasl.webm" type="video/webm">
  <source src="video/ElephantDreams.sasl.mp4"  type="video/mp4">
</video>
<h3>Attribute values:</h3>
<p id="values"></p>
<script>
  var video1 = document.getElementsByTagName("video")[0];
  var video2 = document.getElementsByTagName("video")[1];
  var values = document.getElementById('values');
```

```
function start() {
  setTimeout(function() {
    video1.controller.pause();
    values.innerHTML += "Video1: duration=" + video1.duration + "<br/>";
    values.innerHTML += "Video2: duration=" + video2.duration + "<br/>";
    values.innerHTML += "MediaGroup: " + video1.mediaGroup + "<br/>";
    values.innerHTML += "MediaController: duration="
                        + video1.controller.duration + "<br/>";
    values.innerHTML += "MediaController: paused="
                        + video1.controller.muted + "<br/>";
    values.innerHTML += "MediaController: currentTime="
                        + video1.controller.currentTime;
  }, 10000);
}
video1.addEventListener("play", start, false);
video1.controller.play();
</script>
```

We're synchronizing two video elements—one with ElephantDreams and one with a SASL signer for that same video—together using @mediagroup="sync". In the JavaScript, we let the videos play for 8 seconds and then display the value of the videos' durations in comparison to their controller's duration. You'll notice in the rendering in Figure 4-23 that the controller's duration is the maximum of its slaved media elements. We also print the controller's paused, muted, and currentTime IDL attribute values.

Attribute values:

Video1: duration=653.792
Video2: duration=567.625
MediaGroup: sync
MediaController: duration=653.792
MediaController: paused=false
MediaController: currentTime=8.030998614

Figure 4-23. Rendering of slaved media elements in Safari

Note that Safari is the only browser supporting the @mediagroup attribute and MediaController at this point in time.

@controller

The MediaController object contains the following attributes:

```
enum MediaControllerPlaybackState { "waiting", "playing", "ended" }; [Constructor] interface
MediaController : EventTarget {
    readonly attribute unsigned short readyState;
    readonly attribute TimeRanges buffered;
    readonly attribute TimeRanges seekable;
    readonly attribute unrestricted double duration;
             attribute double currentTime;
    readonly attribute boolean paused;
    readonly attribute MediaControllerPlaybackState playbackState;
    readonly attribute TimeRanges played;
    void pause();
    void unpause();
    void play();
             attribute double defaultPlaybackRate;
             attribute double playbackRate;
             attribute double volume;
             attribute boolean muted;
};
```

The states and attributes of the MediaContoller represent the accumulated states of its slaved media elements. The readyState and playbackState are the lowest value of all slaved media elements. The buffered, seekable, and played TimeRanges are sets and represent the intersection of the same respective attributes on the slaved media elements. Duration is the maximum duration of all slaved media elements. CurrentTime, paused, defaultPlaybackRate, playbackRate, volume, and muted are imposed on all of the MediaController's slaved media elements to keep them all synchronized.

A MediaController also fires the following events, which are somewhat similar to the ones found on the MediaElement:

- **Emptied**: raised when either all slaved media elements have ended or there are no longer any slaved media elements.

- **loadedmetadata**: raised when all slaved media elements have reached at least the HAVE_METADATA readyState.

- **loadeddata**: raised when all slaved media elements have reached at least the HAVE_CURRENT_DATA readyState.

- **canplay**: raised when all slaved media elements have reached at least the HAVE_FUTURE_DATA readyState.

- **canplaythrough**: raised when all slaved media elements have reached at least the HAVE_ENOUGH_DATA readyState.

- **playing**: raised when all slaved media elements are newly playing.

- **ended**: raised when all slaved media elements are newly ended.

- **waiting**: raised when at least one slaved media element is newly waiting.

- **durationchange**: raised when the duration of any slaved media element changes.

- **timeupdate**: raised when the MediaController's currentTime changes.

- **play**: raised when the MediaController's paused state changes.

- **pause**: raised when all media elements move to paused.

- **ratechange**: raised when the defaultPlaybackRate or playbackRate of the MediaController are newly changed.

- **volumechange**: raised when the volume or muted attributes of the MediaController are newly changed.

Listing 4-20 shows an example of a script-created MediaController.

Listing 4-20. Slaving a Main Video and an Audio Description Together Using MediaController

```
<video poster="img/ElephantDreams.png" controls width="50%">
  <source src="video/ElephantDreams.webm" type="video/webm">
  <source src="video/ElephantDreams.mp4"  type="video/mp4">
</video>
<h3>Attribute values:</h3>
<p id="values"></p>
<script>
var values = document.getElementById('values');
var video = document.getElementsByTagName("video")[0];
video.volume = 0.1;
var audio = new Audio();
if (audio.canPlayType('audio/mp3') == "maybe" ||
    audio.canPlayType('audio/mp3') == "probably") {
  audio.src = "video/ElephantDreams.audesc.mp3";
} else {
  audio.src = "video/ElephantDreams.audesc.ogg";
}
audio.volume = 1.0;

var controller = new MediaController();
video.controller = controller;
audio.controller = controller;
controller.play();

controller.addEventListener("timeupdate", function() {
  if (controller.currentTime > 30) {
    values.innerHTML += "MediaController: volume=" + controller.volume;
    values.innerHTML += "MediaController: audio.volume=" + audio.volume;
    values.innerHTML += "MediaController: video.volume=" + video.volume;
    values.innerHTML += "MediaController: currentTime="
                      + controller.currentTime;
    values.innerHTML += "MediaController: audio.currentTime="
                      + audio.currentTime;
    values.innerHTML += "MediaController: video.currentTime="
                      + video.currentTime;
    controller.pause();
  }
}, false);
</script>
```

The `MediaController` synchronizes an audio description with a main video, plays for about 30 seconds, and then displays some IDL attribute values.

Notice, in particular, how we have decided to set the volume of the audio and video objects before slaving them together. By doing this we accommodate the different recording volumes of the resources. Had the volume been set through the `MediaController`, the `MediaController` would force its volume onto all its slaved elements.

Figure 4-24 shows the result.

Attribute values:

MediaController: volume=1
Audio: volume=1
Video: volume=0.1
MediaController: currentTime=40.118032771
Audio: currentTime=39.782047271728516
Video: currentTime=39.69643783569336

Figure 4-24. *MediaController object and its slaved elements in Safari*

Notice the difference in playback position shown for all of the slaved audio and video media elements.

Since Safari is the only browser currently supporting `@mediaGroup` and `MediaController`, you will have to use JavaScript to gain the same functionality with the other browsers. Be careful when doing so, because it's not just a matter of starting playback of two videos at the same time to keep them in sync. They will decode at a different rate and will eventually drift apart. Frequent resynchronization of their timelines is necessary.

Navigation: Accessing Content

As described earlier, providing alt content alone is not sufficient to satisfy all accessibility needs.

A key challenge in creating video for visually impaired users is how to make navigating through the video accessible. The media controls in the browsers contain a timeline navigation bar that seeing users use to click and directly jump to time offsets. This avoids having to watch and wait for a certain piece of interest to come up. The problem is that vision-impaired users cannot see the navigation bar.

In Chapter 2 we discussed the functionality of the default player interfaces and how browsers have made them keyboard accessible. Features like Opera's `CTRL-left/right` arrow navigation by 1/10 of the video duration, or Firefox's left/right arrow navigation using 10-second increments gives vision-impaired users a means to more easily navigate.

What is missing, though, is semantic navigation, which is the ability to directly jump to points of interest, for example, in long-form media files. Most content is structured. This book—just look at the chapters and sections that make up this book's structure—is an example of structured content. Similarly, long-form media files will have a structure. For example, movies on DVDs or Blu-Ray come with chapters that allow direct access to meaningful time offsets. In fact, there is a whole web site dedicated to this subject at http://chapterdb.org/.

We have already seen, earlier in this chapter, how the <track> element can expose text tracks of kind="chapters" and how we can author WebVTT files to provide those chapters. How can we make use of chapters and time offsets for semantic navigation that is also accessible to vision-impaired users?

Listing 4-21 provides an example that uses media fragment URIs to navigate chapters that have been provided via a WebVTT file.

Listing 4-21. Navigating Chapters Using Media Fragment URIs

```
<video poster="img/ElephantDreams.png" controls width="50%">
  <source src="video/ElephantDreams.webm" type="video/webm">
  <source src="video/ElephantDreams.mp4"  type="video/mp4">
  <track src="tracks/ElephantDreams_chapters_en.vtt" srclang="en"
         kind="chapters" default>
</video>
<h3>Navigate through the following chapters:</h3>
<ul id="chapters">
</ul>
<script>
var video = document.getElementsByTagName("video")[0];
var source;
var chapters = document.getElementById('chapters');

function showChapters() {
  source = video.currentSrc;
  var cues = video.textTracks[0].cues;
  for (var i=0; i<cues.length; i++) {
    var li = document.createElement("li");
    var link = document.createElement("a");
    link.href = "#t=" + cues[i].startTime + "," + cues[i].endTime;
    var cue = cues[i].getCueAsHTML();
    cue.textContent = parseInt(cues[i].startTime) + " sec : "
                      + cue.textContent;
    link.appendChild(cue);
    li.appendChild(link);
    chapters.appendChild(li);
  }
  video.removeEventListener("loadeddata", showChapters, false);
}
video.addEventListener("loadeddata", showChapters, false);

function updateFragment() {
  video.src = source + window.location.hash;
  video.load();
  video.play();
}
window.addEventListener("hashchange", updateFragment, false);
</script>
```

After the video has been loaded, we run the showChapters() function to go through the list of chapter cues in the .vtt file and add them to a <ul> list below the video. The list is using the start and end time of the cues to build media fragments: #t=[starttime],[endtime]. These media fragments are provided as URLs for each respective chapter: link.href = "#t=" + cues[i].startTime + "," + cues[i].endTime;.

As the link is being activated, the web page's URL hash changes and activates the updateFragment() function, in which we change the URL to the video element to contain the media fragment: video.src = source + window.location.hash;. Then we reload the video and play it, which activates the change to the video URL and thus navigates the video.

The result can be seen in Figure 4-25 after navigating to the "Emo Creates" chapter.

Navigate through the following chapters:

- 0 sec : Introductory Titles
- 18 sec : The Jack Plugs
- 70 sec : Robotic Birds
- 150 sec : The Phone Room
- 224 sec : Typewriter Dance
- 293 sec : The Elevator
- 428 sec : Emo Creates
- 565 sec : End Titles

Figure 4-25. *Navigating chapters using media fragment URIs in Google Chrome*

Since the anchor element <a> by definition provides keyboard focus for vision-impaired users, this will allow them to navigate the video's chapters. Such direct semantic navigation is actually also really useful to other users, so it's a win-win situation.

Summary

This has been a rather long chapter and we will bet you never considered the fact that there is so much to making media available to people who are either disabled or simply don't speak your language.

The most important lesson in this chapter is that accessibility is not a simple topic. This is simply due to the fact there are so many differing accessibility needs. The easiest way to satisfy them is by providing textual transcripts. The problem is, transcripts provide the worst user experience and should only be used as a fallback mechanism.

The most important accessibility and internationalization needs for media are the following:

- Captions or sign language video for hearing-impaired users,

- Audio or text descriptions for vision-impaired users, and

- Subtitles or dubbed audio tracks for international users.

You've seen how to use WebVTT for authoring text tracks that provide for all of the text-based accessibility needs. You've also seen how to use multitrack media or a `MediaController` to deal with sign language video, audio descriptions, or dubbed audio tracks.

As HTML5 matures and the browser manufacturers continue to keep pace, many of the limited features presented in this chapter will become commonplace.

Speaking of commonplace, smartphones and devices have rapidly moved from novelty to commonplace in a little less than five years. Along with this HTML5 video has blossomed into an interactive and creative medium thanks to the HTML5 Canvas. It is the subject of the next chapter. We'll see you there.

CHAPTER 5

■ ■ ■

HTML5 Video and Canvas

Up to this point in the book video has been treated as a somewhat static medium. As you have discovered, a video is nothing more than a series of images rendered on screen at a specific rate and the user's only interaction with the video is to click a control and/or read a transcript or subtitles. Other than that, there really is nothing more for the user to do than to sit back and enjoy the show. With a bit of JavaScript and the use of the HTML5 canvas, you can actually make this passive medium interactive and, more important, transform it to a creative medium. It all starts with that all-important concept: imaging.

When it comes to drawing images on the screen, HTML5 can render two imaging types: SVG (Scalable Vector Graphics) or Raster Bitmap graphics. SVG images are, to be brief, composed of points, lines, and fills in space. They are commonly driven by code and because of their nature they are device independent, meaning they can be sized and relocated on the screen with no loss in resolution.

Raster Graphics, on the other hand, are pixel-based. They are essentially chained to the pixels in the screen. With the advent of HTML5 video and the canvas element, the screen becomes exactly what the name implies: a blank canvas where you can draw anything from straight lines to complex graphics.

While the SVG environment is a declarative graphics environment dealing with vector-based shapes, the HTML canvas provides a script-based graphics environment revolving around pixels or bitmaps. In comparison with SVG, it is faster to manipulate data entities in canvas, since it is easier to get directly to individual pixels. On the other hand, SVG provides a DOM (Document Object Model) and has an event model not available to canvas. What this should tell you is that applications that need interactive graphics will typically choose SVG, while applications that do a lot of image manipulation will more typically reach for canvas. The available transforms and effects in both are similar, and the same visual results can be achieved with both, but with different programming effort and potentially different performance.

When comparing performance between SVG and canvas, typically the drawing of a lot of objects will eventually slow down SVG, which has to maintain all the references to the objects, while for canvas it's just more pixels to light up. So, when you have a lot of objects to draw and it's not really important that you continue to have access to the individual objects but are just after pixel drawings, you should use canvas.

In contrast, the size of the drawing area of canvas has a huge impact on the speed of a <canvas>, since it has to draw more pixels. So, when you have a large area to cover with a smaller number of objects, you should use SVG.

Note that the choice between canvas and SVG is not fully exclusive. It is possible to bring a canvas into an SVG image by converting it to an image using a function called toDataURL(). This can be used, for example, when drawing a fancy and repetitive background for a SVG image. It may often be more efficient to draw that background in the canvas and include it into the SVG image through the toDataURL() function: which explains why the focus of this chapter is canvas.

Like SVG, the canvas is, at its heart, a visually oriented medium—it doesn't do anything with audio. Of course, you can combine background music with an awesome graphical display by simply using the <audio> element as part of your pages. An amazing example of how audio and canvas come together can be found at 9elements (http://9elements.com/io/?p=153). The project is a stunning a visualization of Twitter chatter through the use of colored and animated circles on a background of music.

If you already have experience with JavaScript, canvas should not be too difficult to understand. It's almost like a JavaScript library with drawing functionality. It supports, in particular, the following function categories:

- **Canvas handling**: creating a drawing area, a 2D context, saving and restoring state.

- **Drawing basic shapes**: rectangles, paths, lines, arcs, Bezier, and quadratic curves.

- **Drawing text**: drawing fill text and stroke text, and measuring text.

- **Using images**: creating, drawing, scaling, and slicing images.

- **Applying styles**: colors, fill styles, stroke styles, transparency, line styles, gradients, shadows, and patterns.

- **Applying transformations**: translating, rotating, scaling, and transformation matrices.

- **Compositing**: clipping and overlap drawing composition.

- **Applying animations**: execute drawing functions over time by associating time intervals and timeouts.

To start let's work with video in canvas.

Video in Canvas

The first step to understanding how to work with video in canvas is to pull the pixel data out of a <video> element and "paint" it on a canvas element. Like any great artist facing a blank canvas, we need to draw an image onto the canvas.

drawImage( )

The `drawImage()` function accepts a video element as well as an image or a canvas element. Listing 5-1 shows how to use it directly on a video. You can follow along with the examples at `http://html5videoguide.net`.

Listing 5-1. Introducing the Video Pixel Data into a Canvas

```
<video controls autoplay height="240" width="360" >
  <source src="video/HelloWorld.mp4"  type="video/mp4">
  <source src="video/HelloWorld.webm" type="video/webm">
</video>

<canvas width="400" height="300" style="border: 1px solid black;">
</canvas>
<script>
var video, canvas, context;
video = document.getElementsByTagName("video")[0];
canvas = document.getElementsByTagName("canvas")[0];
context = canvas.getContext("2d");
video.addEventListener("timeupdate", paintFrame, false);

function paintFrame() {
  context.drawImage(video, 0, 0, 160, 120);
}
</script>
```

The HTML markup is simple. It contains only the <video> element and the <canvas> element into which we are painting the video data.

The JavaScript is pretty uncomplicated. The addEventListener is the key. Every time the video's currentTime updates–timeupdate–the paintFrame function draws the captured pixels onto the canvas using the drawImage() method which is associated with the getContext("2d") object. Those pixels are drawn, as shown in Figure 5-1, in the upper left corner of the <canvas> element (0,0) and fill a space that is 160 × 120. All browsers support this functionality.

Figure 5-1. *Painting a video into a canvas with every timeupdate event*

You will notice that the video is playing at a higher framerate than the canvas. This is because the timeupdate event does not fire for every frame of the video. It fires every few frames—roughly every 100–250 ms. There currently is no function to allow you to reliably grab every frame. We can, however, create a painting loop that is updated every time the screen refreshes using the requestAnimationFrame() function. In typical browsers, that's about 60 times a second and given that most modern videos are about 30 frames a second, it should get most if not all of the frames.

In the next example, we use the play event to start the painting loop when the user starts playback and run until the video is paused or ended. Another option would be to use the canplay or loadeddata events to start the display independently of a user interaction.

Also, let's make the next example a bit more interesting. Since we now know how to capture and draw a video frame to the canvas, let's start to play with that data. In Listing 5-2, we shift the frames by 10 pixels on each of the x- and y-axes each time the canvas redraws.

Listing 5-2. Painting Video Frames at Different Offsets into the Canvas Using requestAnimationFrame

```
<video controls autoplay height="240" width="360" >
  <source src="video/HelloWorld.mp4"  type="video/mp4">
  <source src="video/HelloWorld.webm" type="video/webm">
</video>
<canvas width="400" height="300" style="border: 1px solid black;">
</canvas>
```

```
<script>
var video, canvas, context;
video = document.getElementsByTagName("video")[0];
canvas = document.getElementsByTagName("canvas")[0];
context = canvas.getContext("2d");
video.addEventListener("play", paintFrame, false);
var x = 0, xpos = 10;
var y = 0, ypos = 10;
function paintFrame() {
  context.drawImage(video, x, y, 160, 120);
  if (x > 240) xpos = -10;
  if (x < 0)   xpos =  10;
  x = x + xpos;
  if (y > 180) ypos = -10;
  if (y < 0)   ypos =  10;
  y = y + ypos;
  if (video.paused || video.ended) {
    return;
  }
  requestAnimationFrame(paintFrame);
}
</script>
```

The result, as shown in Figure 5-2, can be rather interesting. The video, itself, seems to be a paintbrush on the canvas as it moves around the canvas painting the video frames into what seems to be random locations. In actual fact, if you carefully follow the paintFrame() function, this is not exactly the case. The size of each image is set to 160 × 120 and the motion of the video is determined by the xpos and ypos values. Every successive frame is offset from the previous one by 10 pixels each to the right and left until it hits the edge of the canvas, when the offset is negated.

Figure 5-2. *Painting a video into a canvas with the requestAnimationFrame function in Chrome*

The framerate at which this example is painted equals the framerate of the requestAnimationFrame() function, which is typically 60Hz. This means that we are now updating the canvas as often or even more often than the video frame.

Since the requestAnimationFrame() method is still fairly new, in older browsers (particularly IE10 and below) you will need to use setTimeout() instead of requestAnimationFrame() to repeatedly grab a frame from the video after a given time interval.

Because the setTimeout() function calls a function after a given number of milliseconds, and we would normally run the video at 24 (PAL) or 30 (NTSC) frames per second, a timeout of 41 ms or 33 ms would be more than appropriate. To be on the safe side, you might want to go with a frame rate equal to the one of requestAnimationFrame(), which equals your typical screen refresh rate of 60Hz. Thus, set the timeout to 1,000/60 = 16 ms to achieve a similar effect to Figure 5-2. For your application, you might want to reduce the frequency even further to make your web page less CPU (Central Processing Unit) intensive.

As you start experimenting with the setTimeout() function, you will notice that it allows us to "render" video frames into a canvas at higher framerates than the original video and than requestAnimationFrame() allows. Let's take the example from Listing 5-2 and rewrite it with setTimeout() and a 0 timeout, so you can see what we mean (see Listing 5-3).

Listing 5-3. Painting Video Frames at Different Offsets into the Canvas Using setTimeout

```
<video controls autoplay height="240" width="360" >
  <source src="video/HelloWorld.mp4"  type="video/mp4">
  <source src="video/HelloWorld.webm" type="video/webm">
</video>
<canvas width="400" height="300" style="border: 1px solid black;">
</canvas>
<script>
var video, canvas, context;
video = document.getElementsByTagName("video")[0];
canvas = document.getElementsByTagName("canvas")[0];
context = canvas.getContext("2d");
video.addEventListener("play", paintFrame, false);
var x = 0, xpos = 10;
var y = 0, ypos = 10;
var count = 0;
function paintFrame() {
  count++;
  context.drawImage(video, x, y, 160, 120);
  if (x > 240) xpos = -10;
  if (x < 0)   xpos =  10;
  x = x + xpos;
  if (y > 180) ypos = -10;
  if (y < 0)   ypos =  10;
  y = y + ypos;
  if (video.paused || video.ended) {
    alert(count);
    return;
  }
  setTimeout(function () {
      paintFrame();
  }, 0);
}
</script>
```

The result, as shown in Figure 5-3, may at first be surprising. We see a lot more video frames being rendered into the canvas than with the requestAnimationFrame() approach. As you think about this some more, you will realize that all we have done is grab a frame from the video into the canvas as quickly as we can and not worry about whether it is a new video frame or not. The visual effect is that we get a higher framerate in the canvas than we have in the video. In fact, in Google Chrome on one of our machines we achieved 210 fps in the canvas. Note that your screen will not render it at that framerate, but still at typically around 60 fps, but with every rendering the canvas has placed three to four new frames, so it looks a lot faster than the previous version.

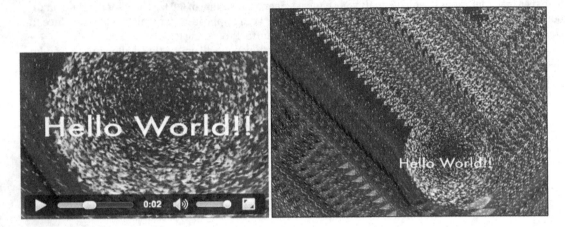

Figure 5-3. *Painting a video into a canvas with the setTimeout event in Chrome*

If you have tried this in a variety of modern browsers you may have noticed each one managed to draw a different number of video frames during the playback of the complete 6-second clip. This is due to the varying speed of their JavaScript engines. They may even get stuck in the middle for a bit before continuing on with drawing more frames. This is because the browser has the ability to delay a setTimeout() call if there is other higher-priority work to do. The requestAnimationFrame() function doesn't suffer from that problem and guarantees an equidistant recurring rendering call, which avoids playback jitter.

■ **Note** Though we have demonstrated one example, don't forget this is code and the neat thing about code is the ability to play with it. For example, a simple thing like changing the xpos and ypos values can yield quite different results from that shown.

Extended drawImage()

So far we have used the drawImage() function to draw the pixels extracted from a video onto the canvas. This drawing also includes scaling that the canvas does for us to fit the pixels into the given width and height dimensions. There is also a version of drawImage() that allows you to extract a rectangular area from the original video and paint it onto a region in the canvas. An example of just such an approach is tiling, where the video is divided into multiple rectangles and redrawn with a gap between the rectangles. Listing 5-4 shows a naïve implementation of this. We only show the new `paintFrame()` function since the remainder of the code is identical to Listing 5-2. We also choose the `requestAnimationFrame()` version of painting because we really don't need to paint at a higher framerate than the video.

Listing 5-4. Naïve Implementation of Video Tiling into a Canvas

```
function paintFrame() {
    in_w = 720; in_h = 480;
    w = 360;    h = 240;
    // create 4x4 tiling
    tiles = 4;
    gap = 5;
    for (x = 0; x < tiles; x++) {
      for (y = 0; y < tiles; y++) {
        context.drawImage(video, x*in_w/tiles, y*in_h/tiles,
                          in_w/tiles, in_h/tiles,
                          x*(w/tiles+gap), y*(h/tiles+gap),
                          w/tiles, h/tiles);
      }
    }
    if (video.paused || video.ended) {
      return;
    }
    requestAnimationFrame(paintFrame);
}
```

The `drawImage()` function with its many parameters allows for the extraction of a rectangular region from any offset in the original video and the drawing of this pixel data into any scaled rectangular region in the canvas. Figure 5-4 shows how this function works. As you can see, a specific region of a video is taken from the source and drawn on to a specific area in the canvas. That specific region for both the source and the destination is set in the `drawimage()` parameters.

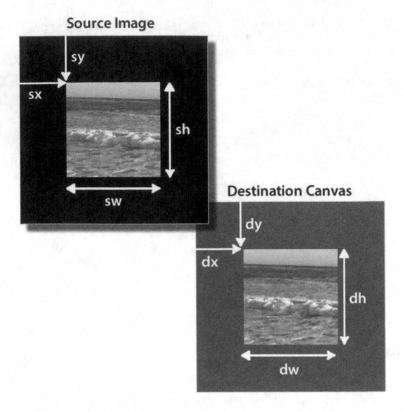

Figure 5-4. *Extracting a rectangular region from a source video into a scaled rectangular region in the canvas using drawImage()*

The parameters are as follows: drawImage(image, sx, sy, sw, sh, dx, dy, dw, dh) (see Figure 5-4). In Listing 5-4 the parameters are used to subdivide the video into tiles whose sizes are set using in_w/tiles by in_h/tiles, where in_w and in_h are the intrinsic width and height of the used video file (i.e., video.videoWidth and video.videoHeight). These tiles are then scaled to size with w/tiles by h/tiles, where w and h are the scaled width and height of the video image in the canvas. Each tile is then placed on the canvas with a 5-pixel gap.

■ **Note**   It is important you understand that the intrinsic width and height of the video resource is used to extract the region from the video and not the potentially scaled video in the video element. If this is disregarded, you may be calculating with the width and height of the scaled video and extract the wrong region. Also note it is possible to scale the extracted region by placing it into a destination rectangle with different dimensions.

Figure 5-5 shows the result of running Listing 5-4. As you can see, the video is broken into a series of tiles on a 4 × 4 grid and spaced 5 pixels from each other. All browsers show the same behavior.

Figure 5-5. *Tiling a video into a canvas in Chrome, video on left, canvas on right*

This implementation is not exactly a best practice because we call the drawImage() function once per tile. If you set the variable tiles to a value of 32, some browsers can't keep up with the canvas rendering and the framerate in the canvas drags to a halt. This is because each call to drawImage() for the video element during the setTimeout function retrieves the pixel data from the video each time it is drawn to the canvas. The result is an overworked browser.

There are three ways to overcome this. All of them rely on getting the video image via the canvas into an intermediate storage area and repainting the image from there. In the first approach you will grab frames and repaint them, in the second you will grab frames but repaint pixels, in the last you will use a second canvas for pixel manipulation.

Frame Grabbing

This approach consists of drawing the video pixels into the canvas, then picking up the pixel data from the canvas with getImageData() and writing it out again with putImageData(). Since putImageData() has parameters to draw out only sections of the picture again, you should be able to replicate the same effect as above. Here is the signature of the function: putImageData(imagedata, dx, dy [, dirtyx, dirtyy, dirtyw, dirtyh]).

Unfortunately, the parameters are not the same as for the drawImage() function. The "dirty" rectangle defines the rectangle from the image data to draw (by default it's the full image). Then the dx and dy allow moving that rectangle from its position further away on the x and y axis. No scaling will happen to the image.

You can see the code in Listing 5-5—again, only the paintFrame() function is provided since the remainder is identical with Listing 5-2.

Listing 5-5. Reimplementation of Video Tiling into a Canvas with putImageData()

```
function paintFrame() {
    in_w = 720; in_h = 480;
    w = 360; h = 240;
    context.drawImage(video, 0, 0, in_w, in_h, 0, 0, w, h);
    frame = context.getImageData(0, 0, w, h);
    context.clearRect(0, 0, w, h);
```

```
    // create 4x4 tiling
    tiles = 4;
    gap = 5;
    for (x = 0; x < tiles; x++) {
      for (y = 0; y < tiles; y++) {
        context.putImageData(frame,
                             x*gap, y*gap,
                             x*w/tiles, y*h/tiles,
                             w/tiles, h/tiles);
      }
    }
    if (video.paused || video.ended) {
      return;
    }
    requestAnimationFrame(paintFrame);
}
```

In this version, the putImageData() function uses parameters to specify the drawing offset, which includes the gap and the size of the cut-out rectangle from the video frame. The frame has already been received through getImageData() as a resized image. Note that the frame drawn with drawImage() needs to be cleared before redrawing with putImageData(), because we don't paint over the 5 px gaps. Figure 5-6 shows the result of running Listing 5-5.

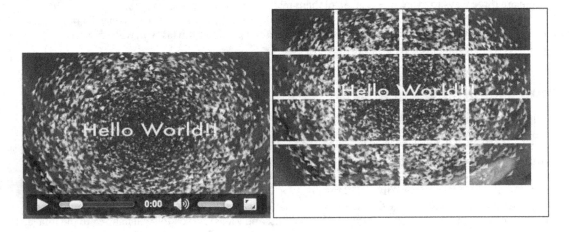

Figure 5-6. Attempted tiling of a video into a canvas using putImageData()

■ **Note**   Note that you have to run this example from a web server, not from a file on your local computer. The reason is that getImageData() does not work cross-site and security checks will ensure it only works on the same http domain. That leaves out local file access.

Pixel Painting

The second approach is to perform the cut-outs manually. Seeing as we have the pixel data available through getImageData(), we can create each of the tiles ourselves and use putImageData() with only the offset attributes to place the tiles. Listing 5-6 shows an implementation of the paintFrame() function for this case.

Listing 5-6. Reimplementation of Video Tiling into a Canvas with createImageData

```
function paintFrame() {
    w = 360; h = 240;
    context.drawImage(video, 0, 0, w, h);
    frame = context.getImageData(0, 0, w, h);
    context.clearRect(0, 0, w, h);

    // create 15x15 tiling
    tiles = 15;
    gap = 2;
    nw = w/tiles;
    nh = h/tiles;

    // Loop over the tiles
    for (tx = 0; tx < tiles; tx++) {
      for (ty = 0; ty < tiles; ty++) {
        output = context.createImageData(nw, nh);

        // Loop over each pixel of output file
        for (x = 0; x < nw; x++) {
          for (y = 0; y < nh; y++) {
            // index in output image
            i = x + nw*y;
            // index in frame image
            j = x + w*y + tx*nw + w*nh*ty;
            // copy all the colours
            for (c = 0; c < 4; c++) {
              output.data[4*i+c] = frame.data[4*j+c];
            }
          }
        }

        // Draw the ImageData object.
        context.putImageData(output, tx*(nw+gap), ty*(nh+gap));
      }
    }

    if (video.paused || video.ended) {
      return;
    }
    requestAnimationFrame(paintFrame);
}
```

First we loop over each of the tiles and call `createImageData()` to create the tile image. To fill the tile with pixel data, we loop through the pixels of the tile image and fill it from the relevant pixels of the video frame image. Then we place the tile using `putImageData()`. Figure 5-7 shows the results with a 15 × 15 grid of tiles.

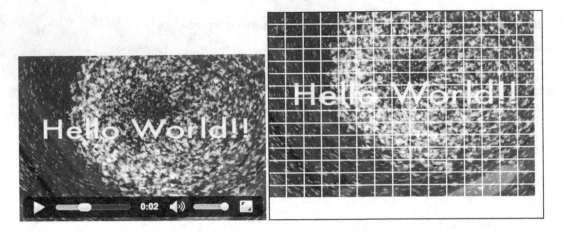

Figure 5-7. *Attempted tiling of a video into a canvas using putImageData() in Chrome*

This could obviously be improved by just writing a single image and placing the gap in between the tiles as we write that one image. The advantage of having an image for each tile is that you can more easily manipulate each individual tile—rotate, translate, or scale it, for example—but you will need to manage the list of tiles (i.e., keep a list of pointers to them).

■ **Note**   That you have to run this example from a web server, not from a file on your local computer. The reason is that `getImageData()` does not work cross-site and security checks will ensure it only works on the same http domain. That leaves out local file access.

Scratch Canvas

The final approach is to store the video images with `drawImage()` into an intermediate canvas–we'll call it the scratch canvas since its only purpose is to hold the pixel data and it is not even displayed visually on screen. Once that is done, you use `drawImage()` with input from the scratch canvas to draw onto the displayed canvas. The expectation is that the image in the canvas is already in a form that can just be copied piece by piece, into the displayed canvas rather than continuous scaling as in the naive approach from earlier. The code in Listing 5-7 shows how to use a scratch canvas.

Listing 5-7. Reimplementation of Video Tiling into a Canvas Using a Scratch Canvas

```
<video controls autoplay height="240" width="360">
  <source src="video/HelloWorld.mp4"  type="video/mp4">
  <source src="video/HelloWorld.webm" type="video/webm">
</video>
<canvas width="400" height="300" style="border: 1px solid black;">
</canvas>
<canvas id="scratch" width="360" height="240" style="display: none;"></canvas>

<script>
  var context, sctxt, video;
  video = document.getElementsByTagName("video")[0];
  canvases = document.getElementsByTagName("canvas");
  canvas = canvases[0];
  scratch = canvases[1];
  context = canvas.getContext("2d");
  sctxt = scratch.getContext("2d");
  video.addEventListener("play", paintFrame, false);
  function paintFrame() {
    // set up scratch frames
    w = 360; h = 240;
    sctxt.drawImage(video, 0, 0, w, h);
    // create 4x4 tiling
    tiles = 4;
    gap = 5;
    tw = w/tiles; th = h/tiles;
    for (x = 0; x < tiles; x++) {
      for (y = 0; y < tiles; y++) {
        context.drawImage(scratch, x*tw, y*th, tw, th,
                          x*(tw+gap), y*(th+gap), tw, th);
      }
    }
    if (video.paused || video.ended) {
      return;
    }
    requestAnimationFrame(paintFrame);
  }
</script>
```

Notice the second canvas with id="scratch" in the HTML. It has to be set large enough to be able to contain the video frame. If you do not give it a width and height attribute, it will default to 300 × 150 and you may lose data around the edges. The purpose of this scratch canvas is to receive and scale the video frames before they are handed off to the canvas. We don't want to display it, which is why it is set to display:none. The tiles are then drawn (see Figure 5-8) into the displayed canvas using the extended drawImage() function shown in Listing 5-4.

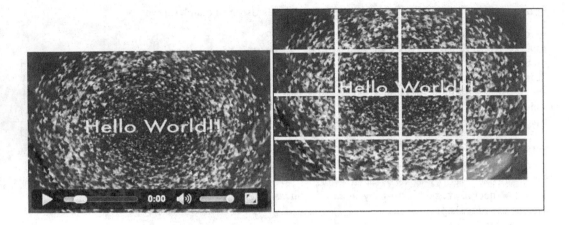

Figure 5-8. *Using the "scratch canvas" technique in Chrome*

■ **Note**   This is the most efficient implementation of the tiling since it doesn't have to repeatedly copy the frames from the video, and it doesn't have to continuously rescale the original frame size. It also works across all browsers, including IE. It also doesn't need to be run on a web server, which is an additional win.

As you may have gathered, tiling a video on the canvas offers some rather interesting creative possibilities. Due to the fact that each tile can be manipulated individually, each tile can use a different transform or other technique. An amazing example of tiling in combination with other canvas effects such as transformations is shown in "Blowing up your video" by Sean Christmann (see http://craftymind.com/factory/html5video/CanvasVideo.html). When you click on the video, the area is tiled and the tiles scatter as shown in Figure 5-9, creating an explosion effect.

You may need to reload the page if video isn't streaming properly. Video courtesy of <u>Big Buck Bunny</u>

Figure 5-9. *Tiling offers you some serious creative possibilities*

Styling

Now that we know how to handle video in a canvas, let's do some simple manipulations to the canvas pixels which will yield some rather interesting results. We'll start by making certain pixels in the video transparent.

Pixel Transparency to Replace the Background

One of the hallmarks of Flash video, before the arrival of HTML5 video, was the ability to use alpha channel video on top of an animation or a static image. This technique can't be used in the HTML5 universe, but manipulation of the canvas allows us to determine which colors are transparent and to overlay that canvas over other content. Listing 5-8 shows a video where all colors but white are made transparent before being projected onto a canvas with a background image. In the browser, pixels consist of a combination of three colors: red, green, and blue. Each of the r, g, and b components can have a value between 0 and 255 equating to 0% to 100% intensity. Black is when all rgb values are 0 and white when all of them are 1. In Listing 5-8, we identify a pixel whose r, g, and b components are all above 180 as close enough to white so we can keep some more "dirty" whites also.

Listing 5-8. Making Certain Colors in a Video Transparent Through a Canvas Manipulation

```
function paintFrame() {
  w = 360; h = 240;
  context.drawImage(video, 0, 0, w, h);
  frame = context.getImageData(0, 0, w, h);
  context.clearRect(0, 0, w, h);
  output = context.createImageData(w, h);

  // Loop over each pixel of output file
  for (x = 0; x < w; x++) {
    for (y = 0; y < h; y++) {
      // index in output image
      i = x + w*y;
      for (c = 0; c < 4; c++) {
        output.data[4*i+c] = frame.data[4*i+c];
      }
      // make pixels transparent
      r = frame.data[i * 4 + 0];
      g = frame.data[i * 4 + 1];
      b = frame.data[i * 4 + 2];
      if (!(r > 180 && g > 180 && b > 180))
        output.data[4*i + 3] = 0;
    }
  }
  context.putImageData(output, 0, 0);
  if (video.paused || video.ended) {
    return;
  }
  requestAnimationFrame(paintFrame);
}
```

Listing 5-8 shows the essential painting function. The rest of the page is very similar to Listing 5-2 with the addition of a background image to the <canvas> styling. All pixels are drawn in exactly the same manner, except for the fourth color channel of each pixel, which is set to 0. This is the a channel, which determines opacity in the rbga color model, so we're making all pixels opaque that are not white. Figure 5-10 shows the result with the stars being the only remaining nontransparent pixels and producing the effect of a firework on the image of Hong Kong.

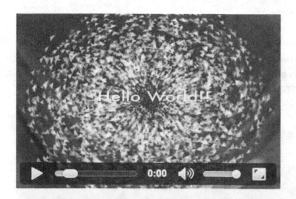

Figure 5-10. *Projecting a masked video onto a background image in the canvas*

■ **Note** This technique can also be applied to a blue or green screen video. In this case the pixels composing solid blue or green background in the video are turned transparent. This will not work if the lighting of the screen is uneven.

Scaling Pixel Slices for a 3D Effect

Videos are often placed in a 3D display to make them look more like real-world screens through the use of perspective. This requires scaling the shape of the video to a trapezoid where both width and height are independently scaled. In a canvas, you can achieve this effect by drawing vertical slices of the video picture with different heights and scaling the width using the drawImage() function. Listing 5-9 shows a great example of this technique.

Listing 5-9. Rendering a Video in the 2D Canvas with a 3D Effect

```
function paintFrame() {
    // set up scratch frame
    w = 270; h = 180;
    sctxt.drawImage(video, 0, 0, w, h);

    // width should be between -500 and +500
    width = -250;
    // right side scaling should be between 0 and 200%
    scale = 2;

    // canvas width and height
    cw = 1000; ch = 400;
    // number of columns to draw
    columns = Math.abs(width);
    // display the picture mirrored?
    mirror = (width > 0) ? 1 : -1;
    // origin of the output picture
    ox = cw/2; oy= (ch-h)/2;
    // slice width
    sw = columns/w;
    // slice height increase steps
    sh = (h*scale-h)/columns;

    // Loop over each pixel column of the output picture
    for (x = 0; x < w; x++) {
      // place output columns
      dx = ox + mirror*x*sw;
      dy = oy - x*sh/2;
      // scale output columns
      dw = sw;
      dh = h + x*sh;
      // draw the pixel column
      context.drawImage(scratch, x, 0, 1, h, dx, dy, dw, dh);
    }
    if (video.paused || video.ended) {
      return;
    }
    requestAnimationFrame(paintFrame);
  }
```

For this example, showing only the paintFrame() function, we use a 1,000 × 400 canvas and a scratch canvas into which we pull the pixel data.

As we pull the video frame into the scratch canvas, we scale the video to the size at which we want to apply the effect. Then we pull pixel column by pixel column into the displayed canvas. As we do that, we scale the width and height of the pixel column to the desired "width" and height of the output image. The width of the output image is given through the width variable. The height of the output image scales between the original height on the left side of the output image and scale times the original height on the right side. A negative width will determine that we are looking through the "back" of the video.

The example is written in such a way that you can achieve innumerable creative effects by simply changing the width and scale variables. For example, you can achieve a book page turning effect by changing the width and scale values synchronously.

Figure 5-11 shows the result in Chrome. All browsers, including IE, support this example and will display the same result.

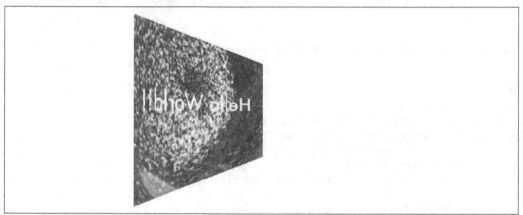

Figure 5-11. *Rendering video in a 3D perspective in Chrome*

Ambient CSS Color Frame

Another nice effect that the canvas can be used for is typically known as an ambient color frame for the video. In this effect, a colored frame or border area is created around the video, and the color of that frame is adjusted according to the average color of the video.

This technique is especially effective if your video needs a border on the page or you want it to be noticed. To that effect, you will frequently calculate the average color of the video and use it to fill a div that sits behind the video and is slightly larger than the video. Listing 5-10 shows an example implementation of this technique.

Listing 5-10. Calculation of Average Color in a Canvas and Display of Ambient Color Frame

```
<style type="text/css">
#ambience {
  transition-property: all;
  transition-duration: 1s;
  transition-timing-function: linear;
  padding: 40px;
  width: 366px;
  outline: black solid 10px;
}
video {
  padding: 3px;
  background-color: white;
}
canvas {
  display: none;
}
</style>
<div id="ambience">
    <video controls autoplay height="240" width="360">
      <source src="video/HelloWorld.mp4"  type="video/mp4">
      <source src="video/HelloWorld.webm" type="video/webm">
    </video>
  </div>
  <canvas id="scratch" width="320" height="160"></canvas>
</div>

<script>
  var sctxt, video, ambience;
  ambience = document.getElementById("ambience");
  video = document.getElementsByTagName("video")[0];
  scratch = document.getElementById("scratch");
  sctxt = scratch.getContext("2d");
  video.addEventListener("play", paintAmbience, false);

  function paintAmbience() {
    // set up scratch frame
    sctxt.drawImage(video, 0, 0, 360, 240);
    frame = sctxt.getImageData(0, 0, 360, 240);
    // get average color for frame and transition to it
    color = getColorAvg(frame);
    ambience.style.backgroundColor =
      'rgb('+color[0]+','+color[1]+','+color[2]+')';
    if (video.paused || video.ended) {
      return;
    }
    // don't do it more often than once a second
    setTimeout(function () {
        paintAmbience();
    }, 1000);
  }
```

```
function getColorAvg(frame) {
  r = 0;
  g = 0;
  b = 0;
  // calculate average color from image in canvas
  for (var i = 0; i < frame.data.length; i += 4) {
    r += frame.data[i];
    g += frame.data[i + 1];
    b += frame.data[i + 2];
  }
  r = Math.ceil(r / (frame.data.length / 4));
  g = Math.ceil(g / (frame.data.length / 4));
  b = Math.ceil(b / (frame.data.length / 4));
  return Array(r, g, b);
}
</script>
```

Though the preceding code block appears to be rather complex, it is also fairly easy to follow.

We start by setting up the CSS style environment such that the video is placed in a separate <div> element whose background color starts with white but will change as the video plays. The video, itself, has a 3 px white padding frame to separate it from the color-changing <div>.

Thanks to the setTimeout() function the color around the video will only change once each second. We decided to use setTimeout() over requestAnimationFrame() for this example to adapt the framing around the video less often. To ensure a smooth color transition, we use CSS transitions to make the change over the course of a second.

The canvas being used is invisible since it is used only to pull an image frame every second and calculate the average color of that frame. The background of the <div> is then updated with that color. Figure 5-12 shows the result.

Figure 5-12. *Rendering of an ambient CSS color frame in Opera*

If you are reading this in the print version, in Figure 5-12 you might see only a dark gray as the background of the video. However, the color actually changes to various shades of the predominant brown in the background.

■ **Note** Though this technique is right up there in the realm of "cool techniques," use it sparingly. If there is a compelling design or branding reason to use it, by all means use it. Using it just because "I can" is not a valid reason.

Video as Pattern

The canvas provides a simple function to create regions tiled with images, another canvas, or frames from a video. The function is createPattern(). This will take an image and copy it into the given region until that region is filled with copies of the image or video. If your video doesn't come in the size that your pattern requires, you will need to use a scratch canvas to resize the video frames first.

Listing 5-11 shows how it's done.

Listing 5-11. Filling a Rectangular Canvas Region with a Video Pattern

```
<video autoplay style="display: none;" >
  <source src="video/HelloWorld.mp4"  type="video/mp4">
  <source src="video/HelloWorld.webm" type="video/webm">
</video>
<canvas width="720" height="480" style="border: 1px solid black;">
</canvas>
<canvas id="scratch" width="180" height="120" style="display:none;">
</canvas>

<script>
  var context, sctxt, video;
  video = document.getElementsByTagName("video")[0];
  canvas = document.getElementsByTagName("canvas")[0];
  context = canvas.getContext("2d");
  scratch = document.getElementById("scratch");
  sctxt = scratch.getContext("2d");
  video.addEventListener("play", paintFrame, false);

  function paintFrame() {
    sctxt.drawImage(video, 0, 0, 180, 120);
    pattern = context.createPattern(scratch, 'repeat');
    context.fillStyle = pattern;
    context.fillRect(0, 0, 720, 480);
    if (video.paused || video.ended) {
      return;
    }
    requestAnimationFrame(paintFrame);
  }
</script>
```

We're hiding the original video element, since the video is already painted 16 times into the output canvas. The scratch canvas grabs a frame roughly every 16 ms (assuming `requestAnimationFrame()` runs at 60 fps), which is then painted into the output canvas using the "repeat" pattern of `createPattern()`.

Each time the `paintFrame()` function is called, the current image in the video is grabbed and used as the replicated pattern in `createPattern()`. The HTML5 canvas specification states if the image (or canvas frame or video frame) is changed after the `createPattern()` function call where it is used, the pattern will not be affected.

Knowing there is no means of specifying scaling on the pattern image being used, we have to first load the video frames into the scratch canvas and then create the pattern from this scratch canvas and apply it to the drawing region.

Figure 5-13 shows the result in Safari. Since all browsers show the same behavior, this is representative for all browsers.

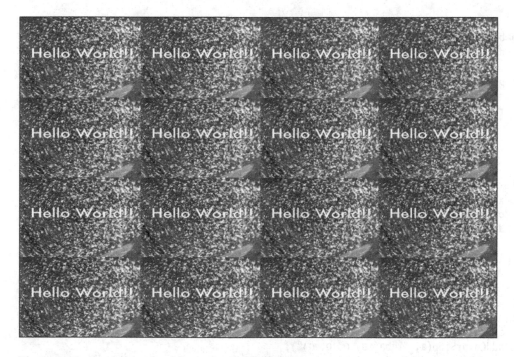

Figure 5-13. *Rendering of a video pattern in Safari*

Gradient Transparency Mask

Gradient masks are used to gradually fade the opacity of an object. Though the availability of transparency masking is quite widespread in practically every video editing application on the market, a gradient mask can also be programmatically added at runtime. This is accomplished by placing the page content–let's assume an image–under the video and applying a grayscale gradient over the video. Using the CSS `mask` property, we can apply transparency to the grayscale mask where the gradient was opaque. We can also do this using the canvas.

With canvas, we have a bit more flexibility, since we can play with the rgba values of the pixels in the gradient. In this example we simply reuse the previous code block and paint the video into the middle of a canvas. The video is blended into the ambient background through use of a radial gradient.

Listing 5-12 shows the key elements of the code.

Listing 5-12. Introducing a Gradient Transparency Mark into the Ambient Video

```
<style type="text/css">
#ambience {
  transition-property: all;
  transition-duration: 1s;
  transition-timing-function: linear;
  width: 420px; height: 300px;
  outline: black solid 10px;
}
#canvas {
  position: relative;
  left: 30px; top: 30px;
}
</style>
<div id="ambience">
  <canvas id="canvas" width="360" height="240"></canvas>
</div>
<video autoplay style="display: none;">
  <source src="video/HelloWorld.mp4"  type="video/mp4">
  <source src="video/HelloWorld.webm" type="video/webm">
</video>
<canvas id="scratch" width="360" height="240" style="display: none;">
</canvas>
<script>
  var context, sctxt, video, ambience;
  ambience = document.getElementById("ambience");
  video = document.getElementsByTagName("video")[0];
  canvas = document.getElementsByTagName("canvas")[0];
  context = canvas.getContext("2d");
  context.globalCompositeOperation = "destination-in";
  scratch = document.getElementById("scratch");
  sctxt = scratch.getContext("2d");
  gradient = context.createRadialGradient(180,120,0, 180,120,180);
  gradient.addColorStop(0, "rgba( 255, 255, 255, 1)");
  gradient.addColorStop(0.7, "rgba( 125, 125, 125, 0.8)");
  gradient.addColorStop(1, "rgba( 0, 0, 0, 0)");
  video.addEventListener("play", paintAmbience, false);

  function paintAmbience() {
    // set up scratch frame
    sctxt.drawImage(video, 0, 0, 360, 240);
    // get average color for frame and transition to it
    frame = sctxt.getImageData(0, 0, 360, 240);
    color = getColorAvg(frame);
    ambience.style.backgroundColor =
      'rgba('+color[0]+','+color[1]+','+color[2]+',0.8)';
    // paint video image
    context.putImageData(frame, 0, 0);
    // throw gradient onto canvas
    context.fillStyle = gradient;
    context.fillRect(0, 0, 360, 240);
```

```
      if (video.paused || video.ended) {
        return;
      }
      requestAnimationFrame(paintAmbience);
    }
</script>
```

We do not repeat the getColorAvg() function, which we defined in Listing 5-10.

We achieve the video masking with a gradient by changing the globalCompositeOperation property of the display canvas to destination-in. This means that we are able to use a gradient that is placed over the video frame to control the transparency of the pixels of the video frame. In this case we use a radial gradient in the initCanvas function and reuse that for every video frame.

Figure 5-14 shows the results in all browsers.

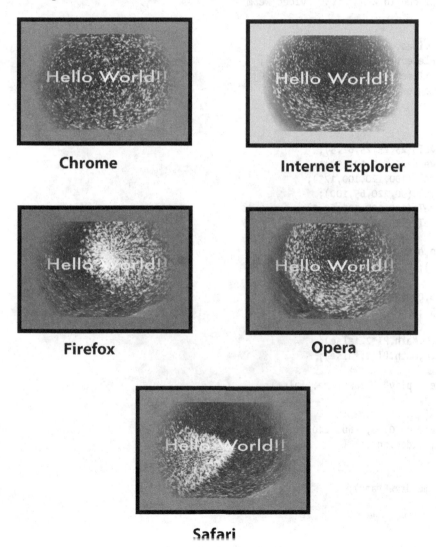

Figure 5-14. Rendering of video with a transparency mask onto an ambient color frame in a variety of browsers

215

Clipping a Region

Another useful compositing effect is to clip out a region from the canvas for display. This will cause everything else drawn onto the canvas afterward to be drawn only in the clipped-out region. For this technique, a path is "drawn" that may also include basic shapes. Then, instead of drawing these paths onto the canvas with the stroke( ) or fill( ) methods, we draw them using the clip( ) method, creating the clipped region(s) on the canvas to which further drawings will be confined. Listing 5-13 shows an example.

Listing 5-13. Using a Clipped Path to Filter out Regions of the Video for Display

```
<canvas id="canvas" width="360" height="240"></canvas>
<video autoplay style="display: none;">
  <source src="video/HelloWorld.mp4"  type="video/mp4">
  <source src="video/HelloWorld.webm" type="video/webm">
</video>
<script>
  var canvas, context, video;
  video = document.getElementsByTagName("video")[0];
  canvas = document.getElementsByTagName("canvas")[0];
  context = canvas.getContext("2d");
  context.beginPath();
  // speech bubble
  context.moveTo(75,25);
  context.quadraticCurveTo(25,25,25,62.5);
  context.quadraticCurveTo(25,100,50,100);
  context.quadraticCurveTo(100,120,100,125);
  context.quadraticCurveTo(90,120,65,100);
  context.quadraticCurveTo(125,100,125,62.5);
  context.quadraticCurveTo(125,25,75,25);
  // outer circle
  context.arc(180,90,50,0,Math.PI*2,true);
  context.moveTo(215,90);
  // mouth
  context.arc(180,90,30,0,Math.PI,false);
  context.moveTo(170,65);
  // eyes
  context.arc(165,65,5,0,Math.PI*2,false);
  context.arc(195,65,5,0,Math.PI*2,false);
  context.clip();
  video.addEventListener("play", drawFrame, false);

  function drawFrame() {
    context.drawImage(video, 0, 0, 360, 240);
    if (video.paused || video.ended) {
      return;
    }
    requestAnimationFrame(drawFrame);
  }
</script>
```

In this example, we don't display the video element but only draw its frames onto the canvas. During setup of the canvas, we define a clip path consisting of a speech bubble and a smiley face. We then set up the event listener for the play event and start playback of the video. In the callback, we only need to draw the video frames onto the canvas.

This is a very simple and effective means of masking out regions of a video. Figure 5-15 shows the results in Chrome. It works in all browsers the same way, including IE.

Figure 5-15. *Rendering of video on a clipped canvas in Google Chrome*

■ **Note**   Keep in mind this example uses a rather simple programmatically drawn shape to mask the video. Using logos or complex shapes to accomplish the same results is a difficult task, at best.

Drawing Text

As you saw in the previous example, simple shapes can be used to create masks for video. We can also use text as a mask for video. This technique is rather simple to both visualize–the text color is replaced with the video–and accomplish. Listing 5-14 shows how it is done with a canvas.

Listing 5-14. Text Filled with Video

```
<canvas id="canvas" width="360" height="240"></canvas>
<video autoplay style="display: none;">
  <source src="video/HelloWorld.mp4"  type="video/mp4">
  <source src="video/HelloWorld.webm" type="video/webm">
</video>
```

```
<script>
  var canvas, context, video;
  video = document.getElementsByTagName("video")[0];
  canvas = document.getElementsByTagName("canvas")[0];
  context = canvas.getContext("2d");
  // paint text onto canvas as mask
  context.font = 'bold 70px sans-serif';
  context.textBaseline = 'top';
  context.fillText('Hello World!', 0, 0, 320);
  context.globalCompositeOperation = "source-in";
  video.addEventListener("play", paintFrame, false);
```

```
function paintFrame() {
  context.drawImage(video, 0, 0, 360, 240);
  if (video.paused || video.ended) {
    return;
  }
  requestAnimationFrame(paintFrame);
}
</script>
```

We have a target canvas and a hidden video element. In JavaScript, we first paint the text onto the canvas. Then we use the globalCompositeOperation property to use the text as a mask for all video frames painted onto the canvas afterward.

Note that we used source-in as the compositing function. This works in all browsers except for Opera, which only briefly paints the text, but afterward ignores the fillText() cut-out and draws the full video frames again. Figure 5-16 shows the results in the other browsers that all support this functionality.

Figure 5-16. *Rendering of video used as a text fill in Google Chrome*

Transformations

The usual transformations supported by CSS are also supported by canvas. These CSS Transforms include translation, rotation, scaling, and transformation matrices. We can apply them to the frames extracted from the video to give the video some special effects.

Reflections

A common visual effect used by web designers and developers is reflections. Reflections are relatively simple to implement and are quite effective, particularly when placed against a dark background. All you need to do is to copy the video frames into a canvas placed underneath the source video, flip the copy, reduce its opacity, and add a gradient, all of which we have learned before.

It would certainly be easier if we were able to create a reflection using a CSS-only approach which uses the box-reflect property. Unfortunately, this property is not yet standardized and therefore only blink and webkit-based browsers implement it. That's the bad news.

The good news is canvas comes to the rescue. By using the canvas we can create consistent reflections in a cross-browser environment, while keeping the copied and source videos in sync.

Listing 5-15 is an example that works in all browsers.

Listing 5-15. Video Reflection Using a Canvas

```
<div style="padding: 50px; background-color: #090909;">
  <video autoplay style="vertical-align: bottom;" width="360">
    <source src="video/HelloWorld.mp4"  type="video/mp4">
    <source src="video/HelloWorld.webm" type="video/webm">
  </video>
  <br/>
  <canvas id="reflection" width="360" height="55"
          style="vertical-align: top;"></canvas>
</div>
<script>
  var context, rctxt, video;
  video = document.getElementsByTagName("video")[0];
  reflection = document.getElementById("reflection");
  rctxt = reflection.getContext("2d");
  // flip canvas
  rctxt.translate(0,160);
  rctxt.scale(1,-1);
  // create gradient
  gradient = rctxt.createLinearGradient(0, 105, 0, 160);
  gradient.addColorStop(0, "rgba(255, 255, 255, 1.0)");
  gradient.addColorStop(1, "rgba(255, 255, 255, 0.3)");
  rctxt.fillStyle = gradient;
  rctxt.rect(0, 105, 360, 160);
  video.addEventListener("play", paintFrame, false);

  function paintFrame() {
    // draw frame, and fill with the opacity gradient mask
    rctxt.drawImage(video, 0, 0, 360, 160);
    rctxt.globalCompositeOperation = "destination-out";
    rctxt.fill();
    // restore composition operation for next frame draw
    rctxt.globalCompositeOperation = "source-over";
    if (video.paused || video.ended) {
      return;
    }
    requestAnimationFrame(paintFrame);
  }
</script>
```

■ **Note** This example uses the <video> element to display the video, though a second canvas could be used for this purpose, as well. If you take this approach be sure to remove the @controls attribute as it breaks the reflection perception.

The example places the video and the aligned canvas underneath the video into a dark <div> element to provide some contrast for the reflection. Also, make sure to give the <video> and the <canvas> elements the same width. Though, in this example, we have given the reflection one-third the height of the original video.

As we set up the canvas, we prepare it as a mirrored drawing area using the scale() and translate() functions. The translation moves it down the height of the video and the scaling mirrors the pixels along the x axis. We then set up the gradient over the bottom 55 pixels of the video frames on the mirrored canvas.

The paintFrame() function applies the reflection effect after the video starts playback and while it is playing back at the maximum speed possible. Because we have decided to have the <video> element display the video, it is possible that the <canvas> cannot catch up with the display, which can result in a slight temporal disconnect between the <video> and its reflection. If that bothers you, the solution is to "paint" the video frames via another canvas and hide the video itself. You just need to set up a second <canvas> element and add a drawImage() function to that canvas above the paintFrame() function.

For the reflection, we "painted" the video frames onto the mirrored canvas. When using two <canvas> elements, you may be tempted to use getImageData() and putImageData() to apply the canvas transformations. However, canvas transformations are not applied to these functions. You have to use a canvas into which you have pulled the video data through drawImage() to apply the transformations.

Now we just need a gradient on the mirrored images.

To apply the gradient, we use a composition function of the gradient with the video images. We have used the composition before to replace the current image in the canvas with the next one. Creating a new composition property changes that. We therefore need to reset the compositing property after applying the gradient. Another solution would be to use the save() and restore() functions before changing the compositing property and after applying the gradient. If you change more than one canvas property or you don't want to keep track of what previous value you have to reset the property to, using save() and restore() is indeed the better approach.

Figure 5-17 shows the resulting renderings.

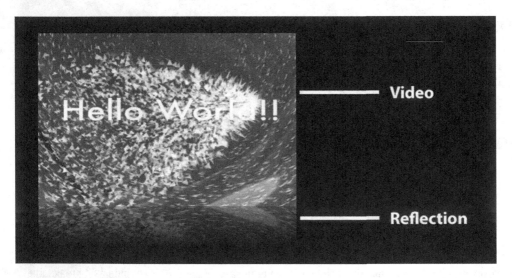

Figure 5-17. *Rendering of video with a reflection*

Spiraling Video

Canvas transformations can make the pixel-based operations that we saw at the beginning of this chapter a lot easier, in particular when you want to apply them to the whole canvas. The example shown in Listing 5-2 and Figure 5-2 can also be achieved with a translate() function, except you will still need to calculate when you hit the boundaries of the canvas to change your translate() function. This accomplished by adding a translate(xpos,ypos) function and always draw the image at position (0,0), which doesn't win you very much.

We want to look here at a more sophisticated example for using transformations. We will use both a translate() and a rotate() to make the frames of the video spiral through the canvas. Listing 5-16 shows how we achieve this.

Listing 5-16. Video Spiral Using Canvas

```
<script>
  var context, canvas, video;
  var i = 0;
  video = document.getElementsByTagName("video")[0];
  canvas = document.getElementsByTagName("canvas")[0];
  context = canvas.getContext("2d");
  // provide a shadow
  context.shadowOffsetX = 5;
  context.shadowOffsetY = 5;
  context.shadowBlur = 4;
  context.shadowColor = "rgba(0, 0, 0, 0.5)";
  video.addEventListener("play", paintFrame, false);

  function paintFrame() {
    context.drawImage(video, 0, 0, 120, 80);
    context.setTransform(1, 0,
                         0, 1,
                         0, 0);
    i += 1;
    context.translate(3 * i , 1.5 * i);
    context.rotate(0.2 * i);
    if (video.paused || video.ended) {
      alert(i);
      return;
    }
    requestAnimationFrame(paintFrame);
  }
</script>
```

The <video> and <canvas> element definitions are unchanged from previous examples. We only need to increase the size of our canvas to fit the full spiral. We also have given the frames being painted into the canvas a shadow, which offsets them from the previously drawn frames.

■ **Note**   Shadows attached to a video element in Chrome don't work at the moment. Google is working on the bug.

The way in which we paint the spiral is such that we paint the new video frame on top of a translated and rotated canvas. In order to apply the translation and rotation to the correct pixels, we need to reset the transformation matrix after painting a frame.

This is very important, because the previous transformations are already stored for the canvas such that another call—to `translate()`, for example— will go along the tilted axis set by the rotation rather than straight down asyou might expect. Thus, the transformation matrix has to be reset; otherwise, the operations are cumulative.

We are also counting the number of frames that we're displaying so we can compare performance between browsers. If you run the video through all the way to the end, you get an alert box with that number for comparison.

Figure 5-18 shows the resulting renderings in Firefox.

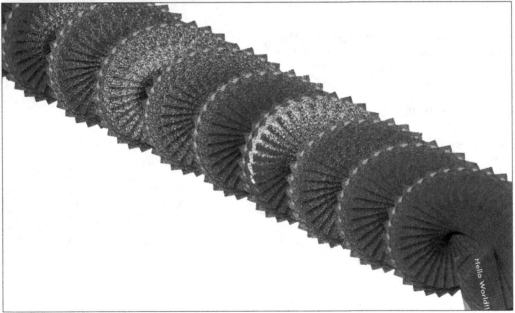

Figure 5-18. *Rendering of spiraling video frames in Firefox*

You may be thinking this is rather neat but what kind of performance "hit" does that lay on the browser? Let's do a small performance comparison between browsers.

The video file has a duration of 6.06 seconds. The requestAnimationFrame() function probes the video at 60Hz, thus in theory picking up about 363 frames over the video duration. Chrome, Safari, Opera, and IE all achieve rendering around that many frames. Firefox achieves only about 165 frames. After some experimentation, it turns out that the size of the canvas is the problem–the larger the canvas that drawImage() has to paint into, the slower Firefox. We hope that this is just a temporary problem that we observed.

This comparison was done on browsers downloaded and installed on Mac OS X without setting up extra hardware acceleration for graphics operations.

The upshot is there has to be a valid reason for using this technique because you have no control over which browser the user chooses.

Animations and Interactivity

We've already used requestAnimationFrame() and setTimeout() to create animated graphics from video frames in sync with the timeline of the video via the canvas. In this section we want to look at another way to animate the canvas: through user interaction.

The key "take-away" here is that the canvas only knows pixels and has no concept of objects. Thus it cannot associate events to a particular shape in the drawing. The canvas as a whole, however, accepts events, which means you can attach a click event to the <canvas> element, and then compare the [x,y] coordinates of the click event with the coordinates of your canvas to identify which object it might relate to.

In this section we will look at an example that is a bit like a simple game. After you start playback of the video through a click, you can click any time again to retrieve a quote from a collection of quotes. Think of it as a fortune cookie gamble. Listing 5-17 shows how we've done it.

Listing 5-17. Fortune Cookie and Video with User Interactivity in Canvas

```
<script>
  var quotes = ["Of those who say nothing,/ few are silent.",
                "Man is born to live,/ not to prepare for life.",
                "Time sneaks up on you/ like a windshield on a bug.",
                "Simplicity is the/ peak of civilization.",
                "Only I can change my life./ No one can do it for me."];
  var canvas, context, video;
  var w = 640, h = 320;
  video = document.getElementsByTagName("video")[0];
  canvas = document.getElementsByTagName("canvas")[0];
  context = canvas.getContext("2d");
  context.lineWidth = 5;
  context.font = 'bold 25px sans-serif';
  context.fillText('Click me!', w/4+20, h/2, w/2);
  context.strokeRect(w/16,h/4,w*7/8,h/2);
  canvas.addEventListener("click", procClick, false);
  video.addEventListener("play", paintFrame, false);
  video.addEventListener("pause", showRect, false);
```

```
function paintFrame() {
  if (video.paused || video.ended) {
    return;
  }
  context.drawImage(video, 0, 0, w, h);
  context.strokeStyle='white';
  context.strokeRect(w/16,h/4,w*7/8,h/2);
  requestAnimationFrame(paintFrame);
}
function isPlaying(video) {
  return (!video.paused && !video.ended);
}

function showRect(e) {
  context.clearRect(w/16,h/4,w*7/8,h/2);
  quote = quotes[Math.floor(Math.random()*quotes.length)].split("/");
  context.fillStyle = 'blue';
  context.fillText(quote[0], w/4+5, h/2-10, w/2-10);
  context.fillText(quote[1], w/4+5, h/2+30, w/2-10);
  context.fillStyle = 'white';
  context.fillText("click again",w/10,h/8);
}

function procClick(e) {
  var pos = canvasPosition(e);
  if ((pos[0] < w/4) || (pos[0] > 3*w/4)) return;
  if ((pos[1] < h/4) || (pos[1] > 3*h/4)) return;
  !isPlaying(video) ? video.play() : video.pause();
}
</script>
```

In this example, we use an array of quotes as the source for the displayed "fortune cookies." Note how the strings have a "/" marker in them to deal with breaking it up into multiple lines. It is done this way for ease of storage in a single string.

We proceed to set up an empty canvas with a rectangle in it that has the text: `Click me!`. Callbacks are registered for the `click` event on the canvas, and also for `pause` and `play` events on the video. The trick is to use the "click" callback to pause and play the video, which will then trigger the respective effects associated with the video pause and play events. We restrict the clickable region to the rectangular region to show how regions can be made interactive in the canvas, even without knowing what shapes there are.

The pause event triggers the display of the fortune cookie within the rectangular region in the middle of the video. The `play` event triggers continuation of the display of the video's frames, thus wiping out the fortune cookie. Note that we do not do anything in `paintFrame()` if the video is paused. This will deal with any potentially queued calls to `paintFrame()` from the `setTimeout()` function.

You may have noticed we are missing a function from the above example–the `canvasPosition()` function. This function is a helper to gain the x and y coordinates of the click within the canvas. It has been extracted into Listing 5-18 (you can find this example at `http://diveintohtml5.org/canvas.html`) because it will be a constant companion for anyone doing interactive work with canvas.

Listing 5-18. Typical Function to Gain the x and y Coordinates of the Click in a Canvas

```
function canvasPosition(e) {
    // from http://www.naslu.com/resource.aspx?id=460
    // and http://diveintohtml5.org/canvas.html
    if (e.pageX || e.pageY) {
      x = e.pageX;
      y = e.pageY;
    } else {
      x = e.clientX + document.body.scrollLeft +
          document.documentElement.scrollLeft;
      y = e.clientY + document.body.scrollTop +
          document.documentElement.scrollTop;
    }
    // make coordinates relative to canvas
    x -= canvas.offsetLeft;
    y -= canvas.offsetTop;
    return [x,y];
  }
```

Figure 5-19 shows the rendering of this example with screenshots from different browsers.

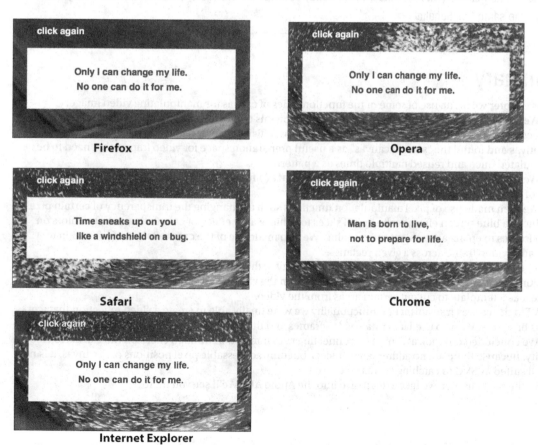

Figure 5-19. Rendering of the fortune cookies example through an interactive canvas with video

225

We can further improve this example by changing the mouse pointer display to a grabber hand while mousing over the box. To that end, we register a callback on the canvas for mousemove events, calling the function in Listing 5-19, which changes the pointer while within the box.

Listing 5-19. Function to Change the Mouse Cursor When over the Top of the White Box

```
function procMove(e) {
  var pos = canvasPosition(e);
  var x = pos[0], y = pos[1];
  if (x > (w/16) && x < (w*15/16) && y > (h/4) && y < (h*3/4)) {
    document.body.style.cursor = "pointer";
  } else {
    document.body.style.cursor = "default";
  }
}
```

You have to reuse the canvasPosition() function from earlier to get the cursor position and then decide whether the cursor is within the box before setting it to "pointer."

■ **Note** Note that the fonts are rendered differently between the browsers, but other than that, they all support the same functionality.

Summary

In this chapter we made use of some of the functionalities of canvas for manipulating video imagery.

We first learned that the drawImage() function allows us to pull images out of a <video> element and into a canvas as pixel data. We then determined the most efficient way of dealing with video frames in the canvas and found the "scratch canvas" as a useful preparation space for video frames that need to be manipulated once and reused multiple times as a pattern.

We identified the getImageData() and putImageData() functions as powerful helpers to manipulate parts of a video's frame data.

We then made use of pixel manipulation functions such as changing the transparency of certain pixels to achieve a blue screen effect, scaling pixel slices to achieve a 3D effect, or calculating average colors on video frames to create an ambient surrounding. We also made use of the createPattern() function to replicate a video frame across a given rectangle.

Then we moved on to the compositing functionality of the canvas to put several of the individual functions together. We used a gradient to fade over from the video to an ambient background, a clip path, and text as a template to cut out certain areas from the video.

With the canvas transformation functionality we were finally able to create a video reflection that works across browsers. We also used it to rotate video frames and thus have them spiral around the canvas.

We concluded our look at canvas by connecting user interaction through clicks on the canvas to video activity. Because there are no addressable objects, but only addressable pixel positions on a canvas, it is not as well suited as SVG to catching events on objects.

In the next chapter, we take a deep dive into the Audio API. We'll see you there.

CHAPTER 6

Manipulating Audio Through the Web Audio API

When it comes to the Web, audio is…'well'…it is just there. This is not to denigrate audio, but, in many respects, audio is treated as either an afterthought or an annoyance. Yet its importance can't be understated. From the simple effects such as click sounds that act as user feedback to voice-over narrations describing products or events, audio is a major communication medium which, as one of the authors likes to say, "seals the deal."

The key aspect of audio is that when it is digitized it can be manipulated. To do this one needs to stop regarding audio as sound and see it for what it really is: data that can be manipulated. And that brings us to the subject of this chapter: how to manipulate sound data in a web browser.

The Web Audio API (Application Programming Interface) complements the features we just learned about for manipulating video data. This enables the development of sophisticated web-based games or audio production applications where the audio can be dynamically created and modified in JavaScript. It also enables the visualization of audio data and the analysis of the data, for example, to determine a beat or identify which instruments are playing or whether a voice you are hearing is female or male.

The Web Audio API (`http://webaudio.github.io/web-audio-api/`) is a specification that is being developed by the W3C Audio Working Group. This specification has been implemented in all major desktop browsers except for Internet Explorer (IE). Microsoft has added it to its development roadmap, so we can assume universal support. Safari is using a `webkit` prefix in its implementation at this point in time. Mozilla used to implement a simpler audio processing specification called the "Audio Data API" but has since replaced this also with the Web Audio API specification.

■ **Note** W3C Audio Working Group has also developed a Web MIDI API specification (`www.w3.org/TR/webmidi/`), but it is currently only available as a trial implementation by Google Chrome, so we won't explain this API at this time.

Before we start it would be useful to review the basics of digital audio.

Bitdepth and Samplerates

We traditionally visualize sound as a sine wave—the closer together the waves, the higher the frequency and therefore the sound. As for the height of the waves, that's called the amplitude of the signal, and the higher the wave, the louder the sound. These waves, an example is shown in Figure 6-1, are called the **waveform**. The horizontal line is time, and if the signal doesn't leave the horizontal line, that's silence.

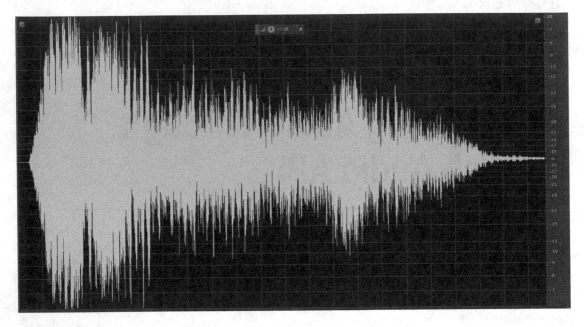

Figure 6-1. *A typical waveform from Adobe Audition CC 2014*

For any sound to be digitized, like a color image in Fireworks or Photoshop, the wave needs to be sampled. A sample is nothing more than a snapshot of a waveform sampled at fixed intervals. An audio CD, for example, is sampled at the frequency of 44,100 times per second, which is traditionally identified as 44.1kHz. The value sampled at the snapshot time is a digital number representing the volume at that time. How often the waveform is sampled each second is called the samplerate. The higher the sampling rate, the more accurately the originally analog sound is represented digitally. The downside to this, of course, is the higher the samplerate, the larger the file size.

Bitdepth is the resolution of the sample value. A bitdepth of 8 bits means that the snapshot is represented as a number ranging from –128 to 127 (i.e., the value fits in 8 bits). A bitdepth of 16 bits means that the number is between –32,768 to 32,767. If you do the math, you see that an 8-bit snapshot has 256 potential values per sample, whereas its 16-bit counterpart has just over 65,000 potential values per sample. The greater the number of potential values of a sample, the greater the dynamic range that the digital file can represent.

Stereo signals have a waveform for each ear. Each of these waveforms gets digitized, individually, into a sequence of samples. They are typically stored as a sequence of pairs, which get separated for playback into their individual channels.

When the numbers are played back in the order in which they were sampled and at the frequency they were sampled, they recreate the sound's waveform. Obviously, a larger bitdepth and higher samplerate mean that the waveform is played back with greater accuracy—the more snapshots taken of the waveform result in a more accurate representation of the waveform. This explains why the songs from an album have such massive file sizes. They are sampled at the highest possible bitdepth.

The three most common samplerates used are 11.025kHz, 22.05kHz, and 44.1kHz. If you reduce the samplerate from 44.1kHz to 22.05kHz, you achieve a reduction of 50% in file size. You obtain an even more significant reduction, another 50%, if the rate is reduced to 11.025kHz. The problem is that reducing the samplerate reduces audio quality. Listening to Beethoven's *Ninth Symphony* at 11.025kHz results in the music sounding as if it were playing from the inside of a tin can.

As a web designer or developer, your prime objective is to obtain the best quality sound at the smallest file size. Though many developers will tell you that 16-bit, 44.1kHz stereo is the way to go, you'll quickly realize this is not necessarily true. For example, a 16-bit, 44.1kHz stereo sound of a mouse click or a sound lasting less than a couple of seconds—such as a whoosh as an object zips across the screen—is a waste of bandwidth. The duration is so short and the frequencies represented in the sound so limited that average users won't realize it if you've made your click an 8-bit, 22.05kHz mono sound. They hear the click and move on. The same holds true for music files. The average user is most likely listening through the cheap speakers that were tossed in when he bought his PC. In this case, a 16-bit, 22.05kHz soundtrack will sound as good as its CD-quality rich cousin.

The HTML5 Audio Formats

In Chapter 1, we already discussed the three audio formats used for HTML 5: MP3, WAV, and OGG Vorbis. These are all encoded audio formats (i.e., the raw samples of an audio waveform are compressed to take up less space and be able to be transmitted faster over the Internet). All of these formats use perceptual encoding, which means they throw away from the audio stream all information that is not typically perceived by humans. When information gets tossed in this way, there is a corresponding decrease in file size. The information tossed for encoding includes sound frequencies your dog may be able to hear but you can't. In short, you hear only the sound a human can perceive (and this sort of explains why animals aren't huge fans of iPods).

All perceptual encoders allow you to choose how much audio is unimportant. Most encoders produce excellent quality files using no more than 16 Kbps to create voice recordings. When you create, for example, an MP3, you need to pay attention to the bandwidth. The format is fine, but if the bandwidth is not optimized for its intended use, your results will be unacceptable, which is why applications that create MP3 files ask you to set the bandwidth along with the samplerate.

In this chapter we deal with the raw audio samples and manipulate them to achieve professional audio effects. The browser takes care of decoding the compressed audio files for us.

So much for generalities; let's get practical and manipulate the ones and zeros that are at the heart of audio data by using the Web Audio API. We start with filter graphs and the `AudioContext`.

Filter Graphs and the AudioContext

The Web Audio API specification is based on the idea of building a graph of connected `AudioNode` objects to define the overall audio rendering. This is very similar to the filter graph idea that is the basis of many media frameworks, including DirectShow, GStreamer, and also JACK the Audio Connection Kit.

The idea behind a **filter graph** is that one or more input signals (in our case: the sound signals) are connected to a destination renderer (the sound output) by sending the input signals through a sequence of filters (sound modifiers) that modify the input data in a specific way.

The term **audio filter** can mean anything that changes the timbre, harmonic content, pitch, or waveform of an audio signal. The specification includes filters for various audio uses including the following:

- Spatialized audio to move sounds in the 3D space.

- A convolution engine to simulate acoustic spaces.

- Real-time frequency analysis to determine the composition of a sound.

- Frequency filters to extract certain frequency regions.

- Sample-accurate scheduled sound playback.

A filter graph in the Web Audio API is contained within an `AudioContext` and consists of connected `AudioNode` objects as demonstrated in Figure 6-2.

AudioContext

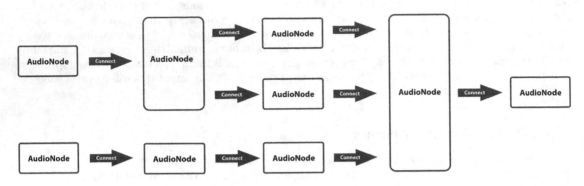

Figure 6-2. *Concept of a filter graph in the Web Audio API*

As you can see, there are AudioNode objects without incoming connections—these are called source nodes. They can also only connect to one AudioNode. Examples are microphone input, media elements, remote microphone inputs (when connected via WebRTC), mere audio samples stored in a memory buffer, or artificial sounds sources like oscillators.

■ **Note** **WebRTC** (Web Real-Time Communication) is an API definition drafted by the World Wide Web Consortium (W3C) that supports browser-to-browser applications for voice calling, video chat, and P2P file sharing without the need of either internal or external plug-ins. It is a huge topic and is beyond the scope of this book.

AudioNode objects without outgoing connections are called destination nodes, and they only have one incoming connection. Examples are audio output devices (speakers) and remote output devices (when connected via WebRTC).

Other AudioNode objects in the middle may have multiple input connections and/or multiple output connections and are intermediate processing nodes.

The developer doesn't have to worry about low-level stream format details when two AudioNode objects are connected; the right thing just happens. For example, if a mono audio filter has a stereo input connected, it will just receive a mix of the left and right channels.

To get you started let's create what could be considered the "Hello World" of web audio applications. To follow along with the examples, they are provided in full at http://html5videoguide.net/. Listing 6-1 shows a simple example, where an oscillator source is connected to the default speaker destination node. You'll hear a sound wave at 1kHz frequency. A word of warning: We will be dealing with audio samples and files and you might want to make sure the volume of your computer is lowered.

Listing 6-1. A Simple Filter Graph of an Oscillator Source Node and a Sound Output Destination Node

```
// create web audio api context
var audioCtx = new (window.AudioContext || window.webkitAudioContext)();

// create Oscillator node
var oscillator = audioCtx.createOscillator();
oscillator.connect(audioCtx.destination);
```

```
oscillator.type = 'square';
oscillator.frequency.value = 1000; // value in hertz

oscillator.start(0);
```

■ **Note**   If you want to hear different tones, simply change the number in `oscillator.frequency.value`. If you don't add a frequency value, the default is 440Hz which, for the musically inclined, is an A above middle C. Why that value? If you have ever been to a symphony and heard the members of the orchestra tune their instruments, that tone has become the standard for concert pitch.

The `oscillator.start()` function has an optional argument to describe at what time in seconds the sound should start playing. Unfortunately, in Safari it is not optional. So make sure you add the 0.

Figure 6-3 shows the filter graph that we have created.

Figure 6-3. *Simple filtergraph examples in the Web Audio API*

Let's dig into the different constructs that the example has just introduced.

The AudioContext Interface

The AudioContext provides the environment in which AudioNode objects are created and connected to each other. All types of AudioNode objects are defined within the AudioContext shown in the following code. There are a lot of AudioNode objects and we'll approach this object in steps and just explain bits of what we need in every step of this chapter.

```
[Constructor]
interface AudioContext : EventTarget {
    readonly    attribute AudioDestinationNode destination;
    readonly    attribute float                sampleRate;
    readonly    attribute double               currentTime;
    Promise                          suspend ();
    Promise                          resume ();
    Promise                          close ();
    readonly    attribute AudioContextState    state;
                attribute EventHandler         onstatechange;
    OscillatorNode                   createOscillator ();
    ...
};
```

```
interface AudioDestinationNode : AudioNode {
    readonly    attribute unsigned long maxChannelCount;
};
enum AudioContextState {
    "suspended",
    "running",
    "closed"
};
```

Every AudioContext contains a single read-only AudioDestinationNode. The destination is typically the computer-connected audio output device such as speakers or headphones. Scripts will connect all audio that is meant to be heard by the user to this node as the "terminal" node in the AudioContext's filter graph. You can see that we've created the oscillator by using the AudioContext object and calling createOscillator() on it and set some of the parameters of the oscillator. Then we've connected it to the destination for speaker/headphone output by calling the connect() function on the oscillator object.

The sampleRate of the AudioContext is fixed for the lifetime of the AudioContext and sets the sampling rate for all AudioNodes in the context. Thus, no samplerate conversion is possible within an AudioContext. By default, the sampleRate is 44,100Hz.

The currentTime of the AudioContext is a time, in seconds, that represents the age of the AudioContext (i.e., it starts at zero when the context is created and increases in real time). All scheduled times are relative to it. It is important to keep in mind that all events in the AudioContext run against this clock and it progresses in fractions of seconds.

The suspend(), resume(), and close() calls will influence the currentTime and suspend, resume, or stop its increase. They also influence whether the AudioContext has control over the audio hardware. After a call to close(), the AudioContext becomes unusable for the creation of new nodes. The AudioContextState represents the state that the AudioContext is in: suspended, running, or closed.

■ **Note**   Browsers do not currently support the suspend(), resume(), and close(), functions and the state attribute.

Listing 6-2 shows a couple of the parameters of an AudioContext with the result displayed in Figure 6-4.

Listing 6-2. The Parameters of the AudioContext

```
<div id="display"></div>
    <script type="text/javascript">
    var display = document.getElementById("display");
    var context = new (window.AudioContext || window.webkitAudioContext)();
    display.innerHTML  = context.sampleRate + " sampling rate<br/>";
    display.innerHTML += context.destination.numberOfChannels
                                        + " output channels<br/>";
    display.innerHTML += context.currentTime + " currentTime<br/>";
    </script>
```

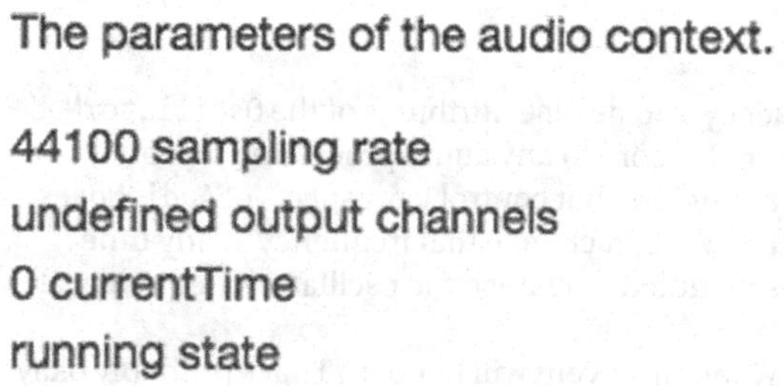

The parameters of the audio context.

44100 sampling rate

undefined output channels

0 currentTime

running state

Figure 6-4. The parameters of the AudioContext by default in Chrome

The number of output channels is unknown until a sound is played through the AudioDestinationNode.

Let's take another look at that oscillator. It's of the type OscillatorNode which contains a few attributes that we can manipulate.

```
interface OscillatorNode : AudioNode {
            attribute OscillatorType type;
    readonly    attribute AudioParam    frequency;
    readonly    attribute AudioParam    detune;
    void start (optional double when = 0);
    void stop (optional double when = 0);
    void setPeriodicWave (PeriodicWave periodicWave);
            attribute EventHandler    onended;
};
enum OscillatorType {
    "sine",
    "square",
    "sawtooth",
    "triangle",
    "custom"
};
```

The first attribute is the OscillatorType, which we set to "square" in our example. You can change it in the example and will notice how the timbre of the tone changes, while its frequency stays the same.

The frequency is an AudioParam object which we'll look at in just a minute. It has a value that can be set—and we set it to 1,000Hz in our example.

The OscillatorNode further has a detune attribute which will offset the frequency by the given percentage amount. Its default is 0. Detuning can help make a note sound more natural.

The start() and stop() methods on the OscillatorNode determine when a oscillator starts and ends in reference to the currentTime of the AudioContext. Note that you can call start() and stop() only once because they define the extent of the sound's existence. You can, however, connect and disconnect the oscillator from the AudioDestinationNode (or whichever is the next AudioNode in the filter graph) to pause/unpause the sound.

The setPeriodicWave() function allows setting a custom oscillator waveform. Use the createPeriodicWave() function of the AudioContext to create a custom waveform using arrays of Fourier coefficients, being the partials of the periodic waveform. Unless you're writing a synthesizer, you probably don't have to understand this.

The AudioParam Interface

The AudioParam object type that we just used for the `frequency` and `detune` attributes of the `OscillatorNode` is actually quite important, so let's try to understand it better. It is core to any audio processing that an AudioNode undertakes in a filter graph, since it holds the parameters that control key aspects of AudioNodes. In our example, it's the frequency at which the oscillator runs. We can change that frequency at any time through the value parameter. That means that an event is scheduled to change the oscillator's frequency at the next possible instant.

Since browsers can be quite busy, it's not foreseeable when this event will happen. That's probably okay in our example, but if you are a musician, you will want to be very accurate with your timing. Therefore, every AudioParam maintains a list of time-ordered change events. The times at which the changes are scheduled are in the time coordinate system of the AudioContext's `currentTime` attribute. The events either initiate changes immediately or start/end them.

Following are the components of the AudioParam interface:

```
interface AudioParam {
            attribute float value;
    readonly    attribute float defaultValue;
    void setValueAtTime (float value, double startTime);
    void linearRampToValueAtTime (float value, double endTime);
    void exponentialRampToValueAtTime (float value, double endTime);
    void setTargetAtTime (float target, double startTime, float timeConstant);
    void setValueCurveAtTime (Float32Array values, double startTime,
                              double duration);
    void cancelScheduledValues (double startTime);
};
```

The event list is maintained internally by the AudioContext. The following methods can change the event list by adding a new event into the list. The type of event is defined by the method. These methods are called *automation* methods.

- **setValueAtTime()** tells the AudioNode to change its AudioParam to *value* at the given startTime.

- **linearRampToValueAtTime()** tells the AudioNode to ramp up its AudioParam value to *value* by a given endTime. This means it either ramps up from "right now" or from the previous event in the event list of the AudioNode.

- **exponentialRampToValueAtTime()** tells the AudioNode to ramp up its AudioParam value using an exponential continuous change from the previous scheduled parameter value to the given value by a given endTime. Parameters representing filter frequencies and playback rate are best changed exponentially because of the way humans perceive sound.

- **setTargetAtTime()** tells the AudioNode to start exponentially approaching the target value at the given startTime with a rate having the given timeConstant. Among other uses, this is useful for implementing the "decay" and "release" portions of an ADSR (Attack-Decay-Sustain-Release) envelope. The parameter value does not immediately change to the target value at the given time, but instead gradually changes to the target value. The larger the timeConstant, the slower the transition.

- **setValueCurveAtTime()** tells the AudioNode to adapt its value following an array of arbitrary parameter values starting at the given startTime for the given duration. The number of values will be scaled to fit into the desired duration.

- **cancelScheduledValues()** tells the AudioNode to cancel all scheduled parameter changes with times greater than or equal to startTime.

Scheduled events are useful for such tasks as envelopes, volume fades, LFOs (low-frequency oscillations), filter sweeps, or grain windows. We're not going to explain these, but professional musicians will know what they are. It is only important you understand that the automation methods provide a mechanism to change a parameter value from one value to another at given time instances and that there are different curves the change can follow. In this way, arbitrary timeline-based automation curves can be set on any AudioParam. We'll see what that means in an example.

Using a timeline, Figure 6-5 shows an automation plan for changing the frequency of an oscillator employing all the preceding introduced methods. In black are the setValueAtTime calls, each with their value as a black cross and their startTime on the currentTime timeline. The exponentialRampToValueAtTime and linearRampToValueAtTime calls have a target value (gray cross) at an endTime (gray line on the timeline). The setTargetAtTime call has a startTime (gray line on the timeline) and a target value (gray cross). The setValueCurveAtTime call has a startTime, a duration, and a number of values it goes through during that time. All of these combine to create the beeping tone and the changes you will hear when you test the code.

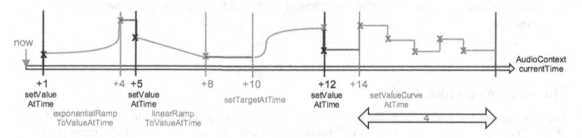

Figure 6-5. *AudioParam automation for oscillator frequency*

Listing 6-3 shows how we adapted Listing 6-1 with this automation.

Listing 6-3. A Frequency Automation for an Oscillator

```
var audioCtx = new (window.AudioContext || window.webkitAudioContext)();
  var oscillator = audioCtx.createOscillator();
  var freqArray = new Float32Array(5);
  freqArray[0] = 4000;
  freqArray[1] = 3000;
  freqArray[2] = 1500;
  freqArray[3] = 3000;
  freqArray[4] = 1500;

  oscillator.type = 'square';
  oscillator.frequency.value = 100; // value in hertz

  oscillator.connect(audioCtx.destination);
  oscillator.start(0);
  oscillator.frequency.cancelScheduledValues(audioCtx.currentTime);
```

```
oscillator.frequency.setValueAtTime(500, audioCtx.currentTime + 1);
oscillator.frequency.exponentialRampToValueAtTime(4000,
                                          audioCtx.currentTime + 4);
oscillator.frequency.setValueAtTime(3000, audioCtx.currentTime + 5);
oscillator.frequency.linearRampToValueAtTime(1000,
                                          audioCtx.currentTime + 8);
oscillator.frequency.setTargetAtTime(4000, audioCtx.currentTime + 10, 1);
oscillator.frequency.setValueAtTime(1000, audioCtx.currentTime + 12);
oscillator.frequency.setValueCurveAtTime(freqArray,
                                          audioCtx.currentTime + 14, 4);
```

AudioNodes can actually process value calculations either on each individual audio sample or on blocks of 128 samples. An AudioParam will specify that it is an **a-rate** parameter, when it needs the value calculation to be done individually for each sample of the block. It will specify that it's a **k-rate** parameter, when only the first sample of the block is calculated and the resulting value is used for the entire block.

The frequency and detune parameters of the oscillator are both a-rate parameters, since each individual audio sample potentially needs adjustment of frequency and detune.

An *a-rate* AudioParam takes the current audio parameter value for each sampleframe of the audio signal.

A *k-rate* AudioParam uses the same initial audio parameter value for the whole block processed (i.e., 128 sampleframes).

The AudioNode Interface

Earlier we became acquainted with the OscillatorNode, which is a type of AudioNode—the building blocks of the filter graph. An OscillatorNode is a source node. We've also become acquainted with one type of destination node in the filter graph: the AudioDestinationNode. It's time we take a deeper look into the AudioNode interface itself, since this is where the connect() function of the OscillatorNode originates from.

```
interface AudioNode : EventTarget {
    void connect (AudioNode destination, optional unsigned long output = 0,
                  optional unsigned long input = 0);
    void connect (AudioParam destination, optional unsigned long output = 0 );
    void disconnect (optional unsigned long output = 0);
    readonly    attribute AudioContext          context;
    readonly    attribute unsigned long         numberOfInputs;
    readonly    attribute unsigned long         numberOfOutputs;
                attribute unsigned long         channelCount;
                attribute ChannelCountMode      channelCountMode;
                attribute ChannelInterpretation channelInterpretation;
};
```

An AudioNode can only belong to a single AudioContext, stored in the context attribute.

The first `connect()` method in `AudioNode` connects it to another `AudioNode`. There can only be one connection between a given output of one specific node and a given input of another node. The `output` parameter specifies the output index from which to connect and similarly the `input` parameter specifies which input index of the destination `AudioNode` to connect to.

The `numberOfInputs` attribute of `AudioNode` provides the number of inputs feeding into the `AudioNode` and the `numberOfOutputs` provides the number coming out of the `AudioNode`. Source nodes have 0 inputs and destination nodes 0 outputs.

An `AudioNode` may have more outputs than inputs; thus fan-out is supported. It may also have more inputs than outputs, which supports fan-in. It is possible to connect an `AudioNode` to another `AudioNode` and back, creating a cycle. This is allowed only if there is at least one `DelayNode` in the cycle or you'll get a `NotSupportedError` exception.

Each input and output of a nonsource and nondestination `AudioNode` has one or more channels. The exact number of inputs, outputs, and their channels depends on the type of `AudioNode`.

The `channelCount` attribute contains the number of channels that the `AudioNode` inherently deals with. By default, it's 2, but that may be overwritten by an explicit new value for this attribute, or through the `channelCountMode` attribute.

```
enum ChannelCountMode {    "max",    "clamped-max",    "explicit" };
```

The values have the following meaning:

- When the `channelCountMode` is "max," the number of channels that the `AudioNode` deals with is the maximum number of channels of all the input and output connections and the `channelCount` is ignored.

- When the `channelCountMode` is "clamped-max," the number of channels that the `AudioNode` deals with is the maximum number of channels of all the input and output connections, but a maximum of `channelCount`.

- When the `channelCountMode` is "explicit," the number of channels that the `AudioNode` deals with is determined by `channelCount`.

For each input, an `AudioNode` does mixing (usually an upmixing) of all connections to that node. When the channels of the inputs need to be down- or upmixed, the `channelInterpretation` attribute determines how this down- or upmixing should be treated.

```
enum ChannelInterpretation { "speakers", "discrete" };
```

When `channelInterpretation` is "discrete," upmixing is done by filling channels until they run out and then zeroing out remaining channels and downmixing by filling as many channels as possible, then dropping remaining channels.

If `channelInterpretation` is set to "speaker," then the upmixing and downmixing are defined for specific channel layouts:

- 1 channel: mono (channel 0)

- 2 channels: left (channel 0), right (channel 1)

- 4 channels: left (ch 0), right (ch 1), surround left (ch 2), surround right (ch 3)

- 5.1 channels: left (ch 0), right (ch 1), center (ch 2), subwoofer (ch 3), surround left (ch 4), surround right (ch 5)

Upmixing works as follows:

- mono: copy to left & right channels (for 2 & 4), copy to center (for 5.1)

- stereo: copy to left and right channels (for 4 and 5.1)

- 4 channels: copy to left and right and surround left and surround right (for 5.1)

Every other channel stays at 0.
Downmixing works as follows:

- Mono downmix:
  - 2 -> 1: 0.5 * (left + right)
  - 4 -> 1: 0.25 * (left + right + surround left + surround right)
  - 5.1 -> 1: 0.7071 * (left + right) + center
  - + 0.5 * (surround left + surround right)
- Stereo downmix:
  - 4 -> 2: left = 0.5 * (left + surround left)
    left = 0.5 * (right + surround right)
  - 5.1 -> 2: left = L + 0.7071 * (center + surround left)
    right = R + 0.7071 * (center + surround right)
- Quad downmix:
  - 5.1 -> 4: left = left + 0.7071 * center
    right = right + 0.7071 * center
    surround left = surround left
    surround right = surround right

Figure 6-6 describes a hypothetical input and output scenario for an AudioNode with diverse sets of channels on each of these. If the number of channels is not in 1, 2, 4, and/or 6, then the "discrete" interpretation is used.

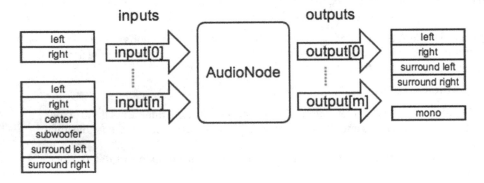

Figure 6-6. Channels and inputs/outputs of an AudioNode

Finally, the second connect() method on the AudioNode object connects an AudioParam to an AudioNode. This means that the parameter value is controlled with an audio signal.

It is possible to connect an AudioNode output to more than one AudioParam with multiple calls to connect(), thus supporting fan-out and controlling multiple AudioParam settings with a single audio signal. It is also possible to connect more than one AudioNode output to a single AudioParam with multiple calls to connect(); thus fan-in is supported and controls a single AudioParam with multiple audio inputs.

There can only be one connection between a given output of one specific node and a specific AudioParam. Multiple connections between the same AudioNode and the same AudioParam are ignored.

An AudioParam will take the rendered audio data from any AudioNode output connected to it and convert it to mono by downmixing (if it is not already mono). Next, it will mix it together with any other such outputs, and the intrinsic parameter value (the value the AudioParam would normally have without any audio connections), including any timeline changes scheduled for the parameter.

We'll demonstrate this functionality via an example of an oscillator that is manipulating a GainNode's gain setting—a so-called LFO. The gain merely means to increase the power of the signal, which results in an increase in its volume. The gain setting of the GainNode is put in between a frequency-fixed oscillator and the destination node and thus causes the fixed tone to be rendered at an oscillating gain (see Listing 6-4).

Listing 6-4. An Oscillator's Gain Is Manipulated by Another Oscillator

```
var audioCtx = new (window.AudioContext || window.webkitAudioContext)();
var oscillator = audioCtx.createOscillator();

// second oscillator that will be used as an LFO
var lfo = audioCtx.createOscillator();
lfo.type = 'sine';
lfo.frequency.value = 2.0; // 2Hz: low-frequency oscillation

// create a gain whose gain AudioParam will be controlled by the LFO
var gain = audioCtx.createGain();
lfo.connect(gain.gain);

// set up the filter graph and start the nodes
oscillator.connect(gain);
gain.connect(audioCtx.destination);
oscillator.start(0);
lfo.start(0);
```

When running Listing 6-3, you will hear a tone of frequency 440Hz (the default frequency of the oscillator) pulsating between a gain of 0 and 1 at a frequency of twice per second. Figure 6-7 explains the setup of the filter graph. Pay particular attention to the fact that the lfo OscillatorNode is connected to the gain parameter of the GainNode and not to the gain node itself.

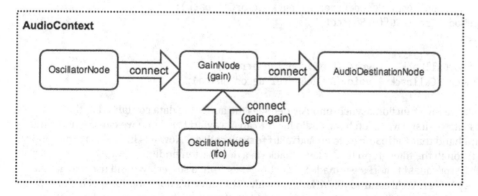

Figure 6-7. *Channels and inputs/outputs of an AudioNode*

We just used another function of the AudioContext to create a GainNode.

```
[Constructor] interface AudioContext : EventTarget {
            ...
            GainNode                    createGain ();
            ...
}
```

For completeness, following is the definition of a GainNode:

```
interface GainNode : AudioNode {
    readonly    attribute AudioParam gain;
};
```

The gain parameter represents the amount of gain to apply. Its default value is 1 (no gain change). The nominal minValue is 0, but may be negative for phase inversion. Phase inversion, in simple terms, is "flipping the signal"—think of the sine waves that we used to explain audio signals at the beginning —to invert their phase means to mirror their value on the time axis. The nominal maxValue is 1, but higher values are allowed. This parameter is a-rate.

A GainNode takes one input and creates one output, the ChannelCountMode is "max" (i.e., it deals with as many channels as it is given) and the ChannelInterpretation is "speakers" (i.e., up- or downmixing is performed for output).

Reading and Generating Audio Data

Thus far we have created audio data via an oscillator. In general, you will, however, want to read an audio file, then take the audio data and manipulate it.

The AudioContext provides functionality to do this.

```
[Constructor] interface AudioContext : EventTarget {
            ...
Promise<AudioBuffer>  decodeAudioData (ArrayBuffer audioData,
                    optional DecodeSuccessCallback successCallback,
                    optional DecodeErrorCallback errorCallback);
AudioBufferSourceNode createBufferSource();
            ...
}
callback DecodeErrorCallback   = void (DOMException error);
callback DecodeSuccessCallback = void (AudioBuffer decodedData);
```

The decodeAudioData() function asynchronously decodes the audio file data contained in the ArrayBuffer. To use it, we first have to fetch the audio file into an ArrayBuffer. Then we can decode it into an AudioBuffer and hand that AudioBuffer to an AudioBufferSourceNode. Now it is in an AudioNode and can be connected through the filter graph (e.g., played back via a destination node).

The XHR (HTMLHttpRequest) interface is made for fetching data from a server). We will use it to get the file data into an ArrayBuffer. We'll assume you're familiar with XHR, since it's not a media-specific interface.

In Listing 6-5, we retrieve the file "transition.wav" using XHR, then decode the received data into an AudioBufferSourceNode by calling the AudioContext's decodeAudioData() function.

■ **Note**   Thanks to CadereSounds for making the "transition.wav" sample available under a Creative Commons license on freesound (see `www.freesound.org/people/CadereSounds/sounds/267125/`).

Listing 6-5. Fetching a Media Resource Using XHR

```
var audioCtx = new (window.AudioContext || window.webkitAudioContext)();
  var source = audioCtx.createBufferSource();

  var request = new XMLHttpRequest();
  var url = 'audio/transition.wav';

  function requestData(url) {
    request.open('GET', url, true);
    request.responseType = 'arraybuffer';
    request.send();
  }

  function receivedData() {
    if ((request.status === 200 || request.status === 206)
        && request.readyState === 4) {
      var audioData = request.response;
      audioCtx.decodeAudioData(audioData,
        function(buffer) {
          source.buffer = buffer;
          source.connect(audioCtx.destination);
          source.loop = true;
          source.start(0);
        },
        function(error) {
          "Error with decoding audio data" + error.err
        }
      );
    }
  }

  request.addEventListener('load', receivedData, false);
  requestData(url);
```

First we define a function that does the XHR request for the file, then the receivedData() function is called after network retrieval. If the retrieval was successful, we hand the resulting ArrayBuffer to decodeAudioData().

■ **Note**   You have to upload this to a web server, because XHR regards file: URLs as not trustable. You could also use the more modern FileReader.readAsArrayBuffer(File) API instead of XHR, which doesn't have the same problems.

Let's look at the involved objects in order.

First, XHR gets the bytes of the audio file from the server and puts them into an ArrayBuffer. The browser can decode data in any format that an <audio> element can decode, too. The decodeAudioData() function will decode the audio data into linear PCM. If that's successful, it will get resampled to the samplerate of the AudioContext and stored in an AudioBuffer object.

The AudioBuffer Interface

```
interface AudioBuffer {
    readonly     attribute float   sampleRate;
    readonly     attribute long    length;
    readonly     attribute double  duration;
    readonly     attribute long    numberOfChannels;
    Float32Array getChannelData (unsigned long channel);
    void         copyFromChannel (Float32Array destination, long channelNumber,
                                  optional unsigned long startInChannel = 0);
    void         copyToChannel (Float32Array source, long channelNumber,
                                optional unsigned long startInChannel = 0);
};
```

This interface represents a memory-resident audio asset (e.g., for one-shot sounds and other short audio clips). Its format is non-interleaved IEEE 32-bit linear PCM with a nominal range of -1 to +1. It can contain one or more channels and may be used by one or more AudioContext objects.

You typically use an AudioBuffer for short sounds—for longer sounds, such as a music soundtrack, you should use streaming with the audio element and MediaElementAudioSourceNode.

The sampleRate attribute contains the samplerate of the audio asset.

The length attribute contains the length of the audio asset in sampleframes.

The duration attribute contains the duration of the audio asset in seconds.

The numberOfChannels attribute contains the number of discrete channels of the audio asset.

The getChannelData() method returns a Float32Array of PCM audio data for the specific channel.

The copyFromChannel() method copies the samples from the specified channel of the AudioBuffer to the destination Float32Array. An optional offset to copy the data from the channel can be provided in the startInChannel parameter.

The copyToChannel() method copies the samples to the specified channel of the AudioBuffer, from the source Float32Array. An optional offset to copy the data from the channel can be provided in the startInChannel parameter.

An AudioBuffer can be added to a AudioBufferSourceNode for the audio asset to enter into a filter network.

You can create an AudioBuffer directly using the AudioContext's createBuffer() method.

```
[Constructor]
interface AudioContext : EventTarget {
    ...
AudioBuffer  createBuffer (unsigned long numberOfChannels,
                           unsigned long length,
                           float sampleRate);
    ...
};
```

It will be filled with samples of the given length (in sample-frames), sampling rate, and number of channels and will contain only silence. However, most commonly, an AudioBuffer is being used for storage of decoded samples.

242

The AudioBufferSourceNode Interface

```
interface AudioBufferSourceNode : AudioNode {
            attribute AudioBuffer? buffer;
    readonly attribute AudioParam  playbackRate;
    readonly attribute AudioParam  detune;
            attribute boolean     loop;
            attribute double      loopStart;
            attribute double      loopEnd;
    void start (optional  double when = 0, optional double offset = 0,
            optional  double duration);
    void stop (optional  double when = 0);
            attribute EventHandler onended;
};
```

An AudioBufferSourceNode represents an audio source node with an in-memory audio asset in an AudioBuffer. As such, it has 0 inputs and 1 output. It is useful for playing short audio assets. The number of channels of the output always equals the number of channels of the AudioBuffer assigned to the buffer attribute, or is one channel of silence if buffer is NULL.

The buffer attribute contains the audio asset.

The playbackRate attribute contains the speed at which to render the audio asset. Its default value is 1. This parameter is k-rate.

The detune attribute modulates the speed at which the audio asset is rendered. Its default value is 0. Its nominal range is [-1,200; 1,200]. This parameter is k-rate.

Both playbackRate and detune are used together to determine a computedPlaybackRate value over time t:

```
computedPlaybackRate(t) = playbackRate(t) * pow(2, detune(t) / 1200)
```

The computedPlaybackRate is the effective speed at which the AudioBuffer of this AudioBufferSourceNode must be played. By default it's 1.

The loop attribute indicates if the audio data should play in a loop. The default value is false.

The loopStart and loopEnd attributes provide an interval in seconds over which the loop should be run. By default, they go from 0 to duration of the buffer.

The start() method is used to schedule when sound playback will happen. The playback will stop automatically when the buffer's audio data has been completely played (if the loop attribute is false), or when the stop() method has been called and the specified time has been reached. start() and stop() may not be issued multiple times for a given AudioBufferSourceNode.

Since the AudioBufferSourceNode is a AudioNode, it has a connect() method to participate in the filter network (e.g., to connect to the audio destination for playback).

The MediaElementAudioSourceNode Interface

Another type of source node that can be used to get audio data into the filter graph is the MediaElementAudioSourceNode.

```
interface MediaElementAudioSourceNode : AudioNode {
};
```

The AudioContext provides functionality to create such a node.

```
[Constructor] interface AudioContext : EventTarget {
          ...
MediaElementAudioSourceNode        createMediaElementSource(HTMLMediaElement
                                                    mediaElement);
          ...
}
```

Together, they allow introducing the audio from an <audio> or a <video> element as a source node. As such, the MediaElementAudioSourceNode has 0 inputs and 1 output. The number of channels of the output corresponds to the number of channels of the media referenced by the HTMLMediaElement, passed in as the argument to createMediaElementSource(), or is one silent channel if the HTMLMediaElement has no audio. Once connected, the HTMLMediaElement's audio doesn't play directly any more but through the filter graph.

The MediaElementAudioSourceNode should be used over an AudioBufferSourceNode for longer media files because the MediaElementSourceNode streams the resource. Listing 6-6 shows an example.

Listing 6-6. Streaming an Audio Element into an AudioContext

```
var audioCtx = new (window.AudioContext || window.webkitAudioContext)();
var mediaElement = document.getElementByTagName('audio')[0];
mediaElement.addEventListener('play', function() {
  var source = audioCtx.createMediaElementSource(mediaElement);
  source.connect(audioCtx.destination);
  source.start(0);
});
```

We have to wait for the play event to fire to be sure that the audio has loaded and has been decoded so the AudioContext can get the data. The audio of the audio element in Listing 6-6 is played back exactly once.

The MediaStreamAudioSourceNode Interface

A final type of source node that can be used to get audio data into the filter graph is the MediaStreamAudioSourceNode.

```
interface MediaStreamAudioSourceNode : AudioNode {
};
```

This interface represents an audio source from a MediaStream, which is basically a live audio input source—a microphone. We will not describe the MediaStream API in this book—it's outside the scope of this book. However, once you have such a MediaStream object, the AudioContext provides functionality to turn the first AudioMediaStreamTrack (audio track) of the MediaStream into an audio source node in a filter graph.

```
[Constructor] interface AudioContext : EventTarget {
          ...
MediaStreamAudioSourceNode        createMediaStreamSource(MediaStream
                                                    mediaStream);
          ...
}
```

As such, the `MediaStreamAudioSourceNode` has 0 inputs and 1 output. The number of channels of the output corresponds to the number of channels of the `AudioMediaStreamTrack`, passed in via the argument to `createMediaStreamSource()`, or is one silent channel if the `MediaStream` has no audio.

Listing 6-7 shows an example.

Listing 6-7. Fetching an Audio Stream's Audio into an AudioContext

```
navigator.getUserMedia = (navigator.getUserMedia ||
                          navigator.webkitGetUserMedia ||
                          navigator.mozGetUserMedia ||
                          navigator.msGetUserMedia);
var audioCtx = new (window.AudioContext || window.webkitAudioContext)();
var mediaElement = document.getElementsByTagName('audio')[0];
var source;

onSuccess = function(stream) {
   mediaElement.src = window.URL.createObjectURL(stream) || stream;
   mediaElement.onloadedmetadata = function(e) {
      mediaElement.play();
      mediaElement.muted = 'true';
   };

   source = audioCtx.createMediaStreamSource(stream);
   source.connect(audioCtx.destination);
};

onError = function(err) {
   console.log('The following getUserMedia error occured: ' + err);
};

navigator.getUserMedia ({ audio: true }, onSuccess, onError);
```

The audio of the audio element in Listing 6-6 is played back through the filter network, despite being muted on the audio element.

■ **Note**   There is also an analogous `MediaStreamAudioDestinationNode` for rendering the output of a filter graph to a `MediaStream` object in preparation for streaming audio via a peer connection to another browser. The `AudioContext`'s `createMediaStreamDestination()` function creates such a destination node. This is, however, currently only implemented in Firefox.

Manipulating Audio Data

By now we have learned how to create audio data for our audio filter graph via four different mechanisms: an oscillator, an audio buffer, an audio file, and a microphone source. Next let's look at the set of audio manipulation functions `AudioContext` provides to the web developer. These are standard audio manipulation functions that will be well understood by an audio professional.

Each one of these manipulation functions is represented in the filter graph via a processing node and is created via a create-function in the AudioContext:

```
[Constructor] interface AudioContext : EventTarget {
...
    GainNode                    createGain ();
    DelayNode                   createDelay(optional double maxDelayTime = 1.0);
    BiquadFilterNode            createBiquadFilter ();
    WaveShaperNode              createWaveShaper ();
    StereoPannerNode            createStereoPanner ();
    ConvolverNode               createConvolver ();
    ChannelSplitterNode         createChannelSplitter(optional unsigned long
                                                numberOfOutputs = 6 );
    ChannelMergerNode           createChannelMerger(optional unsigned long
                                                numberOfInputs = 6 );
    DynamicsCompressorNode      createDynamicsCompressor ();
            ...
}
```

The GainNode Interface

The GainNode represents a change in volume and is created with the createGain() method of the AudioContext.

```
interface GainNode : AudioNode {
    readonly    attribute AudioParam gain;
};
```

It causes a given gain to be applied to the input data before its propagation to the output. A GainNode always has exactly one input and one output, both with the same number of channels:

Number of inputs	1
Number of outputs	1
Channel count mode	"max"
Channel count	2
Channel interpretation	"speakers"

The gain parameter is a unitless value nominally between 0 and 1, where 1 implies no gain change. The parameter is a-rate so the gain is applied to each sampleframe and is multiplied to each corresponding sample of all input channels.

Gain can be changed over time and the new gain is applied using a de-zippering algorithm in order to prevent unaesthetic "clicks" from appearing in the resulting audio.

Listing 6-8 shows an example of manipulating the gain of an audio signal via a slider. Make sure to release the slider so the slider's value actually changes when you try this for yourself. The filter graph consists of a MediaElementSourceNode, a GainNode, and an AudioDestinationNode.

Listing 6-8. Manipulating the Gain of an Audio Signal

```
<audio autoplay controls src="audio/Shivervein_Razorpalm.wav"></audio>
<input type="range"  min="0" max="1" step="0.05" value="1"/>

<script>
var audioCtx = new (window.AudioContext || window.webkitAudioContext)();
var mediaElement = document.getElementsByTagName('audio')[0];

var source = audioCtx.createMediaElementSource(mediaElement);
var gainNode = audioCtx.createGain();
source.connect(gainNode);
gainNode.connect(audioCtx.destination);

var slider = document.getElementsByTagName('input')[0];
slider.addEventListener('change', function() {
  gainNode.gain.value = slider.value;
});
</script>
```

■ **Note**   Remember to upload this example to a web server, because XHR regards file URLs as not trustable.

The DelayNode Interface

The DelayNode delays the incoming audio signal by a certain number of seconds and is created with the createDelay() method of the AudioContext.

```
interface DelayNode : AudioNode {
    readonly    attribute AudioParam dealyTime;
};
```

The default delayTime is 0 seconds (no delay). When the delay time is changed, the transition is smooth without noticeable clicks or glitches.

Number of inputs	1
Number of outputs	1
Channel count mode	"max"
Channel count	2
Channel interpretation	"speakers"

The minimum value is 0 and the maximum value is determined by the maxDelayTime argument to the AudioContext method createDelay.

The parameter is a-rate so the delay is applied to each sampleframe and is multiplied to each corresponding sample of all input channels.

A DelayNode is often used to create a cycle of filter nodes (e.g., in conjunction with a GainNode to create a repeating, decaying echo). When a DelayNode is used in a cycle, the value of the delayTime attribute is clamped to a minimum of 128 frames (one block).

Listing 6-9 shows an example of a decaying echo.

Listing 6-9. Decaying Echo via Gain and Delay Filters

```
<audio autoplay controls src="audio/Big%20Hit%201.wav"></audio>
<script>
var audioCtx = new (window.AudioContext || window.webkitAudioContext)();
var mediaElement = document.getElementsByTagName('audio')[0];

mediaElement.addEventListener('play', function() {
  var source = audioCtx.createMediaElementSource(mediaElement);
  var delay = audioCtx.createDelay();
  delay.delayTime.value = 0.5;

  var gain = audioCtx.createGain();
  gain.gain.value = 0.8;

  // play once
  source.connect(audioCtx.destination);

  // create decaying echo filter graph
  source.connect(delay);
  delay.connect(gain);
  gain.connect(delay);
  delay.connect(audioCtx.destination);
});
</script>
```

The audio is redirected into the filter graph using createMediaElementSource(). The source sound is directly connected to the destination for normal playback and then also fed into a delay and gain filter cycle with the decaying echo being also connected to the destination. Figure 6-8 shows the created filter graph.

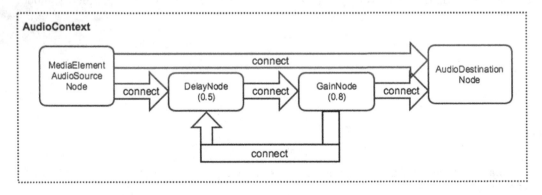

Figure 6-8. *Filter graph of a decaying echo*

■ **Note**   Thanks to robertmcdonald for making the "Big Hit 1.wav" sample available under a Creative Commons license on freesound (see `www.freesound.org/people/robertmcdonald/sounds/139501/`).

The BiquadFilterNode Interface

The BiquadFilterNode represents a low-order filter (see more at http://en.wikipedia.org/wiki/Digital_biquad_filter) and is created with the createBiquadFilter() method of the AudioContext. Low-order filters are the building blocks of basic tone controls (bass, mid, treble), graphic equalizers, and more advanced filters.

```
interface BiquadFilterNode : AudioNode {
            attribute BiquadFilterType  type;
    readonly    attribute AudioParam      frequency;
    readonly    attribute AudioParam      detune;
    readonly    attribute AudioParam      Q;
    readonly    attribute AudioParam      gain;
    void getFrequencyResponse (Float32Array frequencyHz,
                               Float32Array magResponse,
                               Float32Array phaseResponse);
};
```

The filter parameters can be changed over time (e.g., a frequency change creates a filter sweep).

Number of inputs	1
Number of outputs	1
Channel count mode	"max"
Channel count	as many in the output as are in the input
Channel interpretation	"speakers"

Each BiquadFilterNode can be configured as one of a number of common filter types.

```
enum BiquadFilterType {
    "lowpass",
    "highpass",
    "bandpass",
    "lowshelf",
    "highshelf",
    "peaking",
    "notch",
    "allpass"
};
```

The default filter type is lowpass (http://webaudio.github.io/web-audio-api/#the-biquadfilternode-interface).

CHAPTER 6 ■ MANIPULATING AUDIO THROUGH THE WEB AUDIO API

The frequency parameter's default value is 350Hz and starts at 10Hz going up to half the Nyquist frequency (which is 22,050Hz for the default 44.1kHz sampling rate of the AudioContext). It provides frequency characteristics depending on the filter type—for example, the cut-off frequency for the low-pass and high-pass filters, or the center of the frequency band of the bandpass filter.

The detune parameter provides a percentage value for detuning the frequency to make it more natural. It defaults to 0.

Frequency and detune are a-rate parameters and together determine the computed frequency of the filter:

```
computedFrequency(t) = frequency(t) * pow(2, detune(t) / 1200)
```

The Q parameter is the quality factor of the biquad filter with a default value of 1 and a nominal range of 0.0001 to 1,000 (though 1 to 100 is most common).

The gain parameter provides the boost (in dB) to be applied to the biquad filter and has a default value of 0, with a nominal range of -40 to 40 (though 0 to 10 is most common).

The getFrequencyResponse() method calculates the frequency response for the frequencies specified in the frequencyHz frequency array and returns the linear magnitude response values in the magResponse output array and the phase response values in radians in the phaseResponse output array. This is particularly useful to visualize the filter shape.

Listing 6-10 shows an example of the different filter types applied to an audio source.

Listing 6-10. Different Biquad Filter Types Applied to an Audio Source

```
<audio autoplay controls src="audio/Shivervein_Razorpalm.wav"></audio>
<select class="type">
  <option>lowpass</option>
  <option>highpass</option>
  <option>bandpass</option>
  <option>lowshelf</option>
  <option>highshelf</option>
  <option>peaking</option>
  <option>notch</option>
  <option>allpass</option>
</select>

<script>
var audioCtx = new (window.AudioContext || window.webkitAudioContext)();
var mediaElement = document.getElementsByTagName('audio')[0];
var source = audioCtx.createMediaElementSource(mediaElement);
var bass = audioCtx.createBiquadFilter();

// Set up the biquad filter node with a low-pass filter type
bass.type = "lowpass";
bass.frequency.value = 6000;
bass.Q.value = 1;
bass.gain.value = 10;

mediaElement.addEventListener('play', function() {
  // create filter graph
  source.connect(bass);
  bass.connect(audioCtx.destination);
});
```

```
// Update the biquad filter type
var type = document.getElementsByClassName('type')[0];
type.addEventListener('change', function() {
  bass.type = type.value;
});
</script>
```

The input audio file is connected to a biquad filter with a frequency value of 6,000Hz, a quality factor of 1, and a 10 dB boost. The type of filter can be changed with a drop-down between all eight different filters. This way you get a good idea of the effect of these filters on an audio signal.

Using the getFrequencyResponse() method on this example, we can visualize the filter (see also http://webaudio-io2012.appspot.com/#34). Listing 6-11 shows how to draw a frequency–gain graph.

Listing 6-11. Drawing a Frequency-Gain Graph

```
<canvas width="600" height="200"></canvas>
<canvas width="600" height="200" style="display: none;"></canvas>

<script>
var audioCtx = new (window.AudioContext || window.webkitAudioContext)();
var canvas = document.getElementsByTagName('canvas')[0];
var ctxt = canvas.getContext('2d');
var scratch = document.getElementsByTagName('canvas')[1];
var sctxt = scratch.getContext('2d');

var dbScale = 60;
var width = 512;
var height = 200;
var pixelsPerDb = (0.5 * height) / dbScale;
var nrOctaves = 10;
var nyquist = 0.5 * audioCtx.sampleRate;

function dbToY(db) {
  var y = (0.5 * height) - pixelsPerDb * db;
  return y;
}

function drawAxes() {
  ctxt.textAlign = "center";
  // Draw frequency scale (x-axis).
  for (var octave = 0; octave <= nrOctaves; octave++) {
    var x = octave * width / nrOctaves;
    var f = nyquist * Math.pow(2.0, octave - nrOctaves);
    var value = f.toFixed(0);
    var unit = 'Hz';
    if (f > 1000) {
      unit = 'KHz';
      value = (f/1000).toFixed(1);
    }
    ctxt.strokeStyle = "black";
    ctxt.strokeText(value + unit, x, 20);
```

```
            ctxt.beginPath();
            ctxt.strokeStyle = "gray";
            ctxt.lineWidth = 1;
            ctxt.moveTo(x, 30);
            ctxt.lineTo(x, height);
            ctxt.stroke();
        }
        // Draw decibel scale (y-axis).
        for (var db = -dbScale; db < dbScale - 10; db += 10) {
            var y = dbToY(db);
            ctxt.strokeStyle = "black";
            ctxt.strokeText(db.toFixed(0) + "dB", width + 40, y);

            ctxt.beginPath();
            ctxt.strokeStyle = "gray";
            ctxt.moveTo(0, y);
            ctxt.lineTo(width, y);
            ctxt.stroke();
        }
        // save this drawing to the scratch canvas.
        sctxt.drawImage(canvas, 0, 0);
    }
</script>
```

We use two canvases for this so we have a canvas to store the prepared grid and axes. We draw the frequency axis (x-axis) as 10 octaves down from the Nyquist frequency of the audio context. We draw the gain axis (y-axis) from -60 dB to 40 dB. Figure 6-9 shows the result.

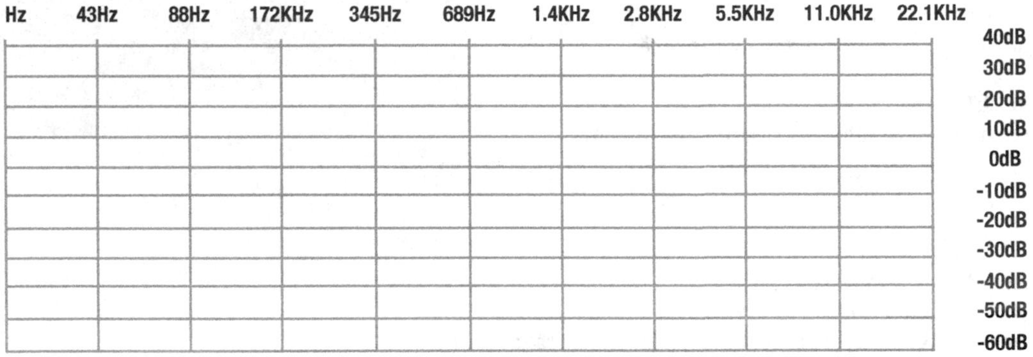

Hz	43Hz	88Hz	172KHz	345Hz	689Hz	1.4KHz	2.8KHz	5.5KHz	11.0KHz	22.1KHz	
											40dB
											30dB
											20dB
											10dB
											0dB
											-10dB
											-20dB
											-30dB
											-40dB
											-50dB
											-60dB

Figure 6-9. *A frequency-gain graph*

Now, all we need to do is draw the frequency response of our filters into this graph. Listing 6-12 shows the function to use for that.

Listing 6-12. Different Biquad Filter Types Applied to an Audio Source

```
function drawGraph() {
  // grab the axis and grid from scratch canvas.
  ctxt.clearRect(0, 0, 600, height);
  ctxt.drawImage(scratch, 0, 0);

  // grab the frequency response data.
  var frequencyHz = new Float32Array(width);
  var magResponse = new Float32Array(width);
  var phaseResponse = new Float32Array(width);
  for (var i = 0; i < width; ++i) {
    var f = i / width;
    // Convert to log frequency scale (octaves).
    f = nyquist * Math.pow(2.0, nrOctaves * (f - 1.0));
    frequencyHz[i] = f;
  }
  bass.getFrequencyResponse(frequencyHz, magResponse, phaseResponse);

  // draw the frequency response.
  ctxt.beginPath();
  ctxt.strokeStyle = "red";
  ctxt.lineWidth = 3;
  for (var i = 0; i < width; ++i) {
    var response = magResponse[i];
    var dbResponse = 20.0 * Math.log(response) / Math.LN10;
    var x = i;
    var y = dbToY(dbResponse);
    if ( i == 0 ) {
        ctxt.moveTo(x, y);
    } else {
        ctxt.lineTo(x, y);
    }
  }
  ctxt.stroke();
}
```

First we grab the earlier graph from the scratch canvas and add it to an emptied canvas. Then we prepare the frequency array for which we want to retrieve the response and call the getFrequencyResponse() method on it. Finally, we draw the curve of the frequency response by drawing lines from value to value. For the full example, combine Listings 6-10, 6-11, and 6-12 and call the drawGraph() function in the play event handler (see http://html5videoguide.net).

Figure 6-10 shows the results for the low-pass filter of Listing 6-10.

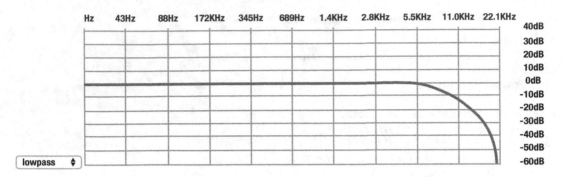

Figure 6-10. *Low-pass filter frequency response of Listing 6-10*

The WaveShaperNode Interface

The WaveShaperNode represents nonlinear distortion effects and is created with the createWaveShaper() method of the AudioContext. Distortion effects create "warm" and "dirty" sounds by compressing or clipping the peaks of a sound wave, which results in a large number of added overtones. This AudioNode uses a curve to apply a waveshaping distortion to the signal.

```
interface WaveShaperNode : AudioNode {
            attribute Float32Array?  curve;
            attribute OverSampleType oversample;
};
```

The curve array contains sampled values of the shaping curve.

The oversample parameter specifies what type of oversampling should be applied to the input signal when applying the shaping curve.

```
enum OverSampleType {
    "none",
    "2x",
    "4x"
};
```

The default value is "none," meaning the curve is applied directly to the input samples. A value of "2x" or "4x" can improve the quality of the processing by avoiding some aliasing, with "4x" yielding the highest quality.

Number of inputs	1
Number of outputs	1
Channel count mode	"max"
Channel count	as many in the output as are in the input
Channel interpretation	"speakers"

The shaping curve is the important construct to understand here. It consists of an extract of a curve in an x-axis interval of [-1; 1] with values only between -1 and 1. At 0, the curve's value is 0. By default, the curve array is null, which means that the WaveShaperNode will apply no modification to the input sound signal.

Creating a good shaping curve is an art form and requires a good understanding of mathematics. Here is a good explanation of how waveshaping works: `http://music.columbia.edu/cmc/musicandcomputers/chapter4/04_06.php`.

We'll use $y = 0.5x^3$ as our waveshaper. Figure 6-11 shows its shape.

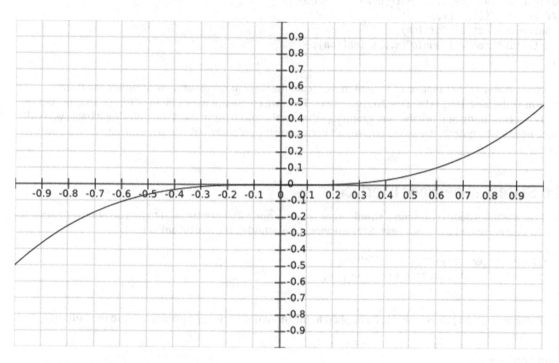

Figure 6-11. *Waveshaper example*

Listing 6-13 shows how to apply this function to a filter graph.

Listing 6-13. Applying a Waveshaper to an Input Signal

```
var audioCtx = new (window.AudioContext || window.webkitAudioContext)();
var mediaElement = document.getElementsByTagName('audio')[0];
var source = audioCtx.createMediaElementSource(mediaElement);

function makeDistortionCurve() {
  var n_samples = audioCtx.sampleRate;
  var curve = new Float32Array(n_samples);
  var x;
  for (var i=0; i < n_samples; ++i ) {
    x = i * 2 / n_samples - 1;
    curve[i] = 0.5 * Math.pow(x, 3);
  }
  return curve;
};
```

```
var distortion = audioCtx.createWaveShaper();
distortion.curve = makeDistortionCurve();
distortion.oversample = '4x';

mediaElement.addEventListener('play', function() {
  // create filter graph
  source.connect(distortion);
  distortion.connect(audioCtx.destination);
});
```

In the makeDistortionCurve() function we create the waveshaping curve by sampling the $0.5x^3$ function at the samplingRate of the AudioContext. Then we create the waveshaper with that shaping curve and 4x oversampling and put the filter graph together on the audio input file. When playing it back, you will notice how much quieter the sound got—that's because this particular waveshaper only has values between -0.5 and 0.5.

The StereoPannerNode Interface

The StereoPannerNode represents a simple stereo panner node that can be used to pan an audio stream left or right and is created with the createStereoPanner() method of the AudioContext.

```
interface StereoPannerNode : AudioNode {
    readonly    attribute AudioParam pan;
};
```

It causes a given pan position to be applied to the input data before its propagation to the output.

Number of inputs	1
Number of outputs	1
Channel count mode	"clamped-max"
Channel count	2
Channel interpretation	"speakers"

This node always deals with two channels and the channelCountMode is always "clamped-max." Connections from nodes with fewer or more channels will be upmixed or downmixed appropriately.

The pan parameter describes the new position of the input in the output's stereo image.

- -1 represents full left

- +1 represents full right

Its default value is 0, and its nominal range is from -1 to 1. This parameter is a-rate.

Pan can be changed over time and thus create the effect of a moving sound source (e.g., from left to right). This is achieved by modifying the gain of the left and right channels.

Listing 6-14 shows an example of manipulating the pan position of an audio signal via a slider. Make sure to release the slider so the slider's value actually changes when you try this for yourself. The filter graph consists of a MediaElementSourceNode, a StereoPannerNode, and an AudioDestinationNode.

Listing 6-14. Manipulating the Pan Position of an Audio Signal

```
<audio autoplay controls src="audio/Shivervein_Razorpalm.wav"></audio>
<input type="range"  min="-1" max="1" step="0.05" value="0"/>

<script>
var audioCtx = new (window.AudioContext || window.webkitAudioContext)();
var mediaElement = document.getElementsByTagName('audio')[0];

var source = audioCtx.createMediaElementSource(mediaElement);
var panNode = audioCtx.createStereoPanner();
source.connect(panNode);
panNode.connect(audioCtx.destination);

var slider = document.getElementsByTagName('input')[0];
slider.addEventListener('change', function() {
  panNode.pan.value = slider.value;
});
</script>
```

As you play this back, you might want to use headphones to get a better feeling of how the slider move affects the stereo position of the signal.

The ConvolverNode Interface

The ConvolverNode represents a processing node, which applies a linear convolution to an AudioBuffer and is created with the createConvolver() method of the AudioContext.

```
interface ConvolverNode : AudioNode {
            attribute AudioBuffer? buffer;
            attribute boolean      normalize;
};
```

We can imagine a linear convolver to represent the acoustic properties of a room and the output of the ConvolverNode to represent the reverberations of the input signal in that room. The acoustic properties are stored in something called an impulse response.

The AudioBuffer buffer attribute contains a mono, stereo, or four-channel impulse response used by the ConvolverNode to create the reverb effect. It is provided as an audio file itself.

The normalize attribute decides whether the impulse response from the buffer will be scaled by an equal-power normalization. It's true by default.

Number of inputs	1
Number of outputs	1
Channel count mode	"clamped-max"
Channel count	2
Channel interpretation	"speakers"

It is possible for a ConvolverNode to take mono audio input and apply a two- or four-channel impulse response to result in a stereo audio output signal. Connections from nodes with fewer or more channels will be upmixed or downmixed appropriately, but a maximum of two channels is allowed.

Listing 6-15 shows an example of three different impulse responses applied to an audio file. The filter graph consists of a MediaElementSourceNode, a ConvolverNode, and an AudioDestinationNode.

Listing 6-15. Applying Three Different Convolutions to an Audio Signal

```
var audioCtx = new (window.AudioContext || window.webkitAudioContext)();
var mediaElement = document.getElementsByTagName('audio')[0];
var source = audioCtx.createMediaElementSource(mediaElement);
var convolver = audioCtx.createConvolver();

// Pre-Load the impulse responses
var impulseFiles = [
  "audio/filter-telephone.wav",
  "audio/kitchen.wav",
  "audio/cardiod-rear-levelled.wav"
];
var impulseResponses = new Array();
var allLoaded = 0;

function loadFile(url, index) {
  var request = new XMLHttpRequest();

  function requestData(url) {
    request.open('GET', url, true);
    request.responseType = 'arraybuffer';
    request.send();
  }

  function receivedData() {
    if ((request.status === 200 || request.status === 206)
        && request.readyState === 4) {
      var audioData = request.response;
      audioCtx.decodeAudioData(audioData,
        function(buffer) {
          impulseResponses[index] = buffer;
          if (++allLoaded == impulseFiles.length) {
              createFilterGraph();
          }
        },
        function(error) {
          "Error with decoding audio data" + error.err
        }
      );
    }
  }
}
```

```
  request.addEventListener('load', receivedData, false);
  requestData(url);
}
for (i = 0; i < impulseFiles.length; i++) {
  loadFile(impulseFiles[i], i);
}

// create filter graph
function createFilterGraph() {
  source.connect(convolver);
  convolver.buffer = impulseResponses[0];
  convolver.connect(audioCtx.destination);
}

var radioButtons = document.getElementsByTagName('input');
for (i = 0; i < radioButtons.length; i++){
  radioButtons[i].addEventListener('click', function() {
    convolver.buffer = impulseResponses[this.value];
  });
}
```

You'll notice that we're loading the three impulse responses as in Listing 6-5 via XMLHttpRequest. Then we store them in an array, which allows us to change between them when the user switches between the input radio buttons. We can only put the filter graph together after all the impulse responses have been loaded (i.e., allLoaded = 2).

The HTML of this will have three input elements as radio buttons to switch between the different impulse responses. As you play with this example, you will notice the difference in reverberation between the "telephone," the "kitchen," and the "warehouse" impulse responses.

The ChannelSplitterNode and ChannelMergeNode Interfaces

The ChannelSplitterNode and the ChannelMergerNode represent AudioNodes for splitting apart and merging back together the individual channels of an audio stream in a filter graph.

The ChannelSplitterNode is created with the createChannelSplitter() method of the AudioContext, which takes an optional numberOfOutputs parameter which signifies the size of the fan-out AudioNodes. It's 6 by default. Which of the outputs will actually have audio data depends on the number of channels available in the input audio signal to the ChannelSplitterNode. For example, fanning out a stereo signal to six outputs creates only two outputs with a signal—the rest are silence.

The ChannelMergerNode is the opposite of the ChannelSplitterNode and created with the createChannelMerger() method of the AudioContext, which takes an optional numberOfInputs parameter, signifying the size of the fan-in AudioNodes. It's 6 by default, but not all of them need to be connected and not all of them need to contain an audio signal. For example, fanning-in six inputs with only the first two having a stereo audio signal each creates a six-channel stream with the first and second input downmixed to mono and the rest of the channels silent.

```
interface ChannelSplitterNode : AudioNode {};
interface ChannelMergerNode   : AudioNode {};
```

	ChannelSplitterNode	ChannelMergeNode
Number of inputs	1	N (default: 6)
Number of outputs	N (default: 6)	1
Channel count mode	"max"	"max"
Channel count	Fan-out to a number of mono outputs	Fan-in a number of downmixed mono inputs
Channel interpretation	"speakers"	"speakers"

For ChannelMergerNode, the channelCount and channelCountMode properties cannot be changed—all inputs are dealt with as mono signals.

One application for ChannelSplitterNode and ChannelMergerNode is for doing "matrix mixing" where each channel's gain is individually controlled.

Listing 6-16 shows an example of matrix mixing on our example audio file. You may want to use headphones to better hear the separate volume control of the left and right channels.

Listing 6-16. Apply Different Gains to Right and Left Channels of an Audio File

```
<audio autoplay controls src="audio/Shivervein_Razorpalm.wav"></audio>
<p>Left Channel Gain:
  <input type="range"  min="0" max="1" step="0.1" value="1"/>
</p>
<p>Right Channel Gain:
  <input type="range"  min="0" max="1" step="0.1" value="1"/>
</p>

<script>
var audioCtx = new (window.AudioContext || window.webkitAudioContext)();
var mediaElement = document.getElementsByTagName('audio')[0];

var source = audioCtx.createMediaElementSource(mediaElement);
var splitter = audioCtx.createChannelSplitter(2);
var merger = audioCtx.createChannelMerger(2);
var gainLeft = audioCtx.createGain();
var gainRight = audioCtx.createGain();

// filter graph
source.connect(splitter);
splitter.connect(gainLeft, 0);
splitter.connect(gainRight, 0);
gainLeft.connect(merger, 0, 0);
gainRight.connect(merger, 0, 1);
merger.connect(audioCtx.destination);

var sliderLeft = document.getElementsByTagName('input')[0];
sliderLeft.addEventListener('change', function() {
  gainLeft.gain.value = sliderLeft.value;
});
```

```
var sliderRight = document.getElementsByTagName('input')[1];
sliderRight.addEventListener('change', function() {
  gainRight.gain.value = sliderRight.value;
});
</script>
```

The example is straightforward with two input sliders individually controlling the volume of the two gain nodes, one for each channel. One thing to understand is the use of the second and third parameters of the AudioNode's connect() methods on the AudioNodes, which allow connecting the separated channels of the ChannelSplitterNode or the ChannelMergerNode.

Figure 6-12 shows the filter graph of the example.

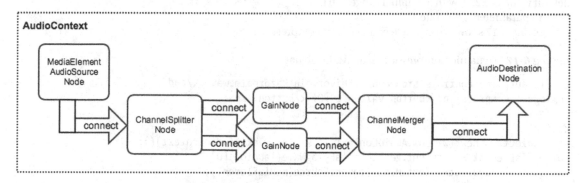

Figure 6-12. *Filter graph of volume control separately for left and right channel*

The DynamicCompressorNode Interface

The DynamicCompressorNode provides a compression effect, which lowers the volume of the loudest parts of the signal to prevent clipping and distortion that can occur when multiple sounds are played and multiplexed together. Overall, a louder, richer, and fuller sound can be achieved. It is created with the createDynamicCompressor() method of the AudioContext.

```
interface DynamicsCompressorNode : AudioNode {
    readonly    attribute AudioParam threshold;
    readonly    attribute AudioParam knee;
    readonly    attribute AudioParam ratio;
    readonly    attribute float       reduction;
    readonly    attribute AudioParam attack;
    readonly    attribute AudioParam release;
};
```

Number of inputs	1
Number of outputs	1
Channel count mode	"explicit"
Channel count	2
Channel interpretation	"speakers"

The threshold parameter provides the decibel value above which the compression will start taking effect. Its default value is -24, with a nominal range of -100 to 0.

The knee parameter provides a decibel value representing the range above the threshold where the curve smoothly transitions to the compressed portion. Its default value is 30, with a nominal range of 0 to 40.

The ratio parameter represents the amount of change in dB needed in the input for a 1 dB change in the output. Its default value is 12, with a nominal range of 1 to 20.

The reduction parameter represents the amount of gain reduction in dB currently applied by the compressor to the signal. If fed no signal the value will be 0 (no gain reduction).

The attack parameter represents the amount of time (in seconds) to reduce the gain by 10 dB. Its default value is 0.003, with a nominal range of 0 to 1.

The release parameter represents the amount of time (in seconds) to increase the gain by 10 dB. Its default value is 0.250, with a nominal range of 0 to 1.

All parameters are k-rate.

Listing 6-17 shows an example of a dynamic compression.

Listing 6-17. Dynamic Compression of an Audio Signal

```
<audio autoplay controls src="audio/Shivervein_Razorpalm.wav"></audio>
<p>Toggle Compression: <button value="0">Off</button></p>

<script>
var audioCtx = new (window.AudioContext || window.webkitAudioContext)();
var mediaElement = document.getElementsByTagName('audio')[0];
var source = audioCtx.createMediaElementSource(mediaElement);

// Create a compressor node
var compressor = audioCtx.createDynamicsCompressor();
compressor.threshold.value = -50;
compressor.knee.value = 20;
compressor.ratio.value = 12;
compressor.reduction.value = -40;

mediaElement.addEventListener('play', function() {
  source.connect(audioCtx.destination);
});

var button = document.getElementsByTagName('button')[0];
button.addEventListener('click', function() {
  if (this.value == 1) {
    this.value = 0;
    this.innerHTML = "Off";
    source.disconnect(audioCtx.destination);
    source.connect(compressor);
    compressor.connect(audioCtx.destination);
  } else {
    this.value = 1;
    this.innerHTML = "On";
    source.disconnect(compressor);
    compressor.disconnect(audioCtx.destination);
    source.connect(audioCtx.destination);
  }
});
</script>
```

In the example, the compressor can be included and excluded from the filter graph by click of a button.

Figure 6-13 plots the compressor used. You can see that below -50 dB no compression is applied. Within the next 20 dB, a smooth transition is made to the compressed curve. The ratio determines how much compression is applied above the threshold and we have chosen a 12 dB change in input for a 1 dB change in output. A 1 dB change would result in no change—the larger the ratio value, the quicker the compression graph flattens out.

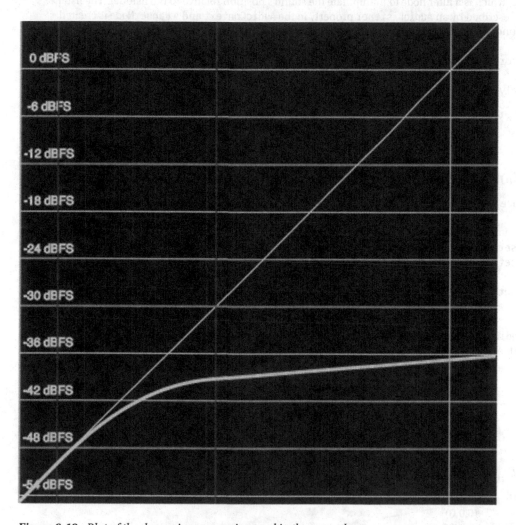

Figure 6-13. *Plot of the dynamic compression used in the example*

The overall effect is that the audio signal is reduced in volume, but only in the previously high volume parts, not in the quieter parts.

This concludes our look at AudioNode interfaces that are standard functions for manipulating diverse aspects of the audio signal including gain, dynamics, delay, waveform, channels, stereo position, and frequency filters.

3D Spatialization and Panning

In this section we will look at the three-dimensional positioning of audio signals, which is of particular use in games when multiple signals need to be mixed together differently depending on the position of the listener. The Web Audio API comes with built-in hardware-accelerated positional audio features.

We deal with two constructs to manipulate 3D audio signals: the position of the listener and the PannerNode, which is a filter node to manipulate the sound's position relative to the listener. The listener's position is described by an AudioListener property in the AudioContext and a PannerNode is created through a function also part of the AudioContext.

```
[Constructor] interface AudioContext : EventTarget {
        ...
    readonly    attribute AudioListener          listener;
    PannerNode               createPanner ();
        ...
}
```

The AudioListener Interface

This interface represents the position and orientation of the person listening to the audio scene.

```
interface AudioListener {
    void setPosition    (float x, float y, float z);
    void setOrientation (float xFront, float yFront, float zFront,
                         float xUp, float yUp, float zUp);
    void setVelocity    (float x, float y, float z);
};
```

The AudioContext assumes a 3D right-handed Cartesian coordinate space in which the listener is positioned (see Figure 6-14). By default, the listener is standing at (0, 0, 0).

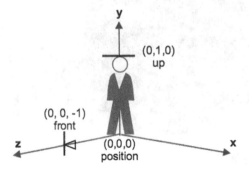

Figure 6-14. *Right-handed Cartesian coordinate space that the listener is standing in*

The setPosition() method allows us to change that position. While the coordinates are unitless, typically you would specify position relative to a particular space's dimensions and use percentage values to specify the position.

The setOrientation() method allows us to change the direction the listener's ears are pointing in the 3D Cartesian coordinate space. Both a Front position and an Up position are provided. In simple human terms, the Front position represents which direction the person's nose is pointing and defaults to (0, 0, -1), indicating that the z-direction is relevant for where the ears are pointing. The Up position represents the direction the top of a person's head is pointing and defaults to (0, 1, 0), indicating that the y-direction is relevant to the person's height. Figure 6-14 also show the Front and Up positions.

The setVelocity() method allows us to change the velocity of the listener, which controls both the direction of travel and the speed in 3D space. This velocity relative to an audio source's velocity can be used to determine how much Doppler shift (pitch change) to apply. The default value is (0, 0, 0), indicating that the listener is stationary.

The units used for this vector are *meters/second* and are independent of the units used for position and orientation vectors. For example, a value of (0, 0, 17) indicates that the listener is moving in the direction of the z-axis at a speed of 17 meters/second.

Listing 6-18 shows an example of the effect of changing listener position and orientation. By default, the audio sound is positioned also at (0, 0, 0).

Listing 6-18. Changing the Listener's Position and Orientation

```
<p>Position:
  <input type="range"  min="-1" max="1" step="0.1" value="0" name="pos0"/>
  <input type="range"  min="-1" max="1" step="0.1" value="0" name="pos1"/>
  <input type="range"  min="-1" max="1" step="0.1" value="0" name="pos2"/>
</p>
<p>Orientation:
  <input type="range"  min="-1" max="1" step="0.1" value="0" name="dir0"/>
  <input type="range"  min="-1" max="1" step="0.1" value="0" name="dir1"/>
  <input type="range"  min="-1" max="1" step="0.1" value="-1" name="dir2"/>
</p>
<p>Elevation:
  <input type="range"  min="-1" max="1" step="0.1" value="0" name="hei0"/>
  <input type="range"  min="-1" max="1" step="0.1" value="1" name="hei1"/>
  <input type="range"  min="-1" max="1" step="0.1" value="0" name="hei2"/>
</p>

<script>
var audioCtx = new (window.AudioContext || window.webkitAudioContext)();
var source = audioCtx.createBufferSource();

var request = new XMLHttpRequest();
var url = 'audio/ticking.wav';
request.addEventListener('load', receivedData, false);
requestData(url);

var inputs = document.getElementsByTagName('input');
var pos = [0, 0, 0];    // position
var ori = [0, 0, -1];   // orientation
var ele = [0, 1, 0];    // elevation

for (i=0; i < inputs.length; i++) {
  var elem = inputs[i];
  elem.addEventListener('change', function() {
```

```
    var type = this.name.substr(0,3);
    var index = this.name.slice(3);
    var value = parseFloat(this.value);

    switch (type) {
      case 'pos':
        pos[index] = value;
        audioCtx.listener.setPosition(pos[0], pos[1], pos[2]);
        break;
      case 'ori':
        ori[index] = value;
        audioCtx.listener.setOrientation(ori[0], ori[1], ori[2],
                                         ele[0], ele[1], ele[2]);
        break;
      case 'ele':
        ele[index] = value;
        audioCtx.listener.setOrientation(ori[0], ori[1], ori[2],
                                         ele[0], ele[1], ele[2]);
        break;
      default:
        console.log('no match');
    }
  });
}
</script>
```

In the example, we're loading a looping sound into an AudioBuffer using functions introduced in Listing 6-5 and we manipulate the three dimensions of the three parameters.

■ **Note**   Thanks to Izkhanilov for making the "Ticking Clock.wav" sample available under a Creative Commons license on freesound (see `www.freesound.org/people/Izkhanilov/sounds/54848/`).

Interestingly, when you replicate our example, you will notice that the parameter changes make no difference to the sound playback. This is because the location of the sound source is not explicitly specified. We believe the AudioContext therefore assumes that the listener and the sound source are co-located. It requires a PannerNode to specify the location of the sound source.

The PannerNode Interface

This interface represents a processing node which positions/spatializes an incoming audio stream in 3D space relative to the listener. It is created with the createPanner() method of the AudioContext.

```
interface PannerNode : AudioNode {
    void setPosition    (float x, float y, float z);
    void setOrientation (float x, float y, float z);
            attribute PanningModelType  panningModel;
            attribute DistanceModelType distanceModel;
            attribute float             refDistance;
            attribute float             maxDistance;
```

```
        attribute float           rolloffFactor;
        attribute float           coneInnerAngle;
        attribute float           coneOuterAngle;
        attribute float           coneOuterGain;
};
```

One way to think of the panner and the listener is to consider a game environment where the antagonist is running through a 3D space and sounds are coming from all sorts of sources across the scene. Each one of these sources would have a `PannerNode` associated with them.

`PannerNode` objects have an orientation vector representing in which direction the sound is projecting. Additionally, they have a sound cone representing how directional the sound is. For example, the sound could be omnidirectional, in which case it would be heard anywhere regardless of its orientation, or it can be more directional and heard only if it is facing the listener. During rendering, the `PannerNode` calculates an azimuth (the angle that the listener has toward the sound source) and elevation (the height above or below the listener). The browser uses thesse values to render the spatialization effect.

Number of inputs	1
Number of outputs	1 (stereo)
Channel count mode	"clamped-max"
Channel count	2 (fixed)
Channel interpretation	"speakers"

The input of a `PannerNode` is either mono (one channel) or stereo (two channels). Connections from nodes with fewer or more channels will be upmixed or downmixed appropriately. The output of this node is hard-coded to stereo (two channels) and currently cannot be configured.

The `setPosition()` method sets the position of the audio source relative to the listener. Default is (0, 0, 0).

The `setOrientation()` method describes which direction the audio source is pointing in the 3D Cartesian coordinate space. Depending on how directional the sound is (controlled by the cone attributes), a sound pointing away from the listener can be very quiet or completely silent. Default is (1, 0, 0).

The `panningModel` attribute specifies which panning model this `PannerNode` uses.

```
enum PanningModelType {
    "equalpower",
    "HRTF"
};
```

The panning model describes how the sound spatialization is calculated. The "equalpower" model uses equal-power panning where the elevation is ignored. The HRTF (head-related transfer function) model uses a convolution with measured impulse responses from human, thus simulating human spatialization perception. The `panningModel` defaults to HRTF.

The `distanceModel` attribute determines which algorithm will be used to reduce the volume of an audio source as it moves away from the listener.

```
enum DistanceModelType {
    "linear",
    "inverse",
    "exponential"
};
```

The "linear" model assumes linear gain reduction as the sound source moves away from the listener. The "inverse" model assumes increasingly smaller gain reduction. The "exponential" model assumes increasingly larger gain reduction. The distanceModel defaults to "inverse."

The refDistance attribute contains a reference distance for reducing volume as source moves further from the listener. The default value is 1.

The maxDistance attribute contains the maximum distance between source and listener, after which the volume will not get reduced any further. The default value is 10,000.

The rolloffFactor attribute describes how quickly the volume is reduced as the source moves away from the listener. The default value is 1.

The coneInnerAngle, coneOuterAngle, and coneOuterGain together describe a cone inside of which the volume reduction is much lower than outside. There is an inner and an outer cone describing the sound intensity as a function of the source/listener angle from the source's orientation vector. Thus, a sound source pointing directly at the listener will be louder than if it is pointed off-axis.

Figure 6-15 describes the sound cone concept visually.

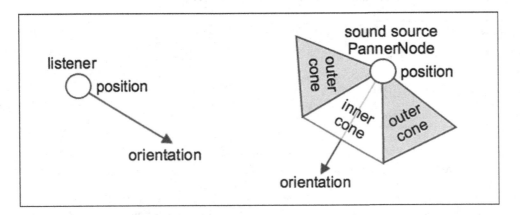

Figure 6-15. *Visualization of the source cone of a PannerNode in relation to the listener*

The coneInnerAngle provides an angle, in degrees, inside of which there will be no volume reduction. The default value is 360, and the value used is modulo 360.

The coneOuterAngle provides an angle, in degrees, outside of which the volume will be reduced to a constant value of coneOuterGain. The default value is 360 and the value is used modulo 360.

The coneOuterGain provides the amount of volume reduction outside the coneOuterAngle. The default value is 0, and the value is used modulo 360.

Let's extend the example of Listing 6-18 and introduce a PannerNode. This has the effect of positioning the sound source at a fixed location distinct from the listener position. We further include a sound cone so we can more easily hear the gain reduction effects. See the changes in Listing 6-19.

Listing 6-19. Introducing a Position and Sound Cone for the Sound Source

```
var audioCtx = new (window.AudioContext || window.webkitAudioContext)();
var source = audioCtx.createBufferSource();
var panner = audioCtx.createPanner();
panner.coneOuterGain = 0.5;
panner.coneOuterAngle = 180;
panner.coneInnerAngle = 90;
source.connect(panner);
panner.connect(audioCtx.destination);
```

Now, as we change the position, orientation, and elevation, we move the listener relative to the sound source, which remains in the middle of the sound scene. For example, as we move the x-value of the position to the right, the sound moves to our left—we have sidestepped the sound to our right. Once we have the sound to our left, as we move the z-value of the orientation between -0.1 and +0.1, the sound moves between left and right—at 0 we are facing the sound, at +0.1 we have turned our right side to it, at -0.1 we have turned our left side to it.

Notice how we haven't actually moved the location of the sound source yet, but only the position of the listener. You use the setPosition() and setOrientation() of the PannerNode for that and you can do this with multiple sounds. We'll leave this as an exercise to the reader.

■ **Note** The Web Audio API specification used to provide a setVelocity() method for the PannerNode which would calculate the Doppler shift for moving sound sources and listener. This has been deprecated and will be removed from Chrome after version 45. There is a plan to introduce a new SpatializerNode interface to replace this. For now, you will need to calculate Doppler shifts yourself, possibly using the DelayNode interface or changing the playbackRate.

JavaScript Manipulation of Audio Data

The current state of implementation of the Web Audio API specification includes an interface called ScriptProcessorNode, which can generate, process or analyze audio directly using JavaScript. This node type is deprecated with an aim of replacing it with the AudioWorker interface, but we will still explain it because it is implemented in current browsers while the AudioWorker interface isn't.

The difference between the ScriptProcessorNode and the AudioWorker interface is that the first one is being run on the main browser thread and therefore has to share processing time with layout, rendering, and most other processing going on in the browser. All other audio nodes of the Web Audio API are running on a separate thread, which makes it more likely that the audio is running uninterrupted from other big tasks. This will change with the AudioWorker, which will also run the JavaScript audio processing on the audio thread. It will be able to run with less latency, because it avoids a change of thread boundaries and having to share resources with the main thread.

This all sounds great, but for now we cannot use the AudioWorker and will therefore look at the ScriptProcessorNode first.

The ScriptProcessorNode Interface

This interface allows writing your own JavaScript code to generate, process, or analyze audio and integrate it into a filter graph.

A ScriptProcessorNode is created through a createScriptProcessor() method on the AudioContext:

```
[Constructor] interface AudioContext : EventTarget {
...
    ScriptProcessorNode createScriptProcessor(
                optional unsigned long bufferSize = 0 ,
                optional unsigned long numberOfInputChannels = 2 ,
                optional unsigned long numberOfOutputChannels = 2 );
...
}
```

It takes only optional parameters and it is recommended to leave the setting of these to the browser. However, following is their explanation:

- a bufferSize in units of sampleframes being one of 256, 512, 1,024, 2,048, 4,096, 8,192, 16,384. This controls how frequently the audio process event is dispatched and how many sampleframes need to be processed in each call.

- the numberOfInputChannels defaults to 2 but can be up to 32.

- the numberOfOutputChannels defaults to 2 but can be up to 32.

The interface of the ScriptProcessorNode is defined as follows:

```
interface ScriptProcessorNode : AudioNode {
                attribute EventHandler onaudioprocess;
    readonly    attribute long         bufferSize;
};
```

The bufferSize attribute reflects the buffer size at which the node was created and the onaudioprocess associates a JavaScript event handler with the node, which is being called when the node is activated. The event that the handler receives is an AudioProcessingEvent.

```
interface AudioProcessingEvent : Event {
    readonly    attribute double       playbackTime;
    readonly    attribute AudioBuffer inputBuffer;
    readonly    attribute AudioBuffer outputBuffer;
};
```

It contains the following read-only data:

- a playbackTime, which is the time when the audio will be played in the same time coordinate system as the AudioContext's currentTime.

- an inputBuffer, which contains the input audio data with a number of channels equal to the numberOfInputChannels parameter of the createScriptProcessor() method.

- an outputBuffer, where the output audio data of the event handler is to be saved. It must have a number of channels equal to the numberOfOutputChannels parameter of the createScriptProcessor() method.

The ScriptProcessorNode does not change its channels or number of inputs.

Number of inputs	1
Number of outputs	1
Channel count mode	"explicit"
Channel count	Number of input channels
Channel interpretation	"speakers"

A simple example use of the ScriptProcessorNode is to add some random noise to the audio samples. Listing 6-20 shows an example of this.

Listing 6-20. Adding Random Noise to an Audio File in a ScriptProcessorNode

```
<audio autoplay controls src="audio/ticking.wav"></audio>

<script>
var audioCtx = new (window.AudioContext || window.webkitAudioContext)();
var mediaElement = document.getElementsByTagName('audio')[0];
var source = audioCtx.createMediaElementSource(mediaElement);

var noiser = audioCtx.createScriptProcessor();
source.connect(noiser);
noiser.connect(audioCtx.destination);

noiser.onaudioprocess = function(event) {
  var inputBuffer = event.inputBuffer;
  var outputBuffer = event.outputBuffer;

  for (var channel=0; channel < inputBuffer.numberOfChannels; channel++) {
    var inputData = inputBuffer.getChannelData(channel);
    var outputData = outputBuffer.getChannelData(channel);

    for (var sample = 0; sample < inputBuffer.length; sample++) {
      outputData[sample] = inputData[sample] + (Math.random() * 0.01);
    }
  }
};
</script>
```

Where we copy the input data to the output data array, we add 10% of a random number between 0 and 1 to the input data, thus creating an output sample with some white noise.

■ **Note** You might want to check out the new AudioWorker interface in the specification and how it replaces the ScriptProcessorNode. We can't describe it here, because at the time of this writing, it was still changing on a daily basis. The principle will be to create a JavaScript file containing the script that an AudioWorkerNode is supposed to execute, then call a createAudioWorker() function on the existing AudioContext to hand this script to a Worker, which executes it in a separate thread. There will be events raised between the AudioWorkerNode and the AudioContext to deal with state changes in each thread and an ability to provide AudioParams to the AudioWorkerNode.

Offline Audio Processing

The OfflineAudioContext interface is a type of AudioContext that doesn't render the audio output of a filter graph to the device hardware but to an AudioBuffer. This allows processing of audio data potentially faster than real time and is really useful if all you're trying to do is analyze the content of your audio stream (e.g. when detecting beats).

```
[Constructor(unsigned long numberOfChannels,
             unsigned long length,
             float sampleRate)]
interface OfflineAudioContext : AudioContext {
             attribute EventHandler oncomplete;
    Promise<AudioBuffer> startRendering ();
};
```

The construction of an OfflineAudioContext works similarly to when you create a new AudioBuffer with the AudioContext's createBuffer() method and takes the same three parameters.

- The numberOfChannels attribute contains the number of discrete channels that the AudioBuffer should have.

- The length attribute contains the length of the audio asset in sampleframes.

- The sampleRate attribute contains the samplerate of the audio asset.

The OfflineAudioContext provides an oncomplete event handler, which is called when processing has finished.

It also provides a startRendering() method. When an OfflineAudioContext is created, it is in a "suspended" state. A call to this function kicks off the processing of the filter graph.

A simple example use of the OfflineAudioContext is to grab audio data from an audio file into an OfflineAudioContext without disturbing the general AudioContext, which may be doing some other work at the time. Listing 6-21 shows how this can be done by adjusting Listing 6-5.

Listing 6-21. Adding Random Noise to an Audio File in a ScriptProcessorNode

```
// AudioContext that decodes data
var offline = new window.OfflineAudioContext(2,44100*20,44100);
var source = offline.createBufferSource();
var offlineReady = false;

// AudioContext that renders data
var audioCtx = new (window.AudioContext || window.webkitAudioContext)();
var sound;

var audioBuffer;

var request = new XMLHttpRequest();
var url = 'audio/transition.wav';

function receivedData() {
  if ((request.status === 200 || request.status === 206)
      && request.readyState === 4) {
    var audioData = request.response;
    offline.decodeAudioData(audioData,
```

```
      function(buffer) {
        source.buffer = buffer;
        source.connect(offline.destination);
        source.start(0);
        offlineReady = true;
      },
      function(error) {
        "Error with decoding audio data" + error.err
      }
    );
  }
}

request.addEventListener('load', receivedData, false);
requestData(url);

function startPlayback() {
  sound = audioCtx.createBufferSource();
  sound.buffer = audioBuffer;
  sound.connect(audioCtx.destination);
  sound.start(0);
}

var stop = document.getElementsByTagName('button')[0];
stop.addEventListener('click', function() {
    sound.stop();
});

var start = document.getElementsByTagName('button')[1];
start.addEventListener('click', function() {
  if (!offlineReady) return;
  offline.startRendering().then(function(renderedBuffer) {
    audioBuffer = renderedBuffer;
    startPlayback();
  }).catch(function(err) {
    // audioData has already been rendered
    startPlayback();
  });
});
```

We've added a second button to the example of Listing 6-5 and are now manually starting the audio file. After downloading the audio file, the offline context is decoding it and starts rendering (when we click the start button). In the rendering routine, we save the decoded AudioBuffer data so we can reload it at a later stage. It's this AudioBuffer data that we hand over to the live AudioContext for playback.

Audio Data Visualization

The final interface that we need to understand is the AnalyserNode interface. This interface represents a node that is able to provide real-time frequency and time-domain sample information. These nodes make no changes to the audio stream, which is passed straight through. They can therefore be placed anywhere in the filter graph. A major use of this interface is for visualizing the audio data.

An AnalyserNode is created through a createAnalyser() method on the AudioContext:

```
[Constructor] interface AudioContext : EventTarget {
...
    AnalyserNode     createAnalyser ();
...
}
```

The interface of the AnalyserNode is defined as follows:

```
interface AnalyserNode : AudioNode {
                attribute unsigned long fftSize;
    readonly    attribute unsigned long frequencyBinCount;
                attribute float         minDecibels;
                attribute float         maxDecibels;
                attribute float         smoothingTimeConstant;
    void getFloatFrequencyData  (Float32Array array);
    void getByteFrequencyData   (Uint8Array array);
    void getFloatTimeDomainData (Float32Array array);
    void getByteTimeDomainData  (Uint8Array array);
};
```

The attributes contain the following information:

- fftSize: the buffer size used for the analysis. It must be a power of 2 in the range 32 to 32,768 and defaults to 2,048.

- frequencyBinCount: a fixed value at half the FFT (Fast Fourier Transform) size.

- minDecibels, maxDecibels: the power value range for scaling the FFT analysis data for conversion to unsigned byte values. The default range is from minDecibels = -100 to maxDecibels = -30.

- smoothingTimeConstant: a value between 0 and 1 that represents the size of a sliding window that smooths results. A 0 represents no time averaging and therefore strongly fluctuating results. The default value is 0.8.

The methods copy the following data into the provided array:

- getFloatFrequencyData, getByteFrequencyData: the current frequency data in different data types. If the array has fewer elements than the frequencyBinCount, the excess elements will be dropped. If the array has more elements than the frequencyBinCount, the excess elements will be ignored.

- getFloatTimeDomainData, getByteTimeDomainData: the current time-domain (waveform) data. If the array has fewer elements than the value of fftSize, the excess elements will be dropped. If the array has more elements than fftSize, the excess elements will be ignored.

The AnalyserNode does not change its channels or number of inputs and the output may be left unconnected:

Number of inputs	1
Number of outputs	1
Channel count mode	"max"
Channel count	1
Channel interpretation	"speakers"

Listing 6-22 shows a simple example of rendering the waveform into a canvas.

Listing 6-22. Rendering Waveform Data of an AudioContext

```
<audio autoplay controls src="audio/ticking.wav"></audio>
<canvas width="512" height="200"></canvas>

<script>
// prepare canvas for rendering
var canvas = document.getElementsByTagName("canvas")[0];
var sctxt = canvas.getContext("2d");
sctxt.fillRect(0, 0, 512, 200);
sctxt.strokeStyle = "#FFFFFF";
sctxt.lineWidth = 2;

// prepare audio data
var audioCtx = new (window.AudioContext || window.webkitAudioContext)();
var mediaElement = document.getElementsByTagName('audio')[0];
var source = audioCtx.createMediaElementSource(mediaElement);

// prepare filter graph
var analyser = audioCtx.createAnalyser();
analyser.fftSize = 2048;
analyser.smoothingTimeConstant = 0.1;
source.connect(analyser);
analyser.connect(audioCtx.destination);

// data from the analyser node
var buffer = new Uint8Array(analyser.frequencyBinCount);

function draw() {
  analyser.getByteTimeDomainData(buffer);

  // do the canvas painting
  var width = canvas.width;
  var height = canvas.height;
  var step = parseInt(buffer.length / width);
  sctxt.fillRect(0, 0, width, height);
  sctxt.drawImage(canvas, 0, 0, width, height);
```

```
  sctxt.beginPath();
  sctxt.moveTo(0, buffer[0] * height / 256);
  for(var i=1; i< width; i++) {
    sctxt.lineTo(i, buffer[i*step] * height / 256);
  }
  sctxt.stroke();
  window.requestAnimationFrame(draw);
}
mediaElement.addEventListener('play', draw , false);
</script>
```

We make use of a canvas into which the wave will be rendered and prepare it with a black background and white drawing color. We instantiate the AudioContext and the audio element for sample input, prepare the analyser and hook it all up to a filter graph.

Once the audio element starts playback, we start the drawing which grabs the waveform bytes from the analyser. These are exposed through a getByteTimeDomainData() method, which fills a provided Uint8Array. We take this array, clear the canvas from the previous drawing, and draw the new array into the canvas as a line connecting all the values. Then call the draw() method again in a requestAnimationFrame() call to grab the next unsigned 8-bit byte array for display. This successively paints the waveform into the canvas.

An alternative and more traditional way to using requestAnimationFrame would have been the use of the setTimeout() function with a 0 timeout. We recommend the use of requestAnimationFrame for all drawing purposes going forward because it is built for rendering and to make sure to properly schedule the drawing at the next possible screen repaint opportunity.

Figure 6-16 shows the result of running Listing 6-22.

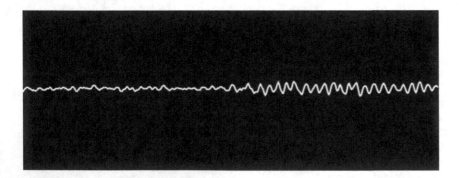

Figure 6-16. *Rendering the audio waveform in the Web audio API*

This concludes our exploration of the Web Audio API.

Summary

In this chapter we learned about the existing proposals for an audio API that gives access to samples, no matter whether they were provided from an algorithmically created audio source, an audio file, or the microphone. The Web Audio API further provides hardware-accelerated manipulation and visualization approaches for such audio data and a means to hook your own JavaScript manipulation routine into an audio filter graph.

Index

Get the eBook for only $5!

Why limit yourself?

Now you can take the weightless companion with you wherever you go and access your content on your PC, phone, tablet, or reader.

Since you've purchased this print book, we're happy to offer you the eBook in all 3 formats for just $5.

Convenient and fully searchable, the PDF version enables you to easily find and copy code—or perform examples by quickly toggling between instructions and applications. The MOBI format is ideal for your Kindle, while the ePUB can be utilized on a variety of mobile devices.

To learn more, go to www.apress.com/companion or contact support@apress.com.